||||BradyGAMES
STRATEGY GUIDES

W9-BYO-003

TABLE OF CONTENTS

GAME BASICS • • • •3

THE CHARACTERS • •8

WALKTHROUGH • • •26

SIDE AREAS • • • •176

BESTIARY • • • • •194

WEAPONS • • • • •212

ARMOR • • • • • •215

ACCESSORIES • • •216

ITEMS • • • • • • •217

MATERIA • • • • •218

WORLD MAP • • •222

OFFICIAL
FINAL FANTASY VII
STRATEGY GUIDE

By David Cassady

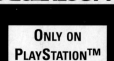

SQUARESOFT®

ONLY ON
PLAYSTATION™

LEGAL STUFF
Official Final Fantasy® VII Strategy Guide

©1997 Brady Publishing

All rights reserved, including the right of reproduction in whole or in part in any form.

Brady Publishing
An Imprint of
Macmillan Computer Publishing USA
201 West 103rd Street
Indianapolis, Indiana 46290

ISBN: 1-56686-714-2

Library of Congress Catalog #: 97-073741

Printing Code: The rightmost double-digit number is the year of the book's printing; the rightmost single-digit number is the number of the book's printing. For example, 97-1 shows that the first printing of the book occurred in 1997.

99 98 10

Manufactured in the United States of America.

BRADY STAFF

PUBLISHER
Lynn Zingraf

EDITOR IN CHIEF
H. Leigh Davis

TITLE/LICENSING MANAGER
David Waybright

MARKETING MANAGER
Janet Cadoff

ACQUISITIONS EDITOR
Debra McBride

CREDITS

DEVELOPMENT EDITOR
David Cassady

PROJECT EDITOR
Tim Cox

SCREENSHOT EDITOR
Michael Owen

CREATIVE DIRECTOR
Jean Bisesi

BOOK DESIGNER
Jean Bisesi

PRODUCTION DESIGNER
Dan Caparo
Max Adamson

Special Thanks

A very special thanks goes to Dan Dunham, who took on the monumental task of creating the various lists for this book. Thanks for your hard work and patience. To Rick Thompson, Fernando, and the entire Quality Assurance Department. Thanks for all your help in uncovering the multitude of secret items and areas, and for all of your helpful suggestions. On behalf of the entire Brady team I'd also like to thank Kenji Mimura, Kyoko Yamashita, Kiomi Murazeki, and Jun Iwasaki for all their assistance on this project. This book wouldn't have been possible without the fantastic staff at Squaresoft. Also, I'd like to thank David Bamberger and everyone at Sony for all their help and support. Thanks also goes to Debra McBride, Tim Cox, Michael Owen, and the design/layout team for all the long hours spent putting this project together. Last, but not least, I'd like to thank Heather Moseman and Carole Cassady for being both my support mechanisms and sometimes my alarm clock. Thanks to everyone for trying their hardest to make this the best book possible.

This book is dedicated to all the gamers about to embark on their first trip into the worlds of Final Fantasy. May there be many more.

GAME BASICS

This section gives you a few tips on exploring, battle, managing your inventory, and equipping your characters. For more specific information, I urge you to check out the training rooms located in the Sector 7 Slums and Junon. There you'll find complete tutorials for all the basics in a graphic demonstration.

GENERAL TIPS

- Save often—you never know what lies around the next turn.

- Talk to everyone—several times. Some characters won't spill their guts the first time you speak to them; however, they'll tell you everything the second and third times around.

- Major events in the game often change what some characters say and do. If something earth-shattering occurs, revisit nearby villages to see if anything has changed.

- After acquiring a vehicle, leave it in a place where you can easily retrieve it. Otherwise, you can easily get completely cut off from your transportation.

- Riding Chocobos is a fun way to get around quickly, but it's not always the best choice. The random battles that occur while traveling between towns are critical for raising your levels and fattening your wallet.

ITEMS

- Carry lots of **Potions**, **Ethers**, and **Phoenix Downs**. These items help the most during battles when your magic runs dry.

- Keep your inventory organized. If things aren't to your liking, situate them so they're easy to find and use. You don't want to waste time in battle searching for an X-Potion that you desperately need.

- Most status effects—either good or bad—only last until the end of a battle. You should carry a few of the items that cure such effects (four or five tops) just to be safe. However, don't waste Gil loading yourself down with a ton of useless supplies.

- Look for special items like **Power Source** and **Guard Source** to give your characters a boost. Each "Source" permanently increases one of your character's statistics by a point.

- There are several items that have no use and just as many that appear useless but aren't. Think about where you might be able to use the odd items that appear. As your levels increase, some items will become less effective. Potions, for example, will no longer heal enough to be worth carrying.

WEAPONS & ARMOR

- Always equip new armor and weapons when you obtain them. You should occasionally check your inventory to make sure you didn't miss the addition of a new item to your inventory.

- The strongest weapon is not always the best choice. Always take into account how much Materia a weapon can store and what kind of effect it has on the Materia's growth rate.

- You don't need to purchase each new weapon and piece of armor you find. You should keep your main party outfitted in the latest gear, but only buy for inactive characters if you have an overabundance of Gil.

- Your armor and accessories can seriously affect the outcome of a battle. For example, an enemy that uses nothing but water-based attacks will have trouble injuring someone equipped with the **Water Ring**.

- Items like the Water Ring enable your party to use normally harmful spells for healing purposes.

- Choose weapons and armor that best fit the roles you've chosen for a character. Fighters need less Materia slots than magic users. If you have a lot of empty Materia slots, you may not be using the best armor or weapon.

MATERIA & SPELLS

- Over the course of your adventure you'll have the opportunity to buy lots of Materia. Although you can find most of it just lying around, you may want to buy a second Materia crystal for essential spells like **Cure** and **Life**.

- **All** is one of the most valuable Materia for eliminating multiple enemies. But it can also be teamed up with a Materia that gives the entire party bonuses, like Restore or Time.

- Each Materia gives the equipped character certain bonuses and penalties. Avoid overloading characters with Materia that have heavy penalties or you may seriously decrease the character's effectiveness.

- **Summon Materia** is sometimes difficult to find. You should search everything and everywhere as you explore. If you can't enter an area at one point in the game, return later and the path may have opened.

- Some of the most valuable spells cause no damage at all and are commonly overlooked. If you want to master Final Fantasy VII, you must learn how to effectively use Materia like **Time** and **Mystify**.

BATTLE

- Characters equipped with short-range weapons (swords, staffs, etc.) cause less damage while standing in the back rank. Even if they're in the front ranks, they still cause less damage if they're forced to attack an opponent's back ranks.

- Characters equipped with long-range weapons can attack from the front or back rank without weakening their attacks. They can also attack an opponent's back rank without a loss of power.

- You can only hit some enemies (mainly bosses) with long-range weapons. Even if your character's best weapon is best suited for close-range attacks, make sure you keep a long-range weapon in your inventory just in case.

- Each player will progress through the game at a different speed. Depending on how quickly you find your way around, you may occasionally need to "build" your levels or fill your pockets with Gil. To accomplish this, roam around a town and fight the local hordes of enemies, resting at an Inn when necessary.

- After becoming familiar with the enemies in an area, take a few moments to re-equip your team. For example, if you're facing ice beasts, equip lots of **Fire Materia** and accessories that protect you from ice attacks.

- Try to focus your party's attention on a single enemy until it's destroyed. This will enable you to quickly eliminate your foes while taking the least amount of damage.

- If the enemy a character was assigned to attack dies before the character can attack, he or she will randomly attack one of the remaining opponents. It's best to measure your attacks and to assign characters to a different monster if it looks like the chosen beast is about to be destroyed. This allows you more control over the situation.

- Be sure to use plenty of defensive magic to make up for weak armor. A solid barrier is sometimes better than a strong piece of armor.

4

- Most creatures have distinct strengths and weaknesses. Pay attention to these things, and do your best to capitalize on them.

- When being attacked from behind, you may want to switch ranks between characters since your front fighters will be in the back, and your back fighters will be in the front. It's not always worth doing, but in longer fights it will pay off in the end.

- When being attacked from behind or when surrounded, you'll take more damage than usual if your opponents hit you in the back. To avoid this in the attacks from behind scenario, tap both L1 and R1 as if to run from the fight. This will turn your characters to face the enemy.

MATERIA COMBINATIONS

The following are some really cool and useful Materia combinations. Equipping any one of them will improve your abilities in battle.

SIMPLE COMBINATIONS

Added Effect +

Added Effect-Transform in a weapon; sometimes transforms monsters when hit with the attack.

Added Effect-Poison In a Weapon

Successful hit may poison creature.

Added Effect-Contain In a Weapon

May petrify, confuse, or stop the creature.

Added Effect-Seal In a Weapon

Silences or puts the enemy to sleep after the attack.

Added Effect-Mystify In a Weapon

Can cause confusion or berserk after the attack.

Added Effect-Time In a Weapon

Sometimes slows or stops a creature.

Added Effect-Destruct In a Weapon

May cause instant death.

NOTE: Placing any of the above combinations in your armor will provide protection from the listed effect.

MEGA-ALL

Mega-All Steal

Allows player to steal from all enemies at once; best with Mug.

Mega-All Deathblow

Player hits all enemies with Deathblow each turn.

ELEMENTAL

Elemental-Most Basic Spells

Adds the element to the attack, or helps defend against such attack.

Elemental-Elemental Summons

Combined with any summons that has an elemental base, it will add the element to your attack or defense.

[COMMAND] COUNTER

[Command] Counter Deathblow

Counters attacks with Deathblow.

[Command] Counter Mime

Counters attack with last action used by party; unpredictable but powerful.

[Command] Counter Morph

Counters with the Morph Command; less powerful, but often useful.

HP ABSORB/MP ABSORB

HP Absorb/MP Absorb Deathblow

Restores more HP/MP than a normal attack.

HP Absorb/MP Absorb Steal [Mug]

Allows you to steal some HP/MP along with an item.

MP Absorb-Most Spells

Cuts down MP consumption by restoring a small portion after the attached spell.

FINAL ATTACK

Final Attack-Revive

Instantly heals a fallen warrior.

QUAD MAGIC

Quad Magic-Most Summons

Casts the attached summon four times in a row.

Quad Magic-Most Spells

Casts the attached spell four times in a row.

COMPLEX COMBINATIONS

Mega-All, Deathblow-HP Absorb/MP Absorb

Restores a large amount of HP/MP while causing damage to all opponents.

Mega-All, Steal [Mug]-HP Absorb/MP Absorb

Damages and steals from all opponents while restoring HP/MP.

Cover, Counter Attack, Counter Attack, [Command] Counter-Deathblow

Covers for other characters and immediately counters three times, finishing with Deathblow.

Knights of the Round-W-Summon, Mime

Can infinitely cast the most powerful summon for only 500 MP. With three Mime, everyone can repeat the summmon for an incredible chain effect.

Sneak Attack-Knights of the Round

Allows you to begin battle by casting Knights of the Round.

Sneak Attack-Deathblow, Mega-Aii

Begins battle by hitting all opponents with Deathblow.

Sneak Attack-Steal [Mug], Mega-All

Begin battle by causing damage to everyone and stealing an item from everyone.

Pre-Emptive, Sneak Attack-Knights of the Round, HP<-->MP

Gives the party the jump on opponents and allows them to begin combat with Knights of the Round. Character with HP<-->MP can use attack repeatedly without a need for rest.

7

CLOUD STRIFE

At age 21, Cloud Strife leads the life of a mercenary for hire. As an ex-member of Shinra's elite squad known as SOLDIER, his fighting skills are in high demand. Cloud joins the rebel group AVALANCHE for their first strike against one of Shinra's huge Mako Reactors that surround the city of Midgar.

The story line of *Final Fantasy VII* revolves around Cloud. In fact, most of the time you're required to have him in your party because he plays a key role in most of the events in the game. Over time Cloud proves to be a great asset, because his powerful sword technique is nearly unmatched. You'll want to keep Cloud in your front line most of the time to take full advantage of his sword technique. His magic skills are solid, but don't overload him with Materia.

CLOUD'S LIMIT BREAKS

LEVEL 1:

BRAVER

Cloud performs a leaping chop that splits a single enemy in two. Unless you're facing a really strong enemy that isn't a boss, this is usually your best Level 1 Limit Break. The attack is stronger than the Cross-Slash, so it usually kills weaker enemies.

CROSS-SLASH

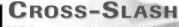

With several powerful slashes, Cloud causes massive damage to a single opponent. If the enemy survives the attack, there is a chance that it may cause paralysis. It can't paralyze enemies who are normally immune to paralysis, like most bosses.

LEVEL 2:

BLADE BEAM

Waves of energy rush from Cloud's sword and collide with a single enemy. The remaining energy then splits into smaller, weaker waves, hitting any remaining enemies. This attack is great against a large group of weaker enemies. Always target the strongest enemy in the group, because the initial wave causes about three times as much damage as the smaller secondary waves.

CLIMHAZZARD

Cloud skewers a single enemy and then leaps high into the sky to cause greater damage. This is best used against a single opponent or any really strong opponents you encounter. Eventually the Blade Beam attack will become ineffective, but the Climhazzard attack should be useful throughout most of the game.

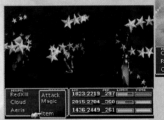

LEVEL 3:

METEORAIN

While leaping into the air, Cloud unleashes a barrage of meteors upon a group of foes causing up to four separate hits. This is actually best used against a single enemy, unless the targeted group is fairly weak. Used against one opponent, this attack can cause as much as 12,000 points of damage.

FINISHING TOUCH

Cloud creates a large whirlwind that sucks a group of opponents into oblivion, which causes them to either immediately perish or suffer extensive damage from falling back to the ground. Most opponents will simply perish, but larger creatures like bosses will always fall back to the ground. Save this Limit Break for groups—it's completely wasted on a single enemy.

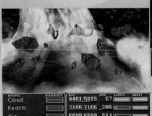

LEVEL 4:

OMNISLASH

Cloud assaults his opponent with a long series of powerful sword attacks. This can be used against a single opponent or a group; either way, this is an extremely powerful attack. With the correct sword in hand, this attack can actually cause just as much, if not more, damage than the fabled "Knights of the Round" Materia.

BARRET WALLACE

Barret is the 35-year-old leader of the rebel team known as AVALANCHE. He leads the team in the quest to stop Shinra's Mako Reactors and save the life of the planet. Although he is truly devoted to the team, Barret often regrets having to leave his young daughter, Marlene, alone or in the care of others. Barret's motives are unclear, but most believe that Shinra was somehow responsible for the death of his wife.

Although he may not look it, Barret is one of the most versatile characters in the game. Unlike most, he has weapons for close- and long-range combat, which enables him to perform well in either rank. You'll want to keep Barret in the back rank most of the time. This enables him to cause heavy damage without taking an equal amount in return. Avoid loading Barret up with Materia that reduces his hit points and strength. You may want to use him as a damage magnet later, and if so he'll need to be as strong as possible.

BARRET'S LIMIT BREAKS

LEVEL 1:

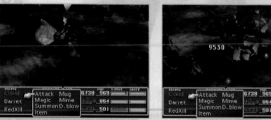

BIG SHOT

Barret fires a large ball of energy from his gun, which causes massive damage to his opponent. For the first portion of the game the Big Shot should come in really handy, but it quickly becomes obsolete as your enemies increase in strength.

MINDBLOW

Barret fires a large ball of blue energy from his gun, which depletes his opponent's magic points. Such attacks often go unappreciated, but the Mindblow can turn a fierce magic user into a helpless wimp.

LEVEL 2:

GRENADE BOMB

Targeting an entire group of enemies, Barret launches a deadly grenade into the enemy ranks. This is typically the Level 2 Limit Break of choice. It causes a decent amount of damage to entire groups of enemies.

HAMMERBLOW

Barret's powerful punch sends an enemy into orbit. Barret can completely remove an enemy from combat with the Hammerblow, but the attack is best used against individual non-Boss monsters. The Hammerblow doesn't cause any direct damage, so it's worthless against Boss creatures.

LEVEL 3:

SATELLITE BEAM

Proving he has friends in high places, Barret calls for the ultimate air strike against a group of enemies. The beams hit for about 3000-4000 points of damage on each creature. Although this attack is great against a group of enemies, it's considerably less effective against a lone attacker.

UNGARMAX

Lock and load! Barret dumps a large amount of ammunition into a group of enemies causing massive damage. The Ungarmax hits more times than the Satellite Beam, but the hits are weaker.

LEVEL 4:

CATASTROPHE

Barret uses his gun arm to hover over a group of enemies, and then burns them to a crisp with a super-heated plasma blast. As you might expect, this is the best of Barret's Limit Breaks. It works well against a group or a single enemy. It does have one downside: Because the attack isn't focused, a single enemy won't feel the full force of the blow.

11

TIFA LOCKHEART

Tifa and Cloud were childhood friends, but parted ways when Cloud left his hometown of Nibelheim to join SOLDIER. When her parents died, Tifa also left Nibelheim and headed for Midgar. Soon after opening her bar, Tifa's Seventh Heaven, she met Barret and joined his ragtag group of rebels known as AVALANCHE. It's her goal to make sure Cloud remains with AVALANCHE after his first mission with the team.

When fighting, Tifa lets her fists do the talking. Her attacks are generally weaker than Cloud's and Barret's, but from early on her chain of Limit Breaks is by far the best thing going. Instead of selecting a single Limit Break, each new attack adds to the chain for a total of seven devastating hits. If she can score "Yeah!" on the twirling slots, she causes extra damage. If she stops a slot on "Miss," she misses with that part of the combo. Tifa should always be a frontline fighter, but may have trouble contributing during some boss fights.

TIFA'S LIMIT BREAKS

LEVEL 1:

BEAT RUSH

Tifa unleashes a quick combo against a single enemy for the first part of her Limit Break combo.

SOMERSAULT

Tifa punishes a single opponent and shows off a little with this flipping kick. The Somersault tacks on another hit to her Limit Break combo.

LEVEL 2:

WATERKICK

The third part of Tifa's combo is a quick elemental wave of water that washes over an opponent.

METEODRIVE

Tifa shows off her brute force by picking up her opponent and delivering a quick backdrop.

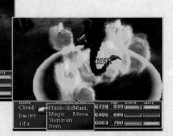

LEVEL 3:

DOLPHIN BLOW

Tifa calls on her fishy friend for this watery uppercut and tacks on hit number five.

METEOR STRIKE

After grabbing her opponent, Tifa jumps into the heavens before slamming down her opponent hard.

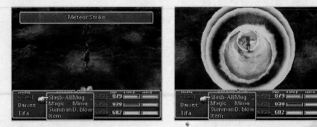

LEVEL 4:

FINAL HEAVEN

Focusing her energies into her fist, Tifa hits the enemy with the force of a nuclear explosion.

13

AERIS GAINSBOROUGH

A beautiful 22-year-old, Aeris is a bright spot in the middle of a dark and dreary town. While selling flowers near AVALANCHE's first target, Aeris' life was forever altered after a chance meeting with Cloud. Because of her mysterious background, Shinra has pursued her for most of her life. Now she must fight against those who would enslave her and destroy what she holds most dear.

Aeris is the closest character *Final Fantasy VII* has to a dedicated magic user. Her physical attacks are fairly weak, but she possesses great skill with Materia and its various forms. Due to this odd balance, you should put her in your back line and load her down with Materia. Let Aeris devote her energies to spell casting while her teammates concentrate on inflicting physical damage. This also takes advantage of her defensive-based Limit Breaks.

AERIS' LIMIT BREAKS

LEVEL 1:

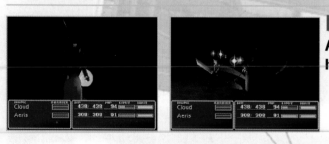

HEALING WIND
Aeris restores the party's lost Hit Points with this heavenly breeze.

SEAL EVIL
Aeris casts a mystic spell on a group of enemies, causing them all to stop and become silenced.

Level 2:

Breath of the Earth

Magical beams of light cure the party of any existing negative statuses.

Fury Brand

Sacrificing her own Limit Attack, Aeris blasts the party with Holy power which instantly fills each of her allies' Limit gauges.

Level 3:

Planet Protector

Aeris forms a protective barrier around the party that makes them temporarily invulnerable.

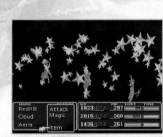

Pulse of Life

With a quick word of prayer, Aeris completely cures the party of any ailments and restores any lost Hit Points or Magic Points.

Level 4:

Great Gospel

Aeris summons the heavenly host and the party is fully recovered and made temporarily invulnerable.

RED XIII

Although his fiery red fur may make him look like a wild animal, Red XIII's intellect is well above that of most humans. Not much is known about Red XIII's origin. He's currently being held captive in Shinra's headquarters where he's forced to participate in their twisted experiments.

Red XIII is strong at both physical and magical combat. His sharp teeth and claws work well with his close-range fighting style, however, this limits his combat options and forces him to take a spot on the front line. There is a long range weapon for Red XIII, but it lacks Materia slots and forces him to act as a fighter. Red XIII makes a solid magic user when loaded down with Materia, but performs best with a more balanced approach. It's best to always take advantage of his physical strength as well as his startling intellect.

RED XIII'S LIMIT BREAKS

LEVEL 1:

SLED FANG

Red XIII charges through an opponent causing a large amount of physical damage. For a while this may be the only long-range attack Red XIII has, so it's sure to come in handy. However, it'll become obsolete by the time you receive Blood Fang.

LUNATIC HIGH

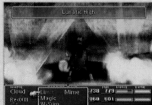

A glowing light covers the party and Haste is cast on everyone. Until you've purchased the "Time" Materia, the Lunatic High should come in handy during major battles.

Level 2:

Blood Fang

Red XIII charges through an opponent causing more physical damage than the Sled Fang attack. He also gains a small amount of Hit Points and Magic Points. This attack isn't much different from the Sled Fang attack, but it's nice for eliminating an opponent and boosting Red XIII's MP.

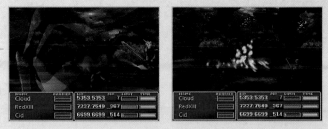

Stardust Ray

Red XII's howl summons a cluster of falling stars, which causes severe damage to groups of enemies. Unless you need the MP boost, stick with the Stardust Ray during fights. It inflicts considerably more damage to a group or a single enemy than the Blood Fang.

Level 3:

Howling Moon

The full moon drives Red XIII into a rage, casting Berserk and Haste on him for the remainder of the battle. This attack has some obvious advantages and disadvantages. Using this attack, Red XIII can attack quickly, but he can no longer aid the party with magic or any kind of special attack.

Earth Rave

Red XIII attacks a group of enemies with a series of five elemental attacks. In the end, the Earth Rave will prove to be more beneficial than the Howling Moon. It does a large amount of direct damage without committing Red XIII to a single attack pattern.

Level 4:

Cosmo Memory

Red XIII summons a huge ball of fire which explodes, engulfing his opponents in a huge ray of super-heated plasma.

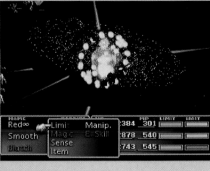

CID HIGHWIND

Cid is an expert pilot and mechanic who dreams of one day becoming the first man in space. His dream would have been fulfilled, but he aborted a launch in order to save the life of one of his crew. Now he spends his time trying to repair his inoperable rocket in the hopes that Shinra may one day reinstate its space program, giving him another chance at fulfilling his dream.

With his lance in hand, Cid is always prepared for battle. His fighting skills are top-notch and come in handy throughout most of the game. His Limit Breaks are very helpful when fighting the evil hordes that threaten to consume the land. You'll notice that they all cause direct damage rather than affecting status or healing the party. Cid's statistics are pretty average all the way around, which can help or hinder his performance depending on how he is equipped.

CID'S LIMIT BREAKS

LEVEL 1:

BOOST JUMP

Cid vaults into the air and crashes down on a single opponent's head. This is a straightforward attack that's your best bet for killing a single enemy early on.

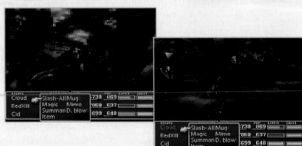

DYNAMITE

Cid produces a large stick of dynamite that he hurls into a group of enemies. Once Cid learns the Dynamite Limit Break, it's unlikely you'll ever use the Boost Jump again. It causes a fair amount of damage to each monster in a group, but the effect isn't cumulative like Big Brawl or Dragon Dive.

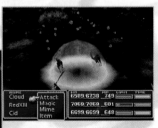

LEVEL 2:

HYPER JUMP

Cid leaps into the air and drives his weapon deep into the ground, causing a huge blue explosion that damages an entire group of enemies. This is basically a more powerful version of the Dynamite Limit Break; it's great against a group, but loses something against individual opponents.

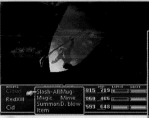
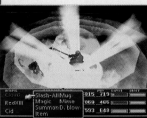

DRAGON

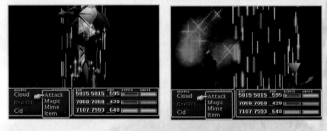

Cid summons a dragon to attack one of his enemies. The dragon injures the victim and transfers the Hit Points and Magic Points back into Cid. This is the best Level 2 attack against a single creature. It's also effective when Cid needs a small boost to his MP; the HP boost is insignificant.

LEVEL 3:

DRAGON DIVE

Cid repeatedly pounces on a group of opponents. Each attack creates a large explosion that causes heavy damage to a single opponent. The Dragon Dive is the stronger of the two Level 3 Limit Breaks, but it connects against the enemy fewer times.

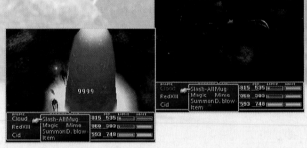

BIG BRAWL

Cid shows off his fighting skills by leaping into a group of enemies and crushing them with a series of blazing-fast attacks. The Big Brawl hits for less each time, but it hits more times than the Dragon Dive. It's difficult to say which attack is better.

LEVEL 4:

HIGHWIND

Cid calls on the Highwind for assistance. The ship's crew answers by unleashing a huge salvo against the opposition. This is a great attack against a single enemy or a huge group. Each missile causes several thousand points of damage to most enemies, plus the total damage is cumulative.

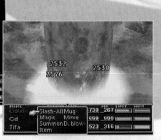

19

YUFFIE KISARAGI

This 16-year-old ninja spent most of her time prey-
ing on helpless travelers until she met up with
Cloud's party. Although she is reluctant to join
AVALANCHE, her ulterior motives give her
reason to tag along, if only temporarily.
Her clever wit and ninja skills coupled
with her selfish ways will either make her a powerful
ally or a serious pain in the neck.

Yuffie isn't one of the strongest team members, but her Limit
Breaks are powerful. Her weapons enable her to attack from
a distance without penalty. Keep her in the back rank and outfit her with plenty of Materia. Although this tactic will lower her
Hit Points, her position in the back rank should keep her safe.

YUFFIE'S LIMIT BREAKS

LEVEL 1:

GREASED LIGHTNING

Yuffie hits a single opponent with a quick attack
that causes massive physical damage. Greased
Lightning does enough damage to eliminate
weaker opponents, but it's well outdated by the
time you receive the first of Yuffie's Level 2 Limit
Breaks.

CLEAR TRANQUIL

A blue orb surrounds each party member and restores a small portion of
each character's Hit Points. Early on, this Limit Break is helpful for curing
your allies, but the amount of damage enemies
cause plus the party's increased HP will soon be too
much for Clear Tranquil to be effective.

Level 2:

Landscaper

Yuffie causes a large tremor that forces the ground beneath a group of opponents to rise and explode, which causes massive damage to her enemies. Use this Limit Break solely against groups of enemies. The damage isn't cumulative, so its effect is drastically reduced against a lone enemy.

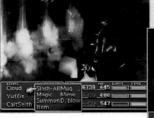

Bloodfest

Yuffie attacks a group of enemies with a series of 10 deadly blows. Unlike the Landscaper, this is effective against a group or a single enemy. The individual attacks are weaker than the Landscaper's single attack, so it's wise to limit its use to small groups.

Level 3:

Gauntlet

Summoning a blue vortex beneath her opponents, Yuffie causes a large amount of damage to an entire group of enemies. Gauntlet causes a large amount of damage, but it's not cumulative. Keep it reserved for large groups of enemies or at least weak groups.

Doom of the Living

Much like the Bloodfest attack, Yuffie moves about the screen and hits her opponents with a long series of deadly blows. The only real difference between the two is the amount of damage inflicted. The damage from this attack is cumulative, which makes it better against a single enemy than Gauntlet.

Level 4:

All Creation

Yuffie blasts her opponents with a huge beam of iridescent light. This attack causes a huge amount of damage to an enemy or enemies.

21

CAIT SITH

Although Cait Sith's fortune telling ability may not impress you, his fighting skills are a sight to be witnessed. The party first bumps into this joker while wandering around the Gold Saucer. Cait Sith eagerly joins the group to see if his predictions prove to be true.

Cait Sith isn't much of a fighter, but his Mog relies on close-range physical attacks. His true strength lies in his various Limit Breaks. You'll notice that he has only two: Dice and Slots. Dice grows with power over time and can prove useful even late in the game. Slots is actually seven separate Limit Breaks. The outcome depends on the combination created when all three slots are stopped. Although these Limit Breaks may seem unpredictable, they can cause serious damage even at the lowest levels. Cait Sith's stuffed body can take quite a bit of damage, so keep this hulk up front unless you decide to load him up with Materia.

CAIT SITH'S LIMIT BREAKS

LEVEL 1:

DICE

Cait Sith throws several dice onto the ground. The resulting score determines how much damage is inflicted to a single enemy. This Limit Break grows over time, making it possible to cause larger amounts of damage.

LEVEL 2:

SLOTS

The gambling cat plays his luck against his own slot machine. There can be many different outcomes, and as you might guess, the more effective outcomes are tougher to get. Occasionally, you'll actually have a particular outcome forced on you. For exmaple, the slots often stop on the Mog Dance and Toy Soldier without the player actually having to time anything. The various effects are:

3 Stars = Mog Dance

A tiny Mog appears and restores the party's HP, MP, and status.

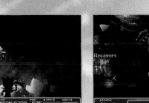

3 Kings = Toy Soldier

Six toy soldiers appear and attack any enemies that are present.

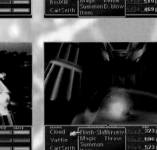

3 Bars = Summon

Cait Sith uses a randomly determined summon spell.

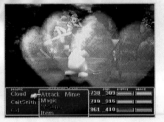

3 Mog = Transform

Cait Sith transforms into a giant version of himself. His teammates disappear for the moment, but return at the end of the battle. Only Cait Sith gains experience from the battle, and the entire party's HP is reduced to 3333 while their MP is reduced to 333.

3 Hearts = Lucky Girl

Party's hit percentage is 100. Ensures perfect attack ratio against all enemies.

2 Cait Sith & a Bar = Death to All

This is the unlucky roll. The entire party is instantly consumed by death... Game over. Don't worry, this is extremely rare.

3 Cait Sith = Instant Victory

All enemies present are instantly killed. This is difficult to get and never seems to be forced on the party.

23

VINCENT VALENTINE

Talk about a dark presence, Vincent sends chills down the toughest person's spine. Although he may look evil at first, there's a good soul trapped beneath his dark exterior. Vincent's plight is yet another example of Shinra's warped experimentation; however, there's more to this story than just bungled scientific research.

Vincent is a strong fighter, much like Barret. He's also quite competent with Materia and makes good use of it from the back row. His Limit Attacks are powerful, but sometimes unpredictable. Once he transforms, you'll no longer be able to control Vincent. Make sure you're familiar with your enemy's strengths and weaknesses before Vincent transforms, or you may end up helping your enemies more than hurting them. Vincent will not join your party on his own. Refer to the section on how to find Vincent Valentine for more information.

VINCENT'S LIMIT BREAKS

LEVEL 1:

GALIAN BEAST

Vincent transforms into a purple beast with horns that attacks with fire-based attacks.

Beast Flare—Launches several orbs that explode and cause damage to a group of enemies.

Berserk Dance—Performs a combo attack against a single enemy.

Level 2:

Death Gigas

Vincent transforms into a Frankenstein creature with powerful physical attacks and a lightning elemental attack.

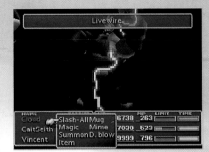

Gigadunk—Hits a single enemy with a powerful punch.

Livewire—Attacks an entire group with an electrical charge.

Level 3:

Hellmasker

Vincent transforms into a chainsaw-bearing maniac who may look very familiar. He can attack with his weapon or he can cause several negative status effects.

Splattercombo—Hits a single enemy five times with his chainsaw.

Nightmare—One enemy is hit with several status effects including Mini, Frog, Sleep, Mute, and Confusion.

Level 4:

Chaos

Vincent transforms into a huge, winged demon. Unlike his other forms, Chaos uses attacks that aren't elemental based. Therefore, you won't find him suddenly healing your opponents.

Chaos Saber—Acts like Slash-All, but doesn't rely on Vincent's weapon to determine damage.

Stan Slam—A large skull is created under the opposition. Any enemies that aren't instantly killed are hit by flaming skulls.

ASSAULT ON MAKO REACTOR No. 1

ITEMS:
Potions (X3) **(A)**, Phoenix Down **(B)**, Restore Materia **(C)**

After meeting several members of the rebel group known as AVALANCHE, Cloud joins their effort to bomb Shinra's Mako Reactor No. 1. Shinra's forces heavily guard the plant, so the group hijacks a train bound for the adjacent slums.

The guards at the station are easily overpowered as the mission quickly gets underway. Cloud exits the train and follows the rest of the team off the platform. Make sure you check the downed guards to collect two **Potions (A)**. Before Cloud can reach the end of the platform, two MPs initiate combat.

MP

Area—Reactor					
LVL 2	HP 30	MP 0	EXP 16	GIL 10	AP 2

Slp	Ret	Con	Sil	Slw	Drk	Trsfr	Stp
Bsk	Psn	Par	Stn	SS	Man	Dth	Imp

MORPH	STEAL	ATTACKS
n/a	n/a	Machine Gun, Punch

MONO DRIVE

Area—Reactor					
LVL 2	HP 28	MP 28	EXP 18	GIL 8	AP 3

Slp	Ret	Con	Sil	Slw	Drk	Trsfr	Stp
Bsk	Psn	Par	Stn	SS	Man	Dth	Imp

MORPH	STEAL	ATTACKS
n/a	n/a	Ram, Fire

1ST RAY

Area—Reactor					
LVL 4	HP 18	MP 0	EXP 12	GIL 5	AP 1

Slp	Ret	Con	Sil	Slw	Drk	Trsfr	Stp
Bsk	Psn	Par	Stn	SS	Man	Dth	Imp

MORPH	STEAL	ATTACKS
n/a	n/a	Laser

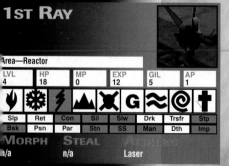

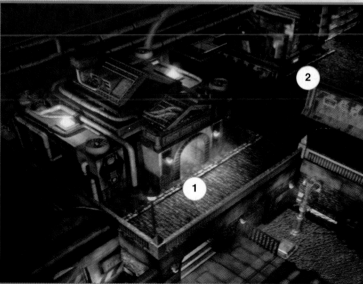

But don't worry, this is one of the few times Cloud has to fight alone. Even so, the MPs aren't much of a threat. Cloud and his companions are more than a match for most of the enemies you'll face in the Mako reactor. After the battle, follow Cloud's companions to the reactor gate and then into the reactor itself.

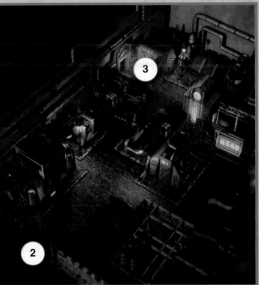

BATTLE TIP: In most of the early battles, you'll only use your characters' normal attacks. You can cut down the selection time by holding the ● button as a character's Time Bar finishes filling. This automatically selects your normal attack and the closest enemy.

Two security doors **(D)** block the only passage in or out of the Mako reactor. Speak with Biggs and Jessie and they'll open the gates. Don't enter the elevator just ahead until after you've picked up the **Phoenix Down (B)** in the control room to the right.

Follow Jessie out of the elevator and into the reactor. After giving you a quick lesson on using ladders, she steps aside as you continue deeper into the factory. Make sure you grab the **Potion (A)** resting just in front of Jessie's sentry position.

NOTE: The party will find many useful items like the **Potion** item lying around different areas of the game. Keep your eyes open or Cloud may run right past one.

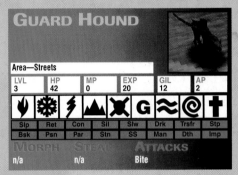

GUARD HOUND

Area—Streets

LVL	HP	MP	EXP	GIL	AP
3	42	0	20	12	2

Slp	Ret	Con	Sil	Slw	Drk	Trsfr	Stp
Bsk	Psn	Par	Stn	SS	Man	Dth	Imp

MORPH	STEAL	ATTACKS
n/a	n/a	Bite

BATTLE TIP: Some enemies have a weakness or immunity to at least one type of element. Ice-based creatures falter against fire, but are healed by any type of ice-based attack. In this area of the game, you'll run into several mechanical enemies, like the Sweeper. You can short-circuit these motored menaces with the **Bolt** spell.

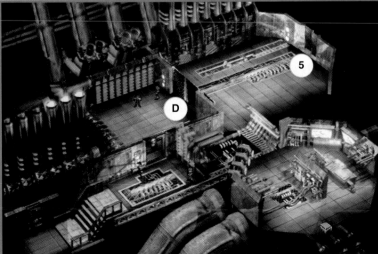

After traveling a little further, the party encounters tougher enemies. Plus, you get your first chance to save your game. Step on the Save Point (E), access the Menu, and then choose Save. You should also use this opportunity to heal the party before moving onward.

As Cloud approaches the Mako reactor, he finds a **Restore Materia (C)** on the floor—unfortunately he can't do anything with it right now. This is another good example of the kind of Materia that can be found lying around.

When you approach the reactor, Barret makes Cloud plant the charges. After the attempted intervention of a mysterious voice, Cloud happily obliges. Unfortunately, their actions trigger an alarm that alerts Shinra's forces to their presence.

BOSS FIGHT: GUARD SCORPION

Although the Guard Scorpion (F) has some deadly attacks, Cloud and Barret's combined strength should be more than enough to punch its ticket.

Start the battle by having Cloud pummel the Scorpion (another mechanical creature) with constant **Bolt** spells while Barret uses his normal attack.

 Battle Tip: Keep your eye on Cloud and Barret's hit points (*HP*). If either falls below 100, use **Potions** to heal them.

After several attacks, the Guard Scorpion raises its tail and begins to shake violently, at which point Cloud warns Barret to be careful. When this occurs, stop your attacks. Attacking the boss during this time period causes it to counterattack with its super weapon,

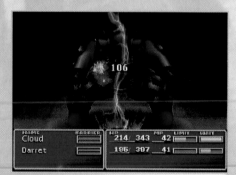

the Tail Laser. This move causes close to 75 points of damage to *both* characters. When the Boss returns to its normal stance, continue your regular attack pattern.

The Guard Scorpion is easily destroyed, but the fight costs the team precious time. Cloud now has only 10 minutes to evacuate the Mako reactor before the bomb explodes.

Before running for the exit, quickly equip Barret with the Assault Gun that the boss leaves behind. You may want to save on your way out just in case something unexpected occurs.

28

NOTE: The timer runs continuously, so you need to quickly finish your battles. If time is short, you can run from your enemies by holding R1 and L1.

As Cloud makes his way through the pipes and support structures, he finds Jessie stuck where he had left her. Help Jessie release her foot and then follow her to the exit. If you fail to rescue Jessie, you won't be able to open the security doors above.

When you reach the security doors, speak with Jessie and Biggs again—they'll release the locks for you. If you made it to this location quickly—and the party is still in good health—use this time to fight some enemies in the area. This is a great opportunity for the characters to easily gain a level. In addition, they will be fully healed when they get outside. When you're ready, run Cloud out of the area and watch Mako Reactor No.1 burn.

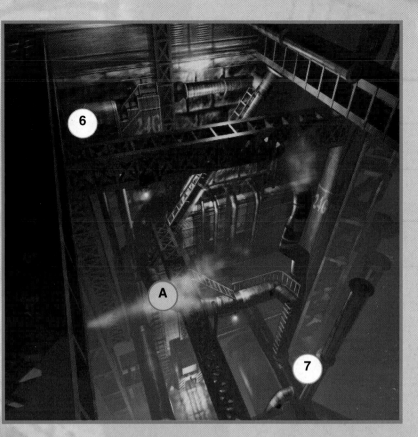

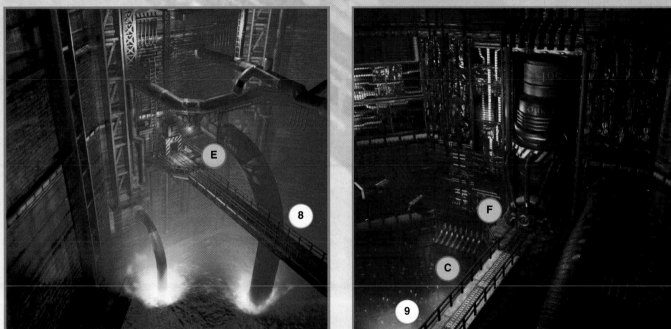

Congratulations on your first successful mission! However, the fight against Shinra has only just begun. There are numerous Mako reactors and AVALANCHE's forces are sparse. This will be a battle not easily won.

29

THE GETAWAY

The team escapes the ruined reactor and prepares to return to their hideout. But first, Barret commands the team to split up and meet at the Sector 8 Station. No problem. The station can't be too far away...right? Even though Barret said to split up, go ahead and follow Barret off-screen.

What's this? Looks like a flower girl has been knocked down in the chaos created by the reactor's explosion. As Cloud

approaches, she stops him in hopes of obtaining some information about the explosion. (Plus, she may even sell another flower!) Take some time to talk to her. You don't need to buy any flowers, but, come on, it's only one Gil! Performing this small deed may even benefit you later in the game. After exchanging pleasantries, follow the flower girl off-screen and into the courtyard.

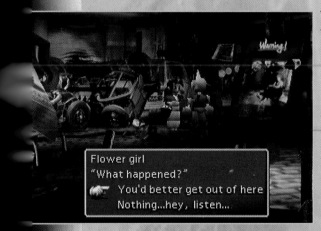

There's not much to do here except talk to a couple of folks and fight a few Guard Hounds. Make sure you grab the **Potion (A)** as you move south toward the next area.

As Cloud hits the streets, he encounters a run-in with the law **(B)**. You have two options in this scenario: *Fight* or *Run*. If you need the experience, you should fight, because none of the MPs present much of a threat.

NOTE: You need to make your decision quickly, because taking too much time is virtually the same as choosing to fight.

The first and second groups in this battle consist of MPs in a normal fight. However, in the third fight, three MPs get the drop on Cloud, forcing him to fight enemies on both sides. Whether you choose to fight or run, Cloud is eventually surrounded and things begin to look bleak. However, Cloud's SOLDIER skills pay off as he hops over a bridge and lands on a train headed for the Sector 7 Slums.

This twist of fate reunites the team, but Barret isn't happy about Cloud's dramatic entrance. Follow the team into the passenger cars and talk to everyone. Jessie takes a moment to explain Midgar's setup and how the trains operate. It seems the team needs fake IDs to get past Shinra's automated security checkpoints. The checkpoints enable Shinra to quickly locate and apprehend any known felons riding the rails.

The train ride goes smoothly and the team quickly arrives at the Sector 7 Slums. Barret orders the team to return to the hideout. Follow them but take a moment to stop and speak with the boy at the base of the pillar (C). These pillar supports keep the city located above from collapsing on the slums below. If one of these structures was ever seriously damaged...

BACK AT H.Q.

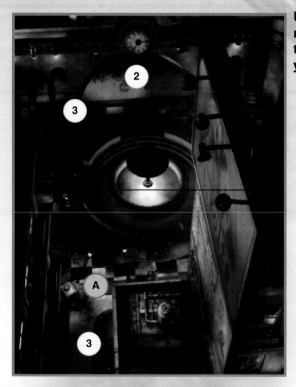

Upon entering the town, Barret clears out the bar and summons the team inside. Take a moment to look around the town if you'd like, but this might annoy Barret. Remember, you'll have plenty of time for sightseein' later.

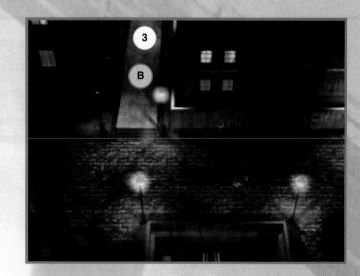

31

Enter the bar and talk to Tifa. If you purchased a flower earlier, you'll get a chance to give the flower to Tifa or Marlene, Barret's daughter. Take a moment to talk to the team and then approach the door. Barret barges in and calls an immediate meeting downstairs. Before attending the meeting, however, speak with Tifa at the bar and join her for a drink. When you're ready, take the pinball machine/elevator to the meeting.

It looks like AVALANCHE's actions have made the news. Already, President Shinra is busy trying to boost the confidence of the local populace in spite of the "terrorist" act. When you speak with Barret, the sparks start to fly. He isn't about to let Cloud forget about his past or forgive him for his involvement with Shinra. Tifa comes to the rescue, but Cloud is already headed for the exit.

Before Cloud can get out the door, Tifa comes running after him. You're not getting out of it that easily, Cloud. When they were kids, Cloud made a promise to protect Tifa should he ever achieve his dream of joining SOLDIER. Now Tifa has every intention of making him keep that promise. Like it or not, you're staying!

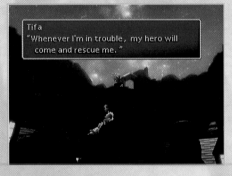

Barret gives Cloud his payment, a paltry 1500 Gil. With some hesitation, he agrees to pay Cloud an additional 2000 Gil for helping with the next mission, an attack on Mako Reactor No. 5. With the team in agreement, everyone rests until morning.

When Cloud awakens, join the team upstairs and prepare to head for the station. Barret asks for a demonstration on how to use Materia. Show him if you know about it, or skip the demonstration altogether by blowing him off. Also note that Tifa tells you to visit the second floor of the Weapons Shop. Looks like it's time to do some slumming.

32

SECTOR 7 SLUMS

As your first order of business, visit the Weapon Shop. Inside, you can purchase new weapons, take a quick rest, and even brush up on your adventuring skills. For now, pick up some **Iron Bangles** and sell the **Bronze Bangles** to the shop owner.

To Sector
7 Station

When you're finished with that task, go upstairs and visit the Beginner's Hall **(1)**. If this is your first Final Fantasy adventure, you should spend some time here talking to everyone. If not, just grab the **"All" Materia** sitting inside the door and then get out.

NOTE: If the team needs to rest, stop and talk to the kid on the first floor **(C)**. For 10 Gil you can use his room for the night. Don't bother giving him anything less.

Now you should stop by the Item Shop **(A)** for some new Materia and **Potions** if you need them. Pick up a **"Fire" Materia** and a **"Restore" Materia**. This should give you three types of attack magic and two ways to cure your fighters. Outfit Cloud's Buster Sword with the **"All" Materia** and the **"Restore" Materia** so that you have a **Cure-All** spell. This will come in handy in future battles.

NOTE: Explore the rest of the town at your leisure and head to the station when you're good and ready. Don't forget to save your game!

ITEMS:
"All" Materia, Ether **(D)**

ITEM SHOP **(A)**

ITEM	COST
Potion	50
Phoenix Down	300
Antidote	80
"Fire"	600
"Ice"	600
"Lightning"	600
"Restore"	750

WEAPON SHOP **(B)**

ITEM	COST
Iron Bangle	160
Assault Gun	350
Grenade	80

REST **(C)**

Boy's Room	10

ITEMS:
Phoenix Down, Hi Potion,
Ether (X2) **(A)**, Potion **(B)**

GRASHTRIKE

Area—Subway

LVL	HP	MP	EXP	GIL	AP
8	42	0	20	20	2

Slp	Ret	Con	Sil	Slw	Drk	Trsfr	Stp
Bsk	Psn	Par	Stn	SS	Man	Dth	Imp

MORPH	STEAL	ATTACKS
n/a	n/a	Silk, Slash

SPECIAL COMBATANT

Area—Reactor2

LVL	HP	MP	EXP	GIL	AP
9	60	0	28	40	3

Slp	Ret	Con	Sil	Slw	Drk	Trsfr	Stp
Bsk	Psn	Par	Stn	SS	Man	Dth	Imp

MORPH	STEAL	ATTACKS
n/a	n/a	Hit, Wave, Beam Gun

ROCKET LAUNCHER

Area—Junon

LVL	HP	MP	EXP	GIL	AP
20	1000	0	600	300	60

Slp	Ret	Con	Sil	Slw	Drk	Trsfr	Stp
Bsk	Psn	Par	Stn	SS	Man	Dth	Imp

MORPH	STEAL	ATTACK
n/a	n/a	Missile

BLUGU

Area—Basement

LVL	HP	MP	EXP	GIL	AP
4	120	0	18	35	2

Slp	Ret	Con	Sil	Slw	Drk	Trsfr	Stp
Bsk	Psn	Par	Stn	SS	Man	Dth	Imp

MORPH	STEAL	ATTACKS
n/a	n/a	Bite, Hell Bubbles

The team hops onto the train and heads out. When you talk to Tifa, an alarm sounds. It looks like Shinra moved the ID check point. The team must run from car to car to avoid getting locked in.

TIP: You may not want to stop and talk to the other passengers during the lockdown, but doing so will get you a few goodies. You must be quick, so make sure your message text speed is set as fast as possible.

In the first car, talk to the bum lying on the seat at the back of the car and he'll give you a **Phoenix Down**. In the second car, talk to the guy closest to the front of the car and he'll give you a **Hi-Potion**. In the third car, a guy walking the opposite direction will sometimes steal something from you. If you run after him, you can force him to give it back, but this takes quite a bit of time. The fifth car, your final destination, has no hidden items.

While you're in the last car, talk to Tifa. The team then jumps off the speeding train and into some tunnels. If you get trapped in the car, Barret blows up the door and the team jumps early. The point in time that the team exits the train determines how far north they must walk to reach the reactor. If you get trapped in the first car, you'll get dropped off next to a station guarded by Special Combatants. You can't get past them, but you can fight them over and over until you get bored and decide to head in the opposite direction.

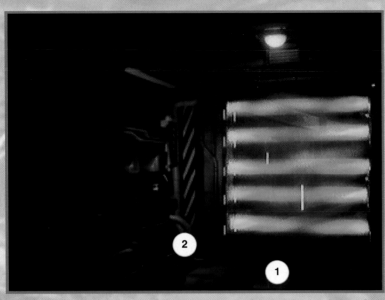

Shinra security sensors block your path at the end of the tunnel. Check the hatch to the left of the sensors and jump inside to bypass them. The chute leads to a large area that resembles a warehouse.

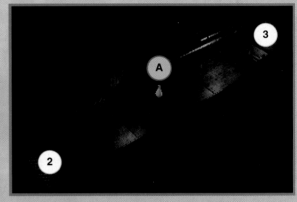

You have two options to go from here, both of which lead to the same place. Talk to the team and they'll guide you in the direction you need to go.

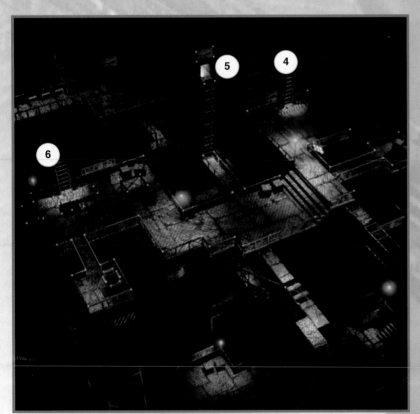

SMOGGER

Area—Reactor2					
LVL	HP	MP	EXP	GIL	AP
8	90	0	32	60	3

❧	❄	⚡	⛰	✖	G	≈	@	✝

Slp	Ret	Con	Sil	Slw	Drk	Trsfr	Stp
Bsk	Psn	Par	Stn	SS	Man	Dth	Imp

MORPH	STEAL	ATTACKS
n/a	n/a	Smog, Hit, Poison

PROTO MACHINEGUN

Area—Reactor2					
LVL	HP	MP	EXP	GIL	AP
4	100	0	16	15	2

❧	❄	⚡	⛰	✖	G	≈	@	✝

Slp	Ret	Con	Sil	Slw	Drk	Trsfr	Stp
Bsk	Psn	Par	Stn	SS	Man	Dth	Imp

MORPH	STEAL	ATTACKS
n/a	n/a	Machine Gun

BLOOD TASTE

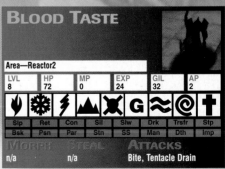

Area—Reactor2					
LVL	HP	MP	EXP	GIL	AP
8	72	0	24	32	2

❧	❄	⚡	⛰	✖	G	≈	@	✝

Slp	Ret	Con	Sil	Slw	Drk	Trsfr	Stp
Bsk	Psn	Par	Stn	SS	Man	Dth	Imp

MORPH	STEAL	ATTACKS
n/a	n/a	Bite, Tentacle Drain

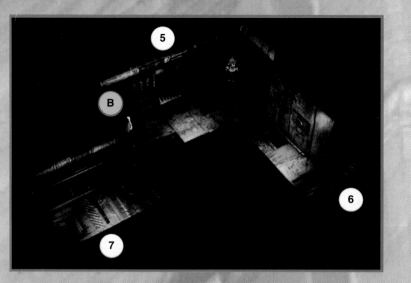

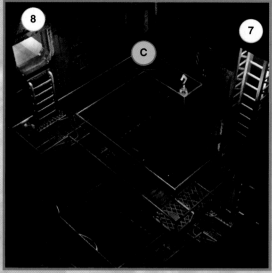

TIP: Make sure you save your game before entering the actual reactor.

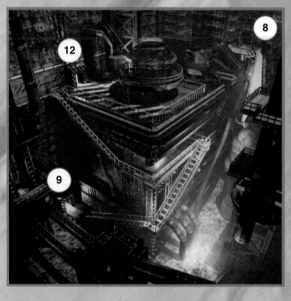

Are things looking familiar? Well, they should be. Use the slide to get down and then head to the reactor core (the path is the same as the first reactor). Just in front of the reactor, Cloud has a flashback of Tifa mourning for her father and swearing to get even with the culprit, Sephiroth. Cloud quickly recovers and sets off the bomb without incident. There's no time limit this time, but the team still needs to quickly head for the exit. You can't go up the slide this time. Instead, you must follow the same path you used to exit the first reactor.

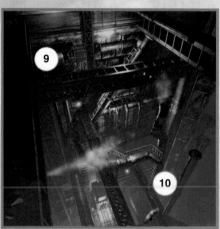

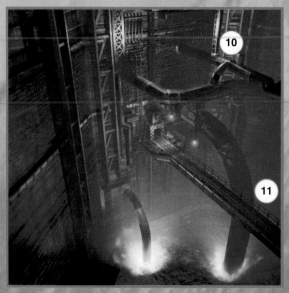

After the elevator, enter the control room **(D)**. To open the security door, the team must press all six switches at once.

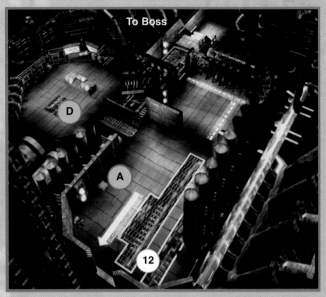

 TIP: This is actually an easy task. All you need to do is count to three and then tap the ● button. Make sure you save the game, and then spend some time building up Cloud's Limit Break before moving on.

The team is cut off by Shinra SOLDIERS on the next screen. President Shinra makes an appearance here—but it's a trap! Before the team can react, the President hops into a chopper for his escape and introduces his latest invention: Air Buster, a techno-soldier!

Boss: Air Buster

Although Air Buster is surrounded, it's still a formidable opponent. Using Limit Break attacks against its back results in a quick fight. In fact, the combined power of Cloud and Barret's Limit Breaks can take down Air Buster in a single turn.

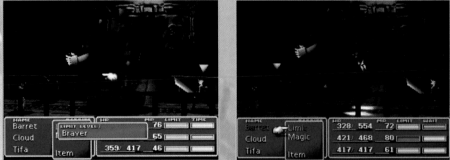

 TIP: Your attacks will be much more effective when you hit Air Buster in the back because it turns and faces its attacker. You'll have much better luck if you can catch it looking the other way.

If you don't have your Limit Breaks built up, use normal attacks against its back and use **Bolt** as much as possible.

WARNING! Watch out for Air Buster's Big Bomber and Counterattack: Rear Gun attacks. Both are surprisingly powerful.

When you defeat the boss, you're rewarded with a Titan Bangle.

As a dramatic finish, when Air Buster is defeated it explodes, leaving Cloud hanging from a jagged piece of metal. There's nothing the team can do for Cloud now. When the reactor explodes, Cloud plummets to the slums below.

THE FLOWER GIRL

The mysterious voice that has haunted Cloud slowly brings him back to consciousness. When he awakens, he finds himself in a bed of flowers located in what appears to be a dilapidated church. The Flower Girl, whom he met earlier, is looking over him. Here, Cloud gets formally introduced to Aeris. He agrees to be her bodyguard—and just in time, too!

Reno of the Turks walks into the church, intent on kidnapping Aeris. As the chase begins, exit through the back of the church and race up the stairs. Aeris will follow Cloud, but is soon cut off by the Shinra soldiers and their trusty machine guns. She falls to the floor below and the soldiers move to intercept. When this occurs, you're given the chance to have Aeris "fight," "run," or "hold on a minute." Choose to have her "wait," and then run up to the next level until you see four barrels, three of which you can use to help Aeris. She will get attacked three times. Push the barrels marked **A**, **B**, and **C** on the map in that order. This will eliminate the threat and Aeris won't be forced to fight alone.

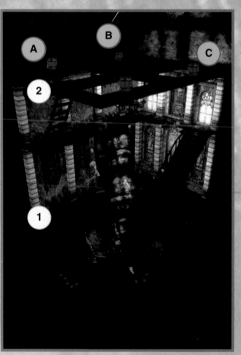

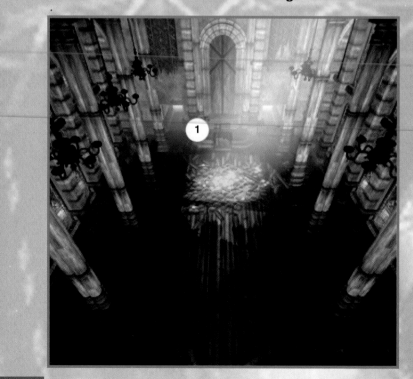

When Aeris is finally safe, quickly escape through the hole in the roof. At this point, she explains Shinra's repeated attempts to kidnap her. After clearing the piles of refuse, Aeris will point the way to her house.

To Sector 5

ITEMS:
5 Gil **(A)**, Ether **(B)**, "Cover" Materia **(C)**, Poison, Phoenix Down

WEAPON SHOP
ITEM	COST
Titan Bangle	280 Gil
Grenande	80 Gil

ITEM SHOP
ITEM	COST
Potion	50 Gil
Phoenix Down	300 Gil
Antidote	80 Gil
Tent	500 Gil

MATERIA SHOP
ITEM	COST
Fire	600 Gil
Ice	600 Gil
Lightning	600 Gil
Restore	750 Gil

WHOLE EATER

Area—Slums					
LVL	HP	MP	EXP	GIL	AP
9	72	0	24	70	2

Slp	Ret	Con	Sil	Slw	Drk	Trsfr	Stp
Bsk	Psn	Par	Stn	SS	Man	Dth	Imp

MORPH	STEAL	ATTACKS
Potion	Potion	Sickle

HEDGEHOG PIE

Area—Church					
LVL	HP	MP	EXP	GIL	AP
6	40	52	6	40	52

Slp	Ret	Con	Sil	Slw	Drk	Trsfr	Stp
Bsk	Psn	Par	Stn	SS	Man	Dth	Imp

MORPH	STEAL	ATTACKS
n/a	n/a	Fire, Charge

VICE

Area—Slums					
LVL	HP	MP	EXP	GIL	AP
7	68	0	24	80	3

Slp	Ret	Con	Sil	Slw	Drk	Trsfr	Stp
Bsk	Psn	Par	Stn	SS	Man	Dth	Imp

MORPH	STEAL	ATTACKS
Potion	Speed Drink	Hit

SECTOR 5 SLUMS

A small distance from the church is the Sector 5 Slums. You can only proceed north for now, because two men have blocked the path to Sector 6. Talk to everyone in the town before moving on to Aeris' house.

To Aeris' Church / Midgar Gate

To Sector 6

NOTE: There's a sleeping boy in the house on the east side of the slums. He mentions a secret drawer in his dresser that contains 5 Gil. Whatever you do, *DON'T TAKE HIS MONEY*! Five Gil is nothing to a warrior like you.

"5 gil."
Take it
Leave it

AERIS' HOUSE

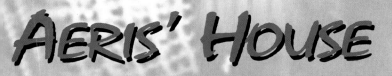

Before you go inside Aeris' house, check the garden for an **Ether** and a **"Cover" Materia**. This is also a good time to save your game.

Inside the house you'll meet Aeris' stepmother, who asks you to leave in the middle of the night without Aeris. Go upstairs to the empty bedroom and rest until that time. Once again, Cloud is taken away by the mysterious voices that haunt him and you see a moment from Cloud's past.

"Would you please leave here, tonight? Without telling Aeris."

When Cloud wakes up, it's time to leave. Aeris hasn't fallen asleep yet, so you need to be quiet. Grab the care package next to the door and slowly walk—don't run—towards the outside edge of the room, sticking close to the railing. When you get outside, head for Sector 6 alone. However, Aeris is one step ahead of you. Guess you'll have to take her along after all!

SECTOR 6

Sector 6 is quite a wreckage, so follow the map until you reach a small playground. Cloud and Aeris take a break, but before long the gate to Sector 7 opens and a Chocobo-drawn cart appears. Is that Tifa in the back of that cart? Follow it to the fabled town of Wall Market.

To Wall Market

To Sector 5

41

WALL MARKET

ITEMS:
Ether **(A)**, Hyper **(B)**,
Phoenix Down **(C)**

REST (E)

Inn	10

ITEM SHOP #1 (A)

Nothing

ITEM SHOP #2 (B)

ITEM	COST
Potion	50
Phoenix Down	300
Antidote	80
Echo Screen	100
Eye Drop	50
Hyper	100
Tranquilizer	100
Hi-Potion	300
Tent	500

WEAPON SHOP (C)

ITEM	COST
Mythril Rod	370
Metal Knuckle	320
Assault Gun	350
Titan Bangle	280
Mythril Armlet	350

MATERIA SHOP (D)

ITEM	COST
Fire	600
Ice	600
Lightning	600
Restore	750
Cover	1000

Wow! Now THIS is a town, but where's Tifa? Looks like you've got some exploring to do. Checking around the southern portion of Wall Market reveals that Tifa's been taken to Don Corneo's Mansion **(F)** for an "interview" with the boss. Why would Tifa want a job at the Honey Bee Inn **(G)**? Well, there's only one way to find out. You'll need to get into Corneo's Mansion and it won't be easy because he has a strict policy of *girls only*. What to do? If Cloud dresses up as a woman, he might be able to sneak into Corneo's Mansion unnoticed. But if Cloud is going to try to fool Don Corneo, he'll need a dress and wig to disguise his manly physique.

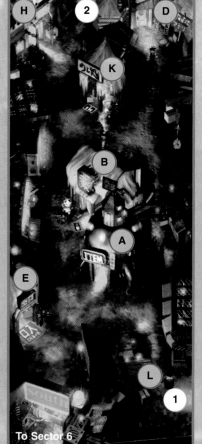

To Sector 6

NOTE: There are several items Cloud can pick up to alter his appearance. However, he only needs to collect a dress and wig to actually get into the Mansion.

TIP: If you want the full Wall Market experience, you'll need to collect *all* of the available items.

Cloud's first stop is the Dress Shop **(H)**. This doesn't start out well, because it appears that the owner can't make any dresses because he's in a bit of a slump. Now he spends his days drinking in a local bar. If you can talk him into returning to work, he may be willing to make Cloud a dress. Go

"Look, the Don's not into men. So don't let me catch you around here again..."

CORNEO'S LACKEY

Area—Brothel							
LVL	HP 42	MP 0	EXP 8	GIL 10	AP 0		

Slp	Ret	Con	Sil	Slw	Drk	Trsfr	Stp
Bsk	Psn	Par	Stn	SS	Man	Dth	Imp.

MORPH	STEAL	ATTACKS
n/a	n/a	Stab, Machine Gun

to the tavern (I) and speak to the owner of the Dress Shop. He'll be happy to make the dress, but you must decide on the type of dress. Here are your choices:

- Something that feels clean or soft

- Something shiny or something that shimmers

Choose "soft" and "shimmers" to get the best dress, which is the Silk Dress. Choosing "clean" and "shiny/shimmers" gets you the Cotton Dress and choosing "soft" and "shiny" gets you the Satin Dress. Now that you have the dress, it's time to find a wig. The shop owner thinks you can get one from the gym (J). Huh?

It looks like Big Bro, the gym's owner, is into cross-dressing and must spend a lot of time at the Dress Shop. He says he'll give you a wig, but first Cloud must defeat one of the muscle-heads in a "squat" contest. To perform the squats, just tap the ■ X ● buttons in order. Don't press the next button until the previous movement has been completed. With a little practice, you can easily find the proper timing. If you mess up during the contest, Cloud will scratch his head and you'll have to start over by pressing the ■ button. You'll get a Blonde Wig when you win the contest. But there's no need to worry if you don't win: You get a Dyed Wig for a tie and a plain Wig that's been stored in a slightly unsanitary spot should you happen to lose.

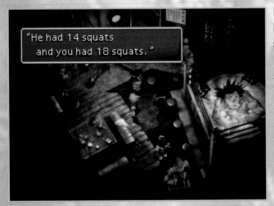

Now it's decision time. You have two options: You can simply proceed to Corneo's Mansion, or you can spend some more time collecting items to make Cloud's disguise more convincing. Why should you continue to collect items? Cloud may look *somewhat* like a woman with his disguise on, but he's not the most attractive woman.

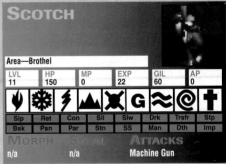

Cloud would look much more appealing to Corneo and his cronies if he had some items like Cologne, Underwear, Make-up, and a Tiara.

 NOTE: If you want to collect the extra items, keep reading. If not, return to the Dress Shop and Cloud will try on his new outfit. Then you can skip ahead to Corneo's Mansion.

First, Cloud needs some Cologne. Remember the guy in the bar doing the "pee-pee dance?" Talk to him and then talk to the lady who seems to be hogging the bathroom. Looks like she needs some medicine, but not any medicine will do. She needs a special medicine that can only be obtained with a pharmacy coupon. You're in luck—it just so happens that the local restaurant (K) is giving out coupons with the purchase of a meal. Go to the restaurant and order any meal, but just make sure you have the money to pay for it.

After you get the coupon, go to the local pharmacy **(B)** and you'll be given a choice of the following medicines: *Disinfectant*, *Deodorant*, or *Digestive*. Select the Digestive and head back to the bar. Hand over the Digestive to the lady in the bathroom and you'll receive the Sexy Cologne. If you choose the Disinfectant, you'll receive Cologne, and if you choose the Deodorant, you'll receive the Flower Cologne.

Now head to the Materia Shop **(D)** and speak to the man behind the counter. He needs a favor and if you're willing to spend the night at the Inn **(E)** and make a small purchase from their vending machine, he'll compensate you for your time. Head to the Inn, but make sure you have *at least* 210 Gil. Pay the 10 Gil for a night's stay and Cloud will go to the vending machine in the middle of the night. Inside the vending machine are three items for sale. Purchase the most expensive item (at 200 Gil) and then return to the Materia Shop in the morning. The owner appreciates the help and gives you a Diamond Tiara for your troubles. You'll receive a Glass Tiara if you spend 50 Gil and a Ruby Tiara if you spend 100 Gil. Now there's only one more item to go!

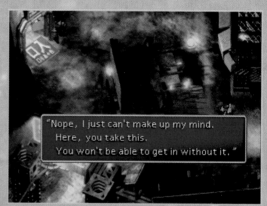

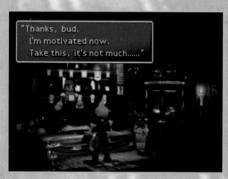

It's time to check out the Honey Bee Inn. Just west of the Honey Bee Inn, there's a guy walking around in circles who just happens to have a Member's Card **(L)**. If you want to get inside, you'll need that card. Fortunately, he turns over his card. Now that you have the card, speak to the man at the entrance and he'll let you inside.

Inside the Inn, you must choose a room for your "activities," but only the two rooms on the left are open.

TIP: You can spy on the two occupied rooms. While looking through the keyhole, you can change your view by pressing left or right on the directional pad. This enables you to keep up with all the action inside.

When you're ready, enter the room of your choice. Regardless of the room you select, you'll walk away with an undergarment of some sort. (Bikini Briefs if you choose the Group Room; Lingerie if you choose the &$#% Room). Before leaving the club, visit the Honey Bees' dressing room and they'll be glad to apply some make-up to Cloud's face.

That's it! Cloud should have everything he needs to complete his disguise. So return to the Dress Shop and try on everything. It's now time to make a return visit to Don Corneo's Mansion.

Upon entering the mansion, you're given a chance to search for Tifa. To find her, enter the open door on the second level. You'll find her alone at the bottom of the stairs. Tifa came here to find out why the Don's goons were casing her bar and is patiently awaiting a chance to speak to the Don. When Don Corneo's guard yells down the stairs, head back up into the Don's chambers. It's in these chambers that Don decides who gets a "fun-filled" evening and who gets thrown to the dogs.

If you collected the Silk Dress, Blonde Wig, Sexy Cologne, Diamond Tiara, an undergarment, and make-up, Corneo will pick Cloud as his lucky guest.

NOTE: Other combinations of items mentioned previously may cause the Don to choose either Aeris or Tifa.

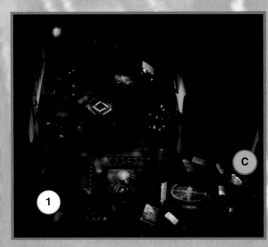

When Cloud is chosen, he goes straight to the Don's bedroom. If he's not chosen, you'll have to deal with Corneo's thugs first.

Cloud is then taken to a side room as a reward to Corneo's faithful few. Run around as much as you like, but the guy guarding the door won't let you leave. You'll need to speak to Scotch and reveal your true gender if you ever want to leave this place. Of course, revealing this instigates a brawl that Cloud *must* win on his own. Scotch is a bit tougher than the other goons, but both fights are really easy. After you escape, either Tifa joins you in the hall or you'll have to retrieve Aeris from the basement before heading for Corneo's bedroom. (This scenario depends upon who was chosen.)

If Cloud gets chosen as Corneo's "friend" for the night, you'll start in his bedroom and get to decide for yourself whether or not you play along with his misguided come-ons.

Eventually, Tifa and Aeris break into the room and together the team forces the Don to spill his guts.

It seems Heidegger of Shinra hired the Don to investigate Barret and locate AVALANCHE'S hideout. Shinra planned on exterminating AVALANCHE after infiltrating the hideout by destroying the Sector 7 support. This would cause the plate above to crush the entire sector, which would cause some severe trouble! Before the team can leave, Don Corneo turns the tables and casts them out of his mansion by using a trap door.

NOTE: Make sure you check behind Corneo's bed to find a well-hidden **Hyper**.

THE SEWERS AND THE TRAIN GRAVEYARD

ITEMS:

Potion **(A)**, "Steal" Materia **(B)**, Hi-Potion **(C)**, Echo Screen **(D)**, Ether **(E)**

SAHAGIN
Shell can protect from physical attacks

Area—Sewers				
LVL 10	HP 150	MP 0	EXP 30	GIL 89	AP 3

Slp	Ret	Con	Sil	Slw	Drk	Trsfr	Stp
Bsk	Psn	Par	Stn	SS	Man	Dth	Imp

MORPH	STEAL	ATTACKS
n/a	Hyper	Water Gun, Trident

CEASAR
Area—Sewers

Area—Sewers				
LVL 8	HP 120	MP 0	EXP 23	GIL 55	AP 2

Slp	Ret	Con	Sil	Slw	Drk	Trsfr	Stp
Bsk	Psn	Par	Stn	SS	Man	Dth	Imp

MORPH	STEAL	ATTACKS
n/a	Tranquilizer	Ram, Bubble

GHOST
Temporarily becomes invisible after being hit

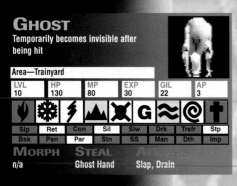

Area—Trainyard				
LVL 10	HP 130	MP 80	EXP 30	GIL 22	AP 3

Slp	Ret	Con	Sil	Slw	Drk	Trsfr	Stp
Bsk	Psn	Par	Stn	SS	Man	Dth	Imp

MORPH	STEAL	ATTACKS
n/a	Ghost Hand	Slap, Drain

DEENGLOW

Area—Trainyard				
LVL 10	HP 120	MP 72	EXP 35	GIL 70	AP 4

Slp	Ret	Con	Sil	Slw	Drk	Trsfr	Stp
Bsk	Psn	Par	Stn	SS	Man	Dth	Imp

MORPH	STEAL	ATTACKS
n/a	Ether	Slash, Demi, Ice

Corneo's trap door deposits the team deep in the sewer system below his mansion. Take a moment to equip Tifa with any new weapons and armor you may have purchased, and give Cloud a Materia crystal or two. Also, consider equipping Aeris with the **"Fire"** Materia before proceeding. However, before the team can fully recover, they get attacked by the Don's hero disposal system, the giant creature known as "Aps."

BOSS FIGHT: APS

Aps is a strange creature. Its strongest attack is the Sewer Tsunami, a water-based attack that causes damage to your entire party. What's interesting about this attack is that it also causes damage to Aps as well. You'll notice that the wave comes from two directions. When coming from behind Aps, it causes more damage to Aps than it causes to the team. If it starts behind the team, it inlficts considerably more damage to the team than to Aps. Regardless, you may find that Aps causes more damage to itself than you can cause to it.

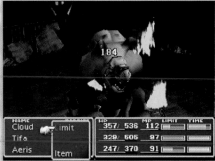

Aps has a definite weakness to Fire, so have your characters equipped with the **"Fire"** Materia. It's best to equip it with Aeris, because you can concentrate on casting the **Fire** spell and healing the party. The other two party members should use normal attacks, magic, and Limit Breaks to knock Aps into submission. If Cloud has his Cross-Slash Limit Break, you'll find Aps much easier to defeat. This Limit Break will often paralyze Aps for most of the fight.

With Aps defeated, the party is ready to make the long trek through the sewers to the Sector 7 Slums. With any luck, they can get there in time to prevent Shinra from destroying the support column.

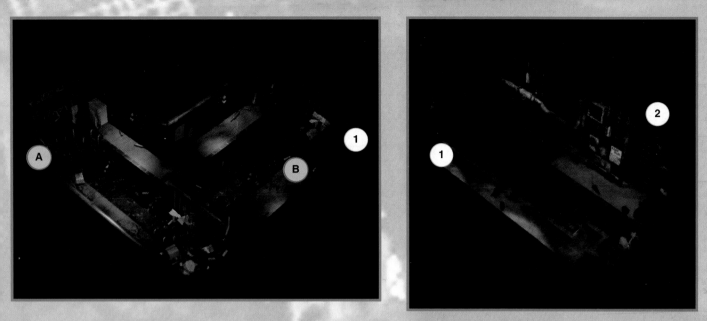

NOTE: There are a few items to pick up in the sewers. The best of which is the **"Steal" Materia (B)**. Equip it immediately, most likely using Tifa. Start filling your inventory with lots of stolen goods.

NOTE: The team may be weak after fighting Aps. You should heal everyone before exploring the sewers.

When you exit the sewers, you'll appear deep inside the Train Graveyard. There are some particularly nasty beasts roaming around here, so save before you attempt to venture through the rusted wreckage.

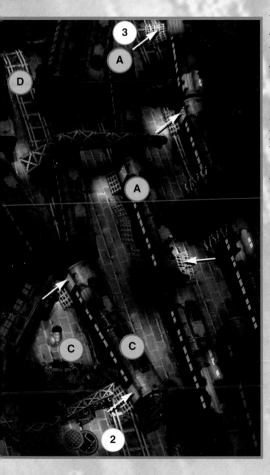

You basically have two ways to get around the train cars: You can either go through the cars or crawl over them. Look for girders and gratings, because they serve as steps into or onto the cars. If you can't get down from a train car, look for an entrance. If you can't go through, look for a way over.

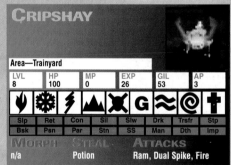

GRIPSHAY							
Area—Trainyard							
LVL 8	HP 100	MP 0	EXP 26		GIL 53	AP 3	
Slp	Ret	Con	Sil	Slw	Drk	Trsfr	Stp
Bsk	Psn	Par	Stn	SS	Man	Dth	Imp
MORPH	**STEAL**		**ATTACKS**				
n/a	Potion		Ram, Dual Spike, Fire				

NOTE: Beware of a creature named Eligor. You can steal a Striking Staff from it, which is Aeris' strongest weapon at this point in the game.

To Sector 7

G

C

F

E

A

3

NOTE: There are lots of items awaiting those willing to search them out, but not all of them are obvious. Make sure you collect the items concealed in the oil barrels that are spread around the Train Graveyard.

A large pile of dirt blocks the exit. Cloud can't go over it or through it, so you'll need to create your own path to reach the exit. Hopping into the first train engine **(F)** causes it to push one of the boxcars to the side. Now hop into the second engine **(G)** and Cloud will move it between two more boxcars. In effect, this creates a bridge to the Sector 7 Station.

ITEM SHOP

Old Man (A)

ITEM	COST
Potion	50g
Phoenix Down	300g
Antidote	80g
Grenade	80g
Hyper	100g
Tranquilizer	100g
Tent	500g

1ST RAY

Area—Reactor

LVL	HP	MP	EXP	GIL	AP
4	18	0	12	5	1

Slp	Ret	Con	Sil	Slw	Drk	Trsfr	Stp
Bsk	Psn	Par	Stn	SS	Man	Dth	Imp

MORPH	STEAL	ATTACKS
n/a	n/a	Laser

THE PILLAR ASSAULT

The team reaches the pillar just in time to fight Shinra. However, the attack is already well under way and Barret is hurting. Aeris briefly leaves the party and goes to make sure Marlene is safe. With Aeris occupied, that means Tifa and Cloud have to quickly scale the tower before Barret succumbs to Shinra's forces. Make sure you save your game before you head out.

1

To Sector 7 Slums

To Train Graveyard

Barret
"Tifa! Cloud!
  You came!"

Climbing the tower isn't very difficult, but during this adventure you'll find Biggs and Jessie seriously wounded and completely removed from the fight. When you reach the top, talk to Barret **(B)** and you'll get a chance to equip before taking on Shinra's forces. Give Barret any new armor you may have picked up, and give him some of the Materia Aeris was using before she left the party. When you're ready, back out of the Menu and get ready to rumble!

It's time again to meet Reno of the Turks. With a press of a button, Reno activates the pillars' self-destruct system. The team might have a chance to stop the bomb, but Reno's not about to let that happen.

Boss Fight: Reno of the Turks

As long as you know what you're doing, this fight shouldn't be too difficult. Reno's best attacks are his Electro-mag Rod and Pyramid. The Electro-mag Rod causes a fair amount of damage and can temporarily stun a victim. If one of your characters gets stunned, there isn't much you can do except heal that person until he/she recovers.

The Pyramid encases Reno's victim in a golden pyramid that keeps the affected player from participating in the battle. It's very similar to the "stone" effect, but you can destroy the pyramid by having one of your unaffected characters target it.

Use your Limit Breaks when they're available and keep your HPs up. If a character gets trapped in a Pyramid, free him/her immediately. **Fire** and **Ice** are also effective against Reno and typically cause twice as much damage as a normal attack. Reno will hold out for quite a while, but he'll bail out when his HP are nearly depleted.

With this fight out of the way, the team attempts to stop the bomb, but to no avail. Tseng of the Turks takes a moment to taunt the team from the safety of his helicopter, and shows off his latest catch—Aeris. There's *nothing* the team can do now but safely escape the blast.

49

AFTERMATH

ITEMS:
"Sense" Materia **(A)**
Turbo Ether

After a daring escape, the team comes to rest in the now ruined playground adjacent to what was Sector 7. Before the team can move on, Barret takes a moment to express his rage over Shinra's actions. Cloud also makes it clear that he wants to know more about the Ancients, which triggers yet another encounter with the mystery voice inside his head. When he recovers, return to Aeris' house in Sector 6 and check on Marlene's safety.

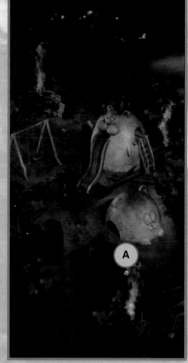

NOTE: There's a **"Sense" Materia** lying on the ground inside the playground. At first you can't collect it, but you can go back for it as soon as Tifa and Barret rejoin the group.

At Aeris' house, you learn more about Aeris and the Ancients. Elmyra, Aeris' stepmother, has plenty to tell the team. Before you leave Aeris' house, take a moment to rest upstairs. When you're ready to leave, the rest of the team will join you in your trip to the Wall Market. Make sure you save before you go.

NOTE: As you pass back through the Sector 5 Slums, stop at the house on the right side of town. The boy upstairs is now awake and will give you a **Turbo Ether**— that is, if you didn't steal his 5 Gil during an earlier visit.

Wall Market has changed a bit since you visited Don Corneo's mansion. The Materia Shop is now open, the Weapon Shop owner's pile of garbage is larger, and you now have a reputation thanks to your stunt at Corneo's. You can tour Corneo's mansion now if you want, but he is nowhere to be found. Kotch, one of Corneo's henchmen, is tied up in the basement. You can release him if you want.

When you first enter the north part of Wall Market, you'll see some kids run off to the right. Follow them and you'll find your way up to Shinra's Headquarters. But before you go to the "Golden Shiny Wire of Hope," you'll need some supplies from the Weapon Shop.

"You goin' up to the plate? You better have a Battery."

The owner has a set of Zinc Batteries you'll need in order to make it up to the top of the plate and he's willing to part with them for a mere 300 Gil.

NOTE: If you don't have the money, get some so you can purchase the batteries. You *must* purchase them in order to reach Shinra's HQ!

GOING UP?

Now it's time for some climbing. Head up the wire and you'll find a huge maze of broken junk. The maze is tricky, so refer to the maps for guidance.

There are sockets scattered throughout the maze. You need to place a Zinc Battery in each socket or you won't be able to get past the various obstacles along the path.

Place a battery in the first socket **(B)** to activate the propeller just ahead. The battery loses its power quickly, but the propeller becomes a bridge to the next pile of junk.

ITEMS:
Ether **(A)**

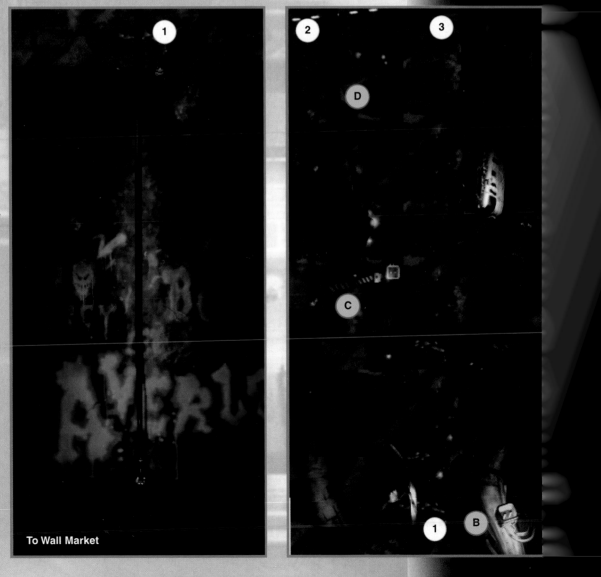

To Wall Market

You must place the second battery in the socket that's connected to the barricade **(C)**. Doing so moves the barricade and creates yet another bridge.

The swing bar **(D)** can be tricky. Press the ● button just before the bar reaches the left side. Don't worry—if you miss, you can try it again.

Placing the third battery **(F)** opens a chest that contains an **Ether**. Placing the last battery isn't necessary, but you have it so you might as well use it. Next stop, Shinra's HQ!

To Shinra HQ

A

F

2

3

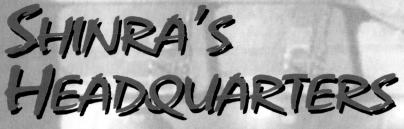

SHINRA'S HEADQUARTERS

Save your game before you do anything. As you start out, you're given a choice as to which path you can take. You can either take the easy, indirect path up the stairs (1) to the side, or you can use the front door (2) and blast through with guns blazing.

NOTE: The paths are *very* different, but both lead to the same place. Check out the walkthrough for your chosen path (*The Stairs* or *In the Front*), and we'll see you on the 59th floor.

GRENADE COMBATANT

Area—Shinra Tower

LVL	HP	MP	EXP	GIL	AP
10	130	0	42	72	4

Slp	Ret	Con	Sil	Slw	Drk	Trsfr	Stp
Bsk	Psn	Par	Stn	SS	Man	Dth	Imp

MORPH	STEAL	ATTACKS
n/a	Tranquilizer	Gun, Hand Grenade

I'm Taking the Stairs!

Prepare for the walk of your life. There are no enemies on the stairs, however, there are nine sets of stairs to climb. It's worth exploring each set of stairs at least once just to see the team's comments.

TIP: There's an **Elixir** on the fifth set of stairs, your only prize for taking the long way.

53

I'm going in the front!

You want a fight, you got a fight! Using the front entrance causes everyone to go running—everyone except a small group of Grenade Combatants. Unlike the rather uneventful stairs path, you'll have to deal with random encounters as you explore the area.

There's an Item Shop on the second tier where you can pick up some supplies and watch a video of the latest in the Shinra Motors line. The

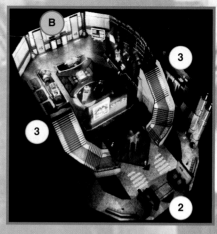

two chests in the back of the store can't be opened...yet. When you're ready, hop on the elevator **(B)** at the back and head for the 59th floor.

The elevator ride isn't a smooth one. An alarm sounds during the trip, which forces the team to fight a series of battles before actually reaching their destination. Don't worry, though, none of the battles are too difficult.

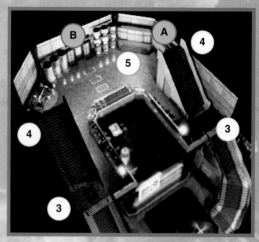

The 59th Floor

There isn't much to do on this floor except collect the Keycard for the 60th floor. To get the Keycard, you must defeat the group of guards near the stairs (the Keycard appears after the battle is won). This Keycard grants you access to the glass elevator **(A)**, which you can use to reach the 60th floor.

NOTE: From this point forward, you can use the glass elevator to reach the next floor if you have the proper Keycard. You can also use it to return to the lobby and rest.

MIGHTY GRUNT

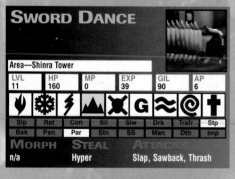

Area—Shinra Tower

LVL	HP	MP	EXP	GIL	AP
12	230	0	50	98	5

Slp	Ret	Con	Sil	Slw	Drk	Trsfr	Stp
Bsk	Psn	Par	Stn	SS	Man	Dth	Imp

MORPH	STEAL	ATTACKS
n/a	Grenade	Gun, Double Gun, Rollerspin

SWORD DANCE

Area—Shinra Tower

LVL	HP	MP	EXP	GIL	AP
11	160	0	39	90	6

Slp	Ret	Con	Sil	Slw	Drk	Trsfr	Stp
Bsk	Psn	Par	Stn	SS	Man	Dth	Imp

MORPH	STEAL	ATTACKS
n/a	Hyper	Slap, Sawback, Thrash

HAMMER BLASTER

Area—Shinra Tower

LVL	HP	MP	EXP	GIL	AP
12	210	0	43	80	5

Slp	Ret	Con	Sil	Slw	Drk	Trsfr	Stp
Bsk	Psn	Par	Stn	SS	Man	Dth	Imp

MORPH	STEAL	ATTACKS
n/a	Echo Screen	Pound

The 60th Floor

This floor is heavily guarded and there's no way past the goons blocking your path. Well, almost no way. If you run into the room to the left **(A)**, you'll break out on your own. You need to access the stairs on the opposite side, but there are four guards ready to stop you. You can get past them, but you must be sneaky.

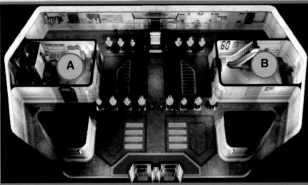

TIP: Using the statues as cover, move from statue to statue whenever the guards turn to walk. The guards follow a definite pattern and there are certain times when it's best to move.

After crossing a section, call over Tifa and Barret. They can't see the guards, so you'll need to tell them the coast is clear. If you mess up, you are forced to fight and then start all over again. When you reach the other side, use the stairs **(B)** to reach the next floor.

The 61st Floor

Your first task is to find a guy **(A)** wandering around near the stairs. This guy gives you the chance to talk about Aeris. You can pry for more information if you want, but it's better to keep your cool. Doing so gets you the Keycard for the 62nd floor. There's nothing else to do here, so move onward.

The 62nd Floor

The first thing you should do is visit Mayor Domino **(A)**. He presents you with the challenge of figuring out the password. Tell him the password and he'll give you his Keycard for the 63rd, 64th, and 65th floors. Hart **(B)** is willing to sell you hints, but each one is offered at a more outrageous price than the last. It's a rip-off, but it's the easiest way to ensure you get the password on the first guess, plus you get to collect the "Elemental" Materia. Of course, you could skip paying Hart and read the tips below at no extra charge.

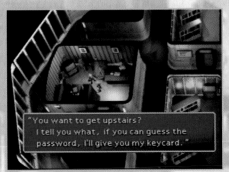

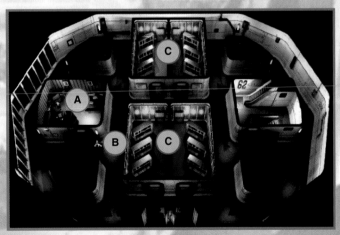

55

*16 Modern history of
Midgar space program vol. 1*

Hart's Tips

There are four research libraries **(C)** on this floor for four different sections of Shinra, Inc. Parts of the password are hidden in each of the libraries. Pay close attention to the files in each room. The name of each library is written on the plaque outside the door. There is one file in each library mixed in from another library. Look carefully at the numbers on each file—there's a number at the beginning of each filename. Of course, there are even numbers on the files that don't belong in that library. You need to match the number with the letters in the title of the file. If the file starts with a 4, then check the fourth letter.

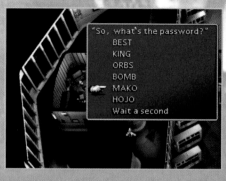

Find all four misplaced files and you'll get the four letters that comprise the password. Now it's just a simple word scramble to figure out the correct answer. The password for each game is different, so you'll need to figure this one out on your own!

The 63rd Floor

This floor is optional, but you can collect some nice items if you're willing to work for them. Visit the computer **(A)** to gain access to three security doors. But there's a problem: You can't collect the three Item Coupons by just opening three doors. To get the coupons, you need to open a couple of doors and then use the duct work to move between rooms. If you mess up, you can reset the doors at the computer only if you've already traded a coupon.

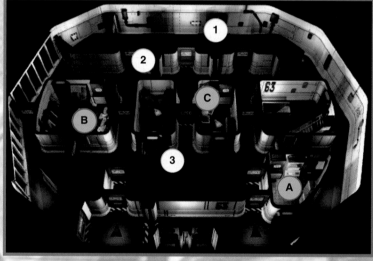

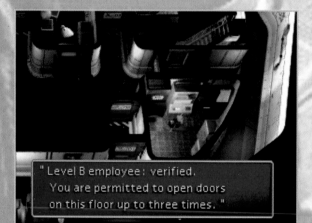

*"Level B employee: verified.
You are permitted to open doors
on this floor up to three times."*

Here's what you need to do: First open Security Doors 1 and 2 (see map). This enables you to enter a room and grab your first Item Coupon **(B)**. Now enter the duct work and crawl to the middle room where the second Item Coupon is located **(C)**. Exit the room and open Security Door 3 to find the last of the Item Coupons. With all three coupons in your possession, return to the computer and trade them in for a **Star Pendant, Four Slot,** and an **"All" Materia.**

56

The 64th Floor

The 64th Floor is a huge recreational area. If you want, you can rest and save your game before moving on (**A**). Visit the locker room and you can steal a couple of items from some unlocked lockers (**B**). There's a **Megaphone** in the back row of lockers, but Cloud won't take something he can't use. Oh well...maybe later.

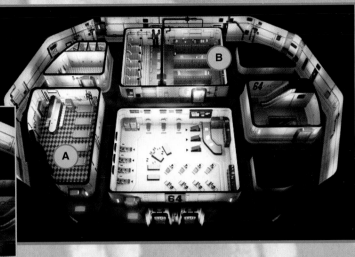

The 65th Floor

There's a huge model of Midgar in the center of this room, but several pieces are missing. The locked chests located in the surrounding rooms each contain a piece of the model; however, you can only collect one piece at a time. Placing a piece in the model unlocks another chest, thus enabling you to get the next piece.

First, grab the piece in Chest A and place it in the spot closest to the door, which unlocks Chest B. Collect that piece and place it in the next spot to the right to unlock the next chest. Continue placing the new pieces in order in a counterclockwise pattern until all five spots have been filled. After placing the fifth piece, the chest in the stairwell unlocks. Inside it is the Keycard for the 66th Floor.

WARNING! There are creatures roaming this floor that you'll need to fight.

57

The 66th Floor

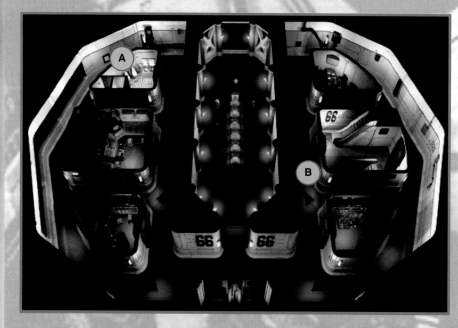

Now it's time for a little spy work. Find the bathroom **(A)**, enter the open stall, and then climb into the duct work that runs over the meeting room in the middle of the floor. From this choice location, you can listen in on the executive meeting below.

You'll learn about Shinra's latest evil doings and the circumstances concerning Aeris' fate. When the meeting is over, back out of the duct work and follow the execs to the stairs **(B)**—it's on to the 67th floor.

The 67th Floor

ITEMS:
Potion (X4) **(A)**
"Enemy-Skill"
Materia **(B)**

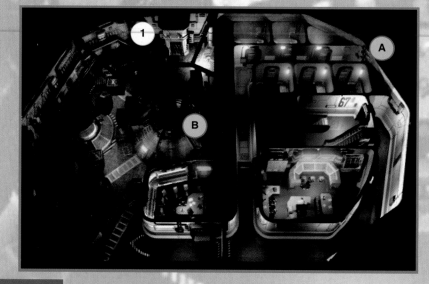

WARNING BOARD

Area—Shinra Tower

LVL	HP	MP	EXP	GIL	AP
12	270	0	38	75	4

Slp	Ret	Con	Sil	Slw	Drk	Trsfr	Stp
Bsk	Psn	Par	Stn	SS	Man	Dth	Imp

MORPH	STEAL	ATTACKS
n/a	n/a	n/a

58

Follow Hojo around the floor and into the stock room **(A)**. When Cloud peers into one of the specimen tanks marked "Jenova," he immediately starts to flip out. When he recovers, head toward the back of the warehouse, where you can save and collect a **"Poison" Materia (B)**. When you're ready, hop on the lift to the 68th floor.

NOTE: If you can find a Moth Slasher or two to fight, you can steal some **Carbon Bangles**, which is a much stronger type of armor. Also, watch for a SOLDIER: 3rd. They're carrying the Hardedge, which is the best weapon for Cloud at this point in the game.

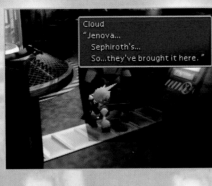

> Cloud
> "Jenova...
> Sephiroth's...
> So...they've brought it here."

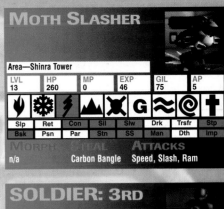

MOTH SLASHER

Area—Shinra Tower

LVL	HP	MP	EXP	GIL	AP
13	260	0	46	75	5

Slp	Ret	Con	Sil	Slw	Drk	Trsfr	Stp
Bsk	Psn	Par	Stn	SS	Man	Dth	Imp

MORPH	STEAL	ATTACKS
n/a	Carbon Bangle	Speed, Slash, Ram

SOLDIER: 3RD

Area—Shinra Tower

LVL	HP	MP	EXP	GIL	AP
13	250	40	54	116	6

Slp	Ret	Con	Sil	Slw	Drk	Trsfr	Stp
Bsk	Psn	Par	Stn	SS	Man	Dth	Imp

MORPH	STEAL
	n/a

The 68th Floor

Hojo is about to begin his next experiment and Aeris is one of the specimens. The team confronts Hojo and frees Aeris, but not before Hojo calls for reinforcements. The "lion-type" specimen, Red XIII, offers his help in defeating Hojo's creation, however, that means you must send one of your characters to the side with Aeris. For now, let Barret stay and send Tifa with Aeris. Also, take a moment to equip Cloud or Barret's armor with the **"Elemental-Poison" Materia** combination. This will help a great deal during the upcoming Boss fight.

> Aeris
> "Cloud, help!"

BOSS FIGHT: SAMPLE: H0512 AND SAMPLE: H0512-OPT

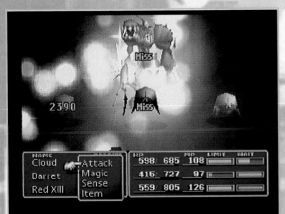

This Boss comes equipped with its own set of henchmen. Normally they wouldn't be much of a problem, but H0512 can reanimate any of its fallen buddies. In effect, this means that regardless of your actions, H0512 will always be in the back rank. Therefore, anyone equipped with a short-range weapon will have trouble causing damage to it. At this point in the game, Barret is the only character with an appropriate long-range weapon.

Focus all of your attention on H0512. If it dies, its friends go with it.

59

BATTLE TIP: Any character who doesn't have a long-range weapon should use spells during the battle, but note that Poison *won't* work in this battle.

Keep an eye on your health—especially those affected by HO512's poison attacks. Defeat the boss and you'll receive a Talisman.

It's time to get out of here. Select your new party and grab the **"Enemy Skill" Materia** that popped into the specimen tank. Hojo's lab assistant is still on the catwalk **(C)**, so stop and harass him to get the Keycard for the 68th floor. Then head for the stairs and walk down to the 66th floor elevators.

Before you go anywhere in the elevator, however, Tseng and Rude cut you off. It's time to pay a visit to President Shinra.

CAUGHT!

The President explains Shinra Corporation's interest in the Ancients, or Cetra. He states that he believes Aeris is the key to the promised land, a land full of Mako Energy. This creates yet another place for Shinra to destroy with its life-sucking Mako Reactors. After the meeting, AVALANCHE is taken to the holding cells on the 67th floor **(A)**.

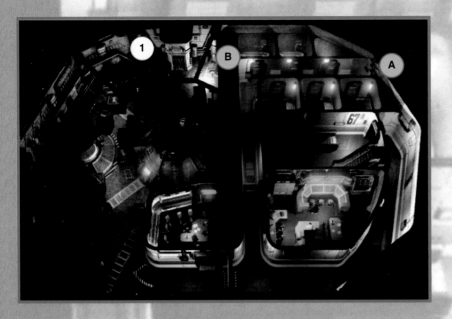

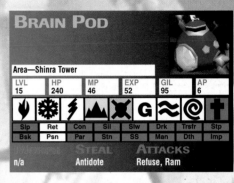

BRAIN POD

Area—Shinra Tower					
LVL 15	HP 240	MP 46	EXP 52	GIL 95	AP 6

🔥	❄	⚡	⛰	✖	G	≈	◎	✝

Slp	Ret	Con	Sil	Slw	Drk	Trsfr	Stp
Bsk	Psn	Par	Stn	SS	Man	Dth	Imp

MORPH	STEAL	ATTACKS
n/a	Antidote	Refuse, Ram

ZENENE

Area—Shinra Tower					
LVL 14	HP 250	MP 93	EXP 58	GIL 60	AP 6

🔥	❄	⚡	⛰	✖	G	≈	◎	✝

Slp	Ret	Con	Sil	Slw	Drk	Trsfr	Stp
Bsk	Psn	Par	Stn	SS	Man	Dth	Imp

MORPH	STEAL	ATTACKS
n/a	Deadly Waste	Ghengana, Tail, Piazzo Shower

While in the cell, approach the door so you can speak to the other characters. When you're finished, take a nap. When you awake from your sleep, you'll notice your cell door is wide open. What the...?

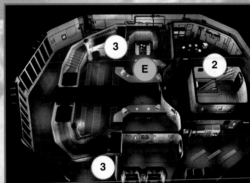

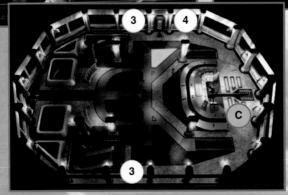

Inspect the downed guard and then wake up Tifa. After getting the cell key from the downed guard, Cloud frees the rest of the team. But something's seriously wrong here: All the lab technicians are dead and Jenova is nowhere to be found **(B)**. To find out what in the world is going on, follow the blood trail to the President's office.

This leads you to the site of President Shinra's body slumped over his desk **(C)**. It looks like Sephiroth is the culprit, but he's nowhere to be found. Soon Rufus, President Shinra's son, lands his helicopter on the roof. Take this opportunity to meet the new leader of Shinra Inc. Cloud will send away the rest of the party when this occurs **(D)**.

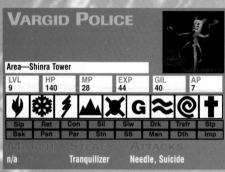

VARGID POLICE

Area—Shinra Tower

LVL	HP	MP	EXP	GIL	AP
9	140	28	44	40	7

Sip	Ret	Con	Sil	Slw	Drk	Trsfr	Stp
Bsk	Psn	Par	Stn	SS	Man	Dth	Imp

MORPH	STEAL	ATTACKS
n/a	Tranquilizer	Needle, Suicide

When Tifa leaves, redistribute your Materia. Give Aeris the **"Lightning"** and **"Restore" Materias** and make sure Red XIII has *at least* one **Spell Materia**.

As soon as you're finished, head for the elevators. As soon as Barret, Aeris, and Red XIII enter the elevator, they get ambushed by Shinra security.

BOSS FIGHT: HUNDRED GUNNER AND HELI GUNNER

The team must fight at long-range against an enemy specially equipped for just such a fight. Barret is the *only* character who can damage the bosses with his normal attack. Everyone else must use magic or Limit Break attacks. The Hundred Gunner is especially weak against Lightning, so cast the Bolt spell as much as possible. After substantially damaging the boss, it transforms and begins charging its super weapon.

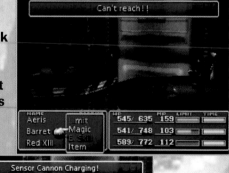

 NOTE: It takes the boss two turns to prepare its cannon, which should give you plenty of time to finish it without taking a hit.

When the Hundred Gunner gets destroyed, a Heli Gunner descends upon the party. This battle is similar to the previous battle. Focus on long-range attacks, Bolt spells, and Limit Breaks. Also, keep a close eye on your HP.

62

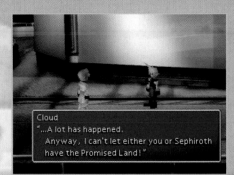

As the Heli Gunner nears death, it transforms and begins unleashing stronger attacks. Keep up your pace and the fight should be over quickly. For defeating both bosses, you're rewarded with a Mythril Armlet.

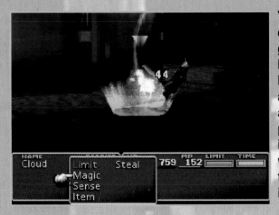

After the boss fight, the scene switches back to Cloud and Rufus. You're given a chance to equip Cloud, which you should accept. Give him a **Restore Materia** and spell Materia combined with the **"All" Materia**. You may also want to place the **"Elemental-Bolt" Materia** combination in his armor. The battle begins whenever you're ready.

Boss Fight: Rufus and Dark Nation

Your first order of business is getting rid of Dark Nation. Its Bolt attacks are powerful and it casts lots of protection spells on itself and Rufus, which tends to make the fight tougher than it has to be.

If you equipped Cloud with the **"Elemental-Lightning" Materia** combination, you won't need to worry about Dark Nation's attacks. Rufus isn't a tough opponent either. Keep your HPs up and use your Limit Breaks when they become available. When Rufus can't take any more, he grabs his chopper and flies away—like father, like son. Survive this battle and you'll receive a Protect Vest and a Guard Source.

With Rufus out of the way, find Tifa **(E)** and then join the rest of the party in the lobby.

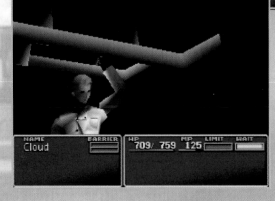

63

THE CHASE

Cloud and the rest of the gang borrow some brand-new Shinra vehicles and hit the highway, but Shinra is in close pursuit. Cloud must defend his friends and their truck by swatting Shinra soldiers off their motorcycles.

However, before you begin, take a moment to equip your party. Make sure you have the **"Lightning" Materia** and several **"Restore" Materia**. You should also equip one character's armor with the **"Elemental-Fire" Materia**

combination. Set your party up in reverse order: Place front row characters in back, and back row characters in front.

During the chase, the Shinra soldiers will attack your truck and cause damage to your friends. You must defend your team and their vehicles by knocking down the Shinra soldiers with your sword. Sounds easy, doesn't it?

There are two types of Shinra Bikers: Red and Orange. The Orange Bikers are decent riders, but they tend to dive right in without thinking, which makes them rather easy to defeat. The Red Bikers pose a much larger threat. Instead of coming towards you, they run from you. Plus, they're always looking for an open spot. The real danger here is that the Red Bikers tend to draw you away from the truck, which enables the other Bikers to cause some damage while your attention is diverted.

BIKE CONTROLS

BUTTON	WHAT IT DOES
D-Pad	Moves bike Forward, Backward, and to the sides
■	Attack to the Left
●	Attack to the Right

BATTLE TIP: Basically, you want to stay close to or behind the truck and hit the enemy bikers as they approach. If one gets past, don't go after him *unless* he attacks the truck. If he backs off (normally only the Red Bikers do), don't chase him—make him come to you.

It's possible to push over enemy Bikers with your hog, but it causes a lot of damage to your bike and it's a much slower process. However, you can also topple enemy Bikers using the "domino effect." If you knock over a Biker in front of another enemy, it causes them to collide. This makes both bikes wreck and makes for an easy kill.

After toppling an enemy bike, you can push it around some as it slides off-screen. Take this opportunity to line up the wrecked bike into the path of oncoming enemy Bikers.

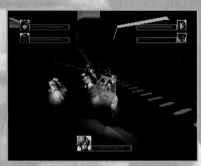

Eventually, the enemy catches up with the party, forcing a fight. Any damage the Shinra motorcycles cause to the party tranfers over to the beginning of the next battle.

Boss Fight: Motor Ball

The boss gets the drop on the party, so it gets to attack first. Don't worry, though, the attack is weak and causes little harm. Immediately start pelting the Boss with everything you have. **Bolt** is extremely effective in this fight and can cause around 250 points of damage with each cast. If a character doesn't have **Bolt**, he or she should use normal attacks and act as the team's medic whenever the need arises.

Speaking of medics, look out for Motor Ball's Rolling Fire attack. Motor Ball only performs this attack while in an upright position. This attack can inflict as much as 250 points of damage to each of your characters, so *keep up your hit points*! When Motor Ball transforms, you really only need to worry about its Twin Burner attack. It only causes about 80-90 points of damage to each character, but it's still a threat. Win the battle and you'll receive a **Star Pendant**.

It's time to leave Midgar and start the search for Sephiroth. You won't be back here for quite a while, so take one last look and then travel to the nearest town, Kalm. Kalm is a small village northeast of Midgar and a good place to begin your search.

NOTE: The game takes a *huge* turn here. Up to this point, the quest has been fairly linear. From now on, you'll have large areas to explore with lots of things to discover. Have fun and take your time when travelling from place to place. After all, half the fun of an RPG is discovery!

65

Kalm: Sephiroth's at Nibelheim

When you reach Kalm, go to the Inn and meet up with the rest of your team on the second floor. Cloud then takes the opportunity to relate his experiences with the infamous Sephiroth.

As the story unfolds, Cloud describes how he and Sephiroth were on their way to investigate a malfunctioning Mako Reactor at Nibelheim, Cloud's hometown. As they approached the reactor, they engaged in combat with a monster created by the Mako Reactor. Cloud was too weak to help in the battle, but Sephiroth easily dispatched of the beast.

When they arrive at Nibelheim, Sephiroth talks about his mother, Jenova (a name that should sound familiar to you). Cloud then gets a chance to wander around and visit everyone.

First, go to Tifa's house and visit her room. You can retrieve a pair of Orthopedic Underwear from her dresser, or you can play a tune on her piano. Pay close attention to the notes, you may want to play the tune again some day:

> Do-Re-Mi-Ti-La
>
> Do-Re-Mi-So-Fa-Do-Re-Do

Next, visit Cloud's house and he'll talk about his mother up until her death. After that, you can visit the rest of the town. For some reason, there seem to be holes in Cloud's memory of his trip to Nibelheim.

In the morning, the team meets up with Tifa, who serves as their guide to the Mako Reactor despite some resistance on Cloud's part. Before you leave, a townsman takes a group photo of Sephiroth, Cloud, and Tifa.

On their way to Mt. Nibel, the team has a close call while crossing a bridge to the Mako Reactor. Cloud must guide the team through the caves and back to the reactor. Along the way, you'll learn more about Materia and the Ancients.

As Sephiroth wonders into the heart of the Mako Reactor, follow him in. Inside, Sephiroth uncovers Hojo's bizarre experiments and begins to realize that he too may have been the result of an experiment. After this strange scenario, Sephiroth vanishes but then later reappears in Shinra Mansion.

Cloud searches the mansion, but cannot find Sephiroth anywhere. In the bedroom, Cloud uncovers a secret door that leads into a dark cavern. At the end of the cavern, Cloud finds Sephiroth in what looks like an old library in which Sephiroth appears to be trying to learn more about Hojo's research.

In the end, what Sephiroth learned drove him mad. He destroyed Nibelheim and slaughtered the villagers, including Cloud's and Tifa's parents. He then returned to the Mako Reactor to free Jenova from its bowels. Tifa was nearly killed as both she and Cloud tried to stop Sephiroth. However, Cloud can't remember what happened when he faced Sephiroth inside Jenova's chamber.

With the story told, the team prepares to rejoin the fight against Shinra. Go back downstairs and you'll receive the PHS. With the PHS in your possession, you can rearrange your party while walking on the World Map—a handy device to say the least. Now go and explore Kalm.

67

KALM TOWN

ITEMS:
Ether (X3) **(A)**,
Peacemaker **(B)**, Guard
Source **(C)**

REST (D)

Inn   20 Gil

ITEM SHOP (E)

ITEM	COST
Potion	50
Phoenix Down	300
Antidote	80
Eye Drop	50
Hyper	100
Tranquilizer	100
Tent	500

MATERIA SHOP (F)

ITEM	COST
Earth	1500
Poison	1500
Steal	1200
Sense	1000
Heal	1500

WEAPON SHOP (G)

ITEM	COST
Mythril Saber	1000
Cannon Ball	950
Mythril Claw	750
Full Metal Staff	800
Mythril Armlet	350

Kalm is a quiet little town set on the outskirts of the wastelands surrounding Midgar. The people here are mainly Mythril miners, but lately no one can mine because of the monsters.

Pick up some supplies in town and talk to everyone—there are plenty of free items to pick up. Make sure you search the houses by looking inside cabinets and stairwells. There's even a treasure chest with a **Peacemaker** inside that you won't be able to use just yet.

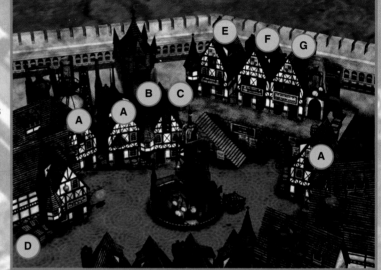

Several townsfolk mention that they've recently seen a man dressed in black carrying a large sword. Hmm, sounds like Sephiroth! A man near the town entrance says he saw him heading east toward the grassy field. Get your team together and go after him.

NOTE: Before dropping 950 Gil on the Cannonball, look for the Custom Sweeper outside Kalm. You can steal the Atomic Scissors from this creature and save yourself the expense.

CHOCOBO RANCH

This is Choco Bill's Chocobo Ranch. Chocobos are bred and raised here for Chocobo racing and for transportation. Take some time to talk to the family.

VEGETABLE STORE

ITEM	C(
"Chocobo Lure" Materia	2
Mimett Greens	
Curiel Greens	
Pahsana Greens	8
Tantal Greens	4
Krakka Greens	2
Gysahl Greens	

NOTE: When you first reach the ranch, talk to the closest Chocobo. The Chocobos will first perform a little dance, and then you'll receive your first summon Materia, the **"Choco/Mog"** **Materia.**

There's only one way to reach the Mythril Mine and that's by crossing the marsh. Choco Billy **(B)** insists that you catch a Chocobo to accomplish this task. Trying to cross the marsh on foot can be dangerous, because there's a huge serpent known as the Midgar Zolom that hunts any- one who enters the area.

Chocobos are faster than the Midgar Zolom, so you should be able to reach the other side unscathed. Choco Bill also mentions that he saw a man in black enter the marsh earlier.

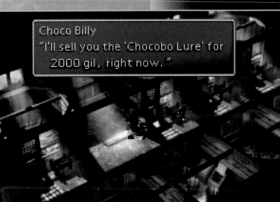

Choco Billy
"I'll sell you the 'Chocobo Lure' for 2000 gil, right now."

Go to the stables and talk to Choco Billy. He doesn't have any Chocobos for sale, but he can sell you the **"Chocobo Lure" Materia**. With this Materia, you can attract and capture a Chocobo by exploring areas near a set of Chocobo tracks. There is one catch: The **"Chocobo Lure" Materia** will cost you 2000 Gil. If you need the Materia, you need to fight some of the monsters around the ranch. You *must* purchase the Materia to continue.

After purchasing the Materia, you can buy **Greens** to aid you in the Chocobo-capturing process. The Greens aren't really necessary, but it's up to you if you decide to purchase them. When you're ready, equip the Materia and go outside.

Look for some Chocobo tracks and walk on them. Eventually, you'll enter a battle and a Chocobo may or may not appear in the enemy group. If the Chocobo is in the enemy group, kill the monster(s) without harming the Chocobo. When done correctly, the Chocobo is yours! If you fail, continue to try until you are successful.

Hop on the Chocobo and ride it through the marsh located to the southwest. Avoid the serpent's shadow or you'll get forced into a fight against the Midgar Zolom.

NOTE: Chocobos have the ability to run away from enemies other than the Midgar Zolom. In fact, as long as you're riding a Chocobo, you won't have to fight any random encounters.

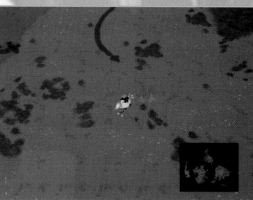

MYTHRIL MINE

ITEMS:

Ether **(A)**
Tent **(B)**
"Long Range" Materia **(C)**
Mind Source **(D)**
Elixer **(E)**
Hi-Potion **(F)**

After crossing the marsh, you'll encounter a Midgar Zolom that has been impaled on a broken tree. Only Sephiroth could have thought of such a gruesome act, so you must be on the right track. The Mythril Mine is just ahead.

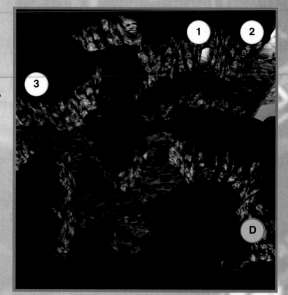

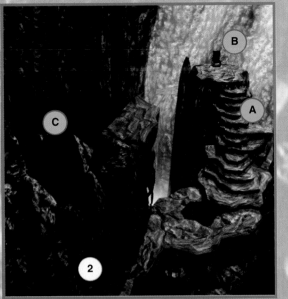

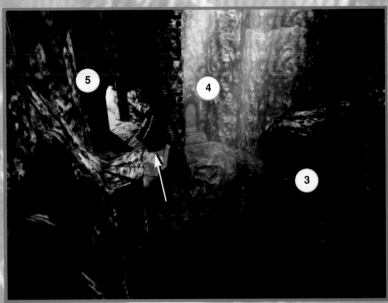

The mine itself is fairly small, so it's quite difficult to get lost in. There are plenty of items to pick up, just refer to the map for exact locations.

 TIP: You can climb some of the vines in the mine. One leads to the exit, and the other leads to a hidden ledge and the **"Long Range" Materia**. This Materia will soon become very useful, so pick it up before you leave.

Before exiting the mine, the team runs into Rude, Elena, and Tseng of the Turks. It appears the Turks are also pursuing Sephiroth. Elena, the newest Turk, slips up and mentions that Sephiroth is headed for Junon Harbor, which isn't far from the mine.

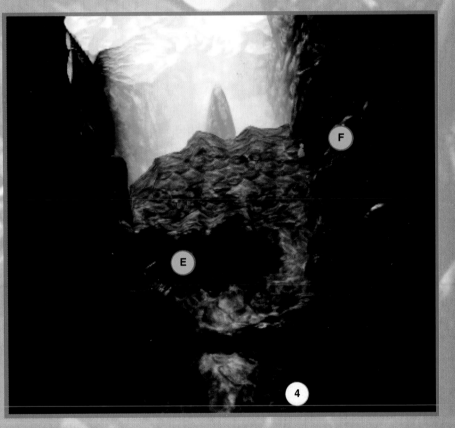

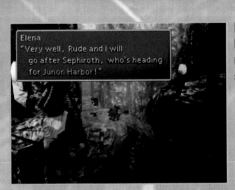

If you follow Tseng out of the mine, you'll see a large condor on a nearby hill. You've come across Fort Condor, home of a small band of rebels fighting against Shinra. Take the opportunity to stop by and get some rest before moving on to Junon Harbor.

71

ITEM SHOP (A)

ITEM	COST
Potion	50
Phoenix Down	300
Hyper	100
Tranquilizer	100
Tent	500

MATERIA SHOP (B)

ITEM	COST
Fire	600
Lightning	600
Ice	600
Restore	750

REST (C)

Lower Bedroom	Free

There's not much you can do here at this point. However, you can visit the shops, rest, and learn a bit about Fort Condor and the fight against Shinra. You can even help out by talking to the man at the top of Fort Condor, which is actually a strategy-based mini-game in which you can take part. This is *completely* optional at this point, but it's good practice. If you want to know more about the Fort Condor mini-game, check the dedicated section in the back of the book.

Outside

NOTE: You won't be able to rest or buy items until you've agreed to join the fight to save the Condors. Speak with the man in the middle of Fort Condor **(D)** to do so.

When you're done here, leave the fort and continue northwest to Junon Harbor.

"When we can't stand up to the attack any longer, the Shinra will take both the condors and our lives, as well as all the materia within the reactor."

TIP: Before venturing to Junon, go find Yuffie, a new ally. Check the "Finding Yuffie" section in the back of the book for tips on locating her.

JUNON HARBOR

WARNING! Junon Harbor may be difficult to find on your first trip. It's located right against the ocean and behind a small cliff. It's easy to find on the map, so just walk around in that area until you see something unusual.

At first, there's not much to do. You can talk to the villagers and perhaps even visit the Weapon Shop. There's also a beach, but instead of taking it easy, take a moment to re-equip your characters.

BATTLE TIP: First things first: Put Barret in your party if he isn't already. Give Cloud the **"Long Range" Materia** and switch Barret to a long-range weapon if he's currently using a short-range one. Also, equip your remaining character with the **"Choco/Mog" Materia**. Now you're ready to hit the beach.

At the beach, you'll meet a little girl named Priscilla **(C)**. She is good with animals and not very fond of Shinra. She asks you to leave, but a monster attacks the party leaving Priscilla in the middle of everything.

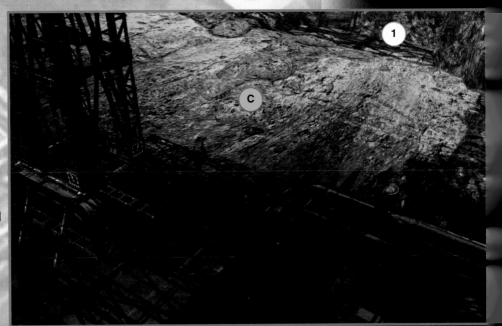

To Junon

Cloud
"Hey! Hold on, we're coming!"

BOSS FIGHT: BOTTOMSWELL

Bottomswell is a flying boss, so only characters equipped with long-range weapons can hit it with their normal attacks. This is the main reason you need Barret in your party during this battle. Also, this is why Cloud needs to have the **"Long Range" Materia** equipped. Have Barret and Cloud attack Bottomswell with their normal attacks and magic, but have your third character concentrate on healing the party and using attack spells.

BATTLE TIP: Bottomswell has two attacks that you should be aware of. The Water Bubble attack encases one of your characters in a bubble, which prevents that character from participating in the battle. This attack is very similar to Reno's Pyramid; however, you can only pop the bubbles with magic.

TIP: It's best to use a magic attack that can hit both the Boss and the bubble at the same time. In effect, you're conserving MP without wasting a turn. Act quickly—the bubble slowly suffocates its victim. Also, use an "All" Materia with a Magic Materia; this affects both the Boss and the bubbles.

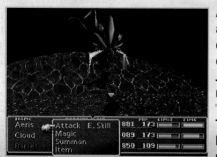

Also, watch for the Big Wave attack. This hits your entire party and causes around 100 points of damage to *each* character. Normally this isn't a big deal, but Bottomswell gets to use the Big Wave as a final attack. So basically, when you kill it, it'll cast Big Wave in hopes of taking you down with it. Just keep your HP above 150. When you defeat Bottomswell, you're rewarded with a Power Wrist.

This latest threat is out of the way, but Priscilla isn't breathing! Cloud must perform CPR on the little girl to save

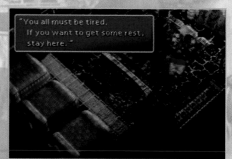

her life. The trick is to let your lungs fill up as much as possible before exhaling—just don't wait too long or you'll accidentally exhale. This sounds easy, but it may take several tries. Press the ● button and Cloud will slowly begin to fill his lungs with air. When the meter reaches the top of the lungs, press the ● button a second time and Cloud will breath into her mouth. This should be enough to bring Priscilla around.

The lady who owns the house at the entrance to the town is thankful for your assistance, so she lets you use her home any time you need a rest. Take her up on the offer and spend the night.

Cloud has another visit from the mysterious voice and is prompted to ask Tifa about Nibelheim. She's reluctant to answer Clouds inquiries, but there's no time to argue. Pay a visit to Priscilla and investigate what the ruckus is about.

Priscilla gives Cloud the **"Shiva" Materia** for saving her life, and says that Shinra is throwing a celebration for Rufus. You must get up to that city, but how? Priscilla has the answer.

Mr. Dolphin can launch Cloud up to a safe part of the tower. To do so, find the spot you want to jump from and then call Mr. Dolphin. He'll leap high into the air with Cloud on his nose. If you find the right spot, you'll land safely on the bar overhead. The accompanying screenshot shows the best location.

74

When you land on the pole, Cloud will climb up to the Junon Airport. Walk west to the lift and take it down to the door below. Inside this room the soldiers are going crazy as they try to prepare for Rufus' arrival. One of the captains sees Cloud and assumes he's just out of uniform. Follow him into the locker room and Cloud will don a Shinra uniform. You must also learn the proper greeting procedure, because you're now part of the reception committee. You just need to stay in step during the march, plus you'll have to "shoulder" your rifle by pressing the ● button when the other soldiers do.

The parade is already in progress, so you'll need to jump in. Follow your new commander through a shortcut to the parade route. When he gives the sign,

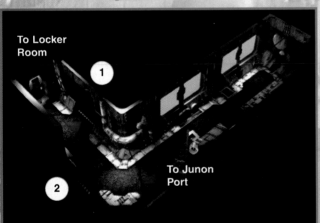

To Locker Room

1

2

To Junon Port

run around the marching soldiers and retake your position in the back. When the Shinra soldiers raise their guns, you should raise yours as well. The same holds true when they shoulder their guns. There's a definite rhythm to it. Depending on how well you perform, the TV Producer will send you an item. Refer to the sidebar for the items.

PERCENT

29% or

30-39%

40%-49%

50% or

"Hey!
You still dressed like that!?
Come 'ere!"

"Now!! 4......!"

Live TV Ratings 35%

Rufus and Heidegger get into it after the parade and you learn that Sephiroth is indeed here; however, you can't go looking for him just yet. First, you must attend Rufus' send-off and your commander isn't about to let you go without a little practice.

Heidegger "......Gya haa haa!"

"Hey!"

NOTE: The short send-off procedure that you learn here isn't the one you use later. It's important to remember this when you get to the dock.

Easy enough, right? Not really, the timing is the difficult part. The commander will bark an order, promting you to respond correctly. You'll notice that the other soldiers hesitate a little, but you can't hesitate or you'll throw off the whole thing. Practice your timing a bit and then head out.

PPER JUNON SHOPS

REE ITEMS

1/35 Soldier **(A)**
Mind Source **(B)**
Luck Source **(C)**
Power Source **(D)**
Guard Source **(E)**
"Enemy Skill" Materia **(F)**

IATERIA SHOP (G)

EM	COST
Sense	1000
Seal	3000
Restore	750
Heal	1500
Revive	3000

JEAPON SHOP (H)

EM	COST
Hardedge	1500
Grand Glove	1200
Atomic Scissors	1400
Striking Staff	1300
Diamond Pin	1300
Boomerang	1400

EM SHOP (I)

EM	COST
Potion	50
Hi-Potion	300
Phoenix Down	300
Antidote	80
Eye Drop	50
Echo Screen	100
Hyper	100
Tranquilizer	100
Tent	500

There's plenty to do in Junon. Visit the shops along the main strip as you head toward the dock. You can get all sorts of new stuff and a few special items if you look hard enough. Don't forget to stop at the Respectable Inn. It's a lot like Beginner's Hall, but you can learn a lot of advanced information about many things. Also, you'll want to pick up the **"Enemy-Skill" Materia** lying on the floor. Don't forget to talk to the sailor in the cross section. He mentions a Submarine Dock and an Underwater Mako Reactor beneath Junon. This information might prove to be useful later.

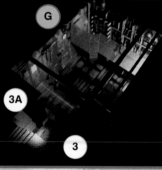

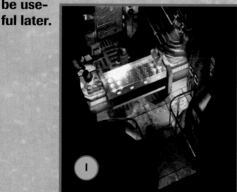

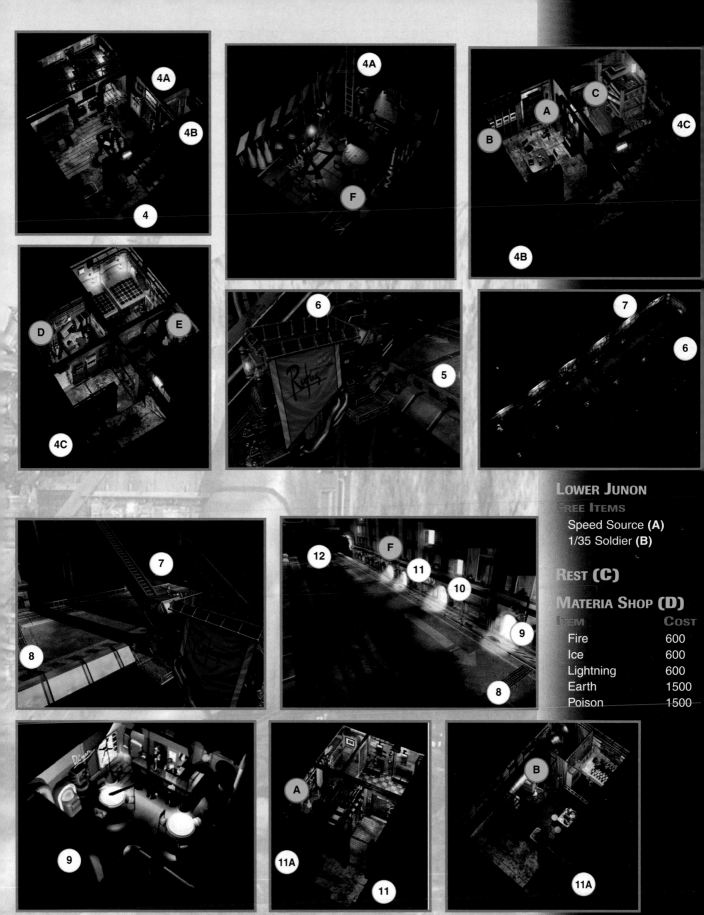

LOWER JUNON

FREE ITEMS
Speed Source **(A)**
1/35 Soldier **(B)**

REST (C)

MATERIA SHOP (D)

ITEM	COST
Fire	600
Ice	600
Lightning	600
Earth	1500
Poison	1500

SORY SHOP (E)

	COST
Glasses	3000
and	3000

N SHOP (F)

	COST
Saber	1000
n Ball	950
Claw	750
etal Staff	800
Clip	800

As soon as you reach the dock, the send-off begins. (Hey! Isn't that Red XIII hiding over there?) Follow your commander's orders and try to make Rufus happy. Depending on how you perform, Heidegger will give you a prize.

"Right: Right Face!"

President's Mood Gauge 040

MOOD	ITEM
0-50	Silver Glasses
60-90	"HP Plus" Materia
100 or higher	Force Stealer (sword)

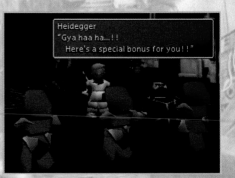

Heidegger
"Gya haa ha...!!
    Here's a special bonus for you!!"

NOTE: The send-off is always random, so the commander's orders are always different.

TIP: When you're dismissed, follow Rufus and Heidegger onto the boat. They're looking for Sephiroth, so you don't want to be far behind.

SHINRA BOAT

The boat departs without a hitch. Thought you were alone, huh? You'll soon learn that the entire team has sneaked onboard. Locate them all and collect any items along the way.

If you can't find Barret, check the front of the boat. You'll find him trying to eavesdrop on Rufus and Heidegger. The longer you talk to him, the more it seems like he might get out of control. But then an alarm sounds! Sephiroth must be onboard! Organize your party and get down to the cargo hold.

ITEMS:
- Ether **(A)**
- "All" Materia **(B)**
- Wind Slash **(C)**
- "Ifrit" Materia **(D)**

ITEM SHOP **(E)**

ITEM	COST
Potion	50
Phoenix Down	300

REST

Invisible Alpha	250

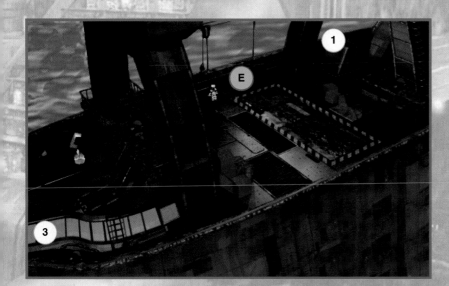

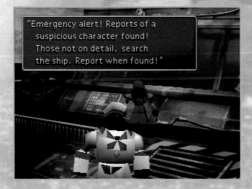

"Emergency alert! Reports of a suspicious character found! Those not on detail, search the ship. Report when found!"

MARINE

Area—Shinra Boat

LVL	HP	MP	EXP	GIL	AP
16	300	20	75	150	8

Slp	Ret	Con	Sil	Slw	Drk	Trsfr	Stp	
Bsk	Psn	Par	Stn	SS	Man	Dth	Imp	

MORPH	STEAL	ATTACKS
n/a	Shin-Ra Defense	Sleep, Gun, Grenade

SCRUTIN EYE

Area—Shinra Boat

LVL	HP	MP	EXP	GIL	AP
15	240	60	80	120	8

Slp	Ret	Con	Sil	Slw	Drk	Trsfr	Stp	
Bsk	Psn	Par	Stn	SS	Man	Dth	Imp	

MORPH	STEAL	ATTACKS
n/a	Ether	Fire2, Ice2, Ram

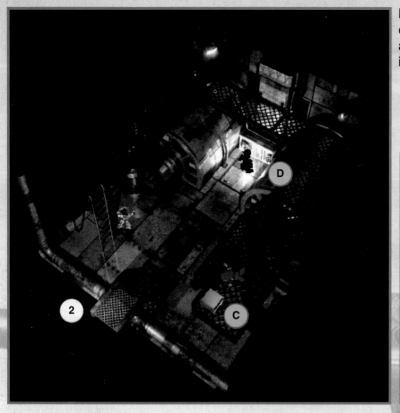

It must be Sephiroth, because most of the crew is either dead or dying. Those who aren't are out to kill anything that isn't wearing a Shinra uniform... and that means you!

 NOTE: Shinra Marines are carrying a piece of armor called **Shinra Beta**. It's a decent piece of armor and well worth stealing.

In the back of the boat it's more of the same. Also, don't forget to pick up the Wind Slash. Approaching the standing guard prompts Sephiroth's appearance. He looks the same, but he's obviously more powerful than ever. Sephiroth beats a hasty retreat and leaves the team with a nasty surprise.

Boss Fight: Jenova-BIRTH

Although this is a pretty straightforward fight, keep in mind that Jenova is considerably more powerful than you. Its Tail Laser is its strongest attack and can easily knock down each of your fighters by about 200 HPs (400 if it does it twice in a row). Jenova can also tip the odds in its favor by casting **Stop** on one of your characters.

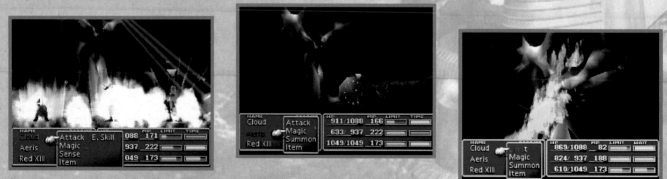

Use your most powerful spells and Limit Breaks against it. The enemy skill **Flamethrower** is particularly effective during this battle, but only if you learned it in the Mythril Mines. Also, use your **Summon Materia** to cause some serious damage to Jenova with solid hits from "Choco/Mog" and "Shiva." Defeat Jenova and you'll receive a White Cape.

It looks like Sephiroth may be preparing to take over the planet. If Jenova is alive and Sephiroth's power has grown, this could be a really long fight.

Costa del Sol is quickly approaching. Grab the "Ifrit" Materia left behind by Jenova and return to the deck.

80

COSTA DEL SOL

Ah, a tropical resort! Too bad the team doesn't have time for a vacation. That's okay though, when Rufus learns that AVALANCHE was onboard the boat, Heideggar will provide all the entertainment you could ask for.

There's not much for you to do here. You can visit all the shops and stock up on supplies if you're low. If you have plenty of money (fat chance!), you can purchase President Shinra's beach house for the not so low price of 300,000 Gil. Just because you can't afford it doesn't mean you shouldn't take the items in the basement.

ITEMS:

Motor Drive (**A**), Fire Ring (**B**), Power Source (**C**)

WEAPON SHOP (D)

ITEM	COST
Platinum Bangle	1800
Carbon Bangle	800
Four Slots	1300
Molotov	400

MATERIA SHOP (E)

ITEM	COST
Heal	1500
Revive	3000
Restore	750
Seal	3000
Fire	600
Ice	600
Lightning	600

ITEM SHOP (F)

ITEM	COST
Potion	50
Hi-Potion	300
Phoenix Down	300
Soft	150
Antidote	80
Eye Drop	50
Hyper	100
Tranquilizer	100
Tent	500

REST (G)

Inn	200

NOTE: Just for fun, kick the soccer ball at Red XIII and watch what happens.

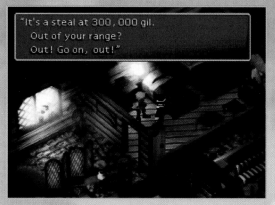
"It's a steal at 300,000 gil. Out of your range? Out! Go on, out!"

When you've looked around town, go to the beach and you'll find Hojo lounging around with a bunch of bikini-clad women. Who would've guessed Hojo was such a ladies man? The only important information he has is that you need to head for Mt. Corel to the south.

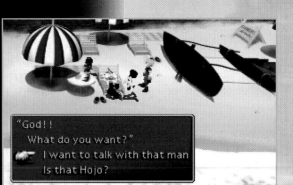
"God!! What do you want?" I want to talk with that man Is that Hojo?

NOTE: There's a reason Softs are the town's specialty. Mt. Corel is filled with monsters that can cast the Stone spell. Make sure you pick up a few before you leave.

After exploring all of Costa del Sol, head to the Inn for a solid night's rest, because in the morning you're off to Mt. Corel and the Gold Saucer.

MT. COREL

ITEMS:

Wizard Staff **(A)**
Star Pendant **(B)**
W Machine Gun **(C)**
Turbo Ether **(D)**
"Transform" Materia **(E)**
Phoenix Down (x10) **(F)**
Power Source **(G)**
Mind Source **(H)**
Tent **(I)**

Head west from Costa del Sol to find Mt. Corel, which is at the end of a winding path through the mountains. Mt. Corel is pretty much a straight path, but it's full of surprisingly strong enemies. Keep a close eye on each character's health during battles.

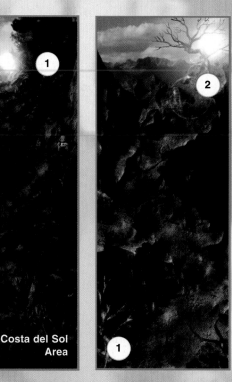

Costa del Sol Area

1

You'll see another Mako Reactor shortly after entering Mt. Corel. You just can't seem to get away from these things. There's nothing to do here at the moment, but make a mental note of its location.

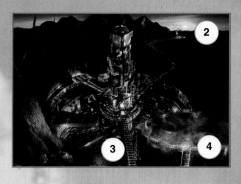

When you exit the reactor area, you'll start walking on some old railroad tracks that occasionally break. If you fall, hold Left or

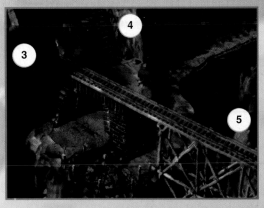

Right on the D-pad and tap the ● button as fast as possible. This enables you to pick up one of two items as you climb back up. The item on the left side is the Wizard Staff; the item on the right is a Star Pendant. You'll get three chances, but you can only pick up each item once.

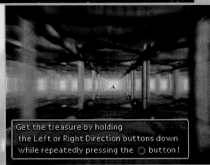

It's impossible to get across the low bridge at the end of the tracks because someone left the draw bridge up. Instead, go back and take the high road over the water. This path leads to a dead end, but it also leads to the bridge's controls **(J)**.

Next to the bridge controls you'll hear the sound of chirping. Climb up the wall at that spot **(F)** and you'll see a bird's nest resting on some treasure chests. You can take the treasure (10 **Phoenix Downs**) if you're conscience allows it, but you'll disappoint your partners, plus you'll have to fight a Cokatolis.

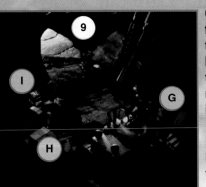

Go back down to the lower tracks and follow your partners. As they turn to the right, you need to take the left split because buried in the hill under the tracks is a cave with an out-of-work miner. You can pick up several useful items along the way.

Now jump back on the tracks and follow the path until you reach a small town named North Corel.

50

)

COST

50
300
500

(C)

COST

5000
150
150
150
100
100

(D)

COST

800
2200
400

Welcome to North Corel. Long ago this was a beautiful coal mining town. Now it's nothing but a burned-up version of what it used to be. It's also Barret's hometown.

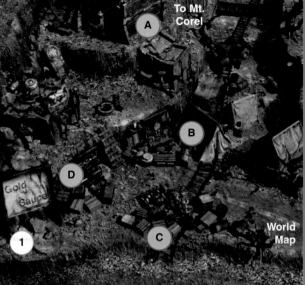

Upon entering North Corel, Barret receives a rather cold reception. It's not exactly what you'd expect, but there's more going on here than you might have guessed.

Talk to everyone and visit the shops. Also, step outside the town and save before you go to the Ropeway to the west.

Before boarding the Ropeway (E), Barret will stop the party and relate to them the story of North Corel. There was an explosion at the Corel Reactor and Shinra blamed the people of North Corel for what they felt was a terrorist attack. Shinra burned the entire town, killing nearly everyone there.

"Look at this place! It's all your fault North Corel turned into a garbage heap!"

...My hometown, Corel's always been a coal mining town.

When Barret finishes his story, hop on the Ropeway and ride up to the Gold Saucer.

Barret
"But listen, Dyne.
No one uses coal nowadays.
It's the sign of the times."

GOLD SAUCER

The approach to Gold Saucer is something you don't want to miss. This giant amusement park/casino has everything. Inside you can bet on Chocobo Races, fight in the Battle Arena, visit the Ghost Hotel, play at the arcade, and even participate in a stage play. There is one small catch—admission to the park is a whopping *3000 Gil* for a one-day pass, or *30,000 Gil* for a lifetime pass. For now you'll probably only be able to afford the one-day pass, but you'll want to pick up a lifetime pass at some point.

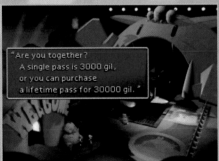

"Are you together?
A single pass is 3000 gil,
or you can purchase
a lifetime pass for 30000 gil."

ITEM SHOP (
ITEM
Potion
Phoenix Down
Ether
Antidote
Maiden's Kiss
Cornucopia
Soft
Echo Screen
Hyper
Tranquilizer

REST (B)
Inn

NOTE: There are two things you should know about the entrance to the Gold Saucer. First, it costs 5 GP (not Gil) to use the save point. Second, you can occasionally purchase GP from a man who hides in the hut behind the Ropeway car. He'll sell you 1 GP for 100 Gil, up to a maximum of 100 GP. He's not there each time you enter the Gold Saucer, but once you have a lifetime pass you can run in and out of the entrance until he appears.

Most of the attractions here use GP instead of Gil. You can win GP at the Chocobo Races and at Wonder Square. Just remember that GP is useless outside of the Gold Saucer, so it's a really bad idea to convert your entire fortune into GP.

NOTE: If you'd like specific information on the various rides and attractions at the Gold Saucer, refer to the Gold Saucer section in the back of the book.

It looks like everyone—well, almost everyone—is up for a little fun. Pick your partner and explore the park.

First, you should visit Speed Square. Here you'll meet Dio, the owner of the Gold Saucer. Dio mentions that someone wearing a black cape with the number 1 tattooed on it came through earlier asking about a Black Materia. It sounds like Sephiroth was here, but he's probably already left.

Next, stop by Wonder Square. Here you'll meet a rather poor fortune teller named Cait Sith. He'll give you a fortune, and then join your party to see if his predictions come true. After the encounter, you can enter the arcade and mess around, or you can head over to Battle Square.

What's this? A dead Shinra soldier lays on the steps to the entrance of the Battle Arena. Inside it's more of the same. Who could have done such a thing? The bodies are riddled with bullet holes. No...it couldn't be. Barret was mad, but not THAT mad.

"How 'bout it?
Want me to read your fortune!?
A bright future! A happy future!"

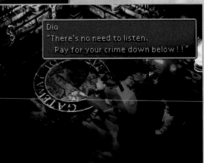

Dio
"There's no need to listen.
Pay for your crime down below!!"

Talk about being in the wrong place at the wrong time. Dio walks in and the next thing you know, the team is getting thrown out of the Gold Saucer for a crime they didn't commit.

"Ugh...ugh...a man
with a gun...on his arm......"

COREL PRISON

(A)

Cost
50
300
500

The team ends up in Corel Prison at the base of the Gold Saucer. There's no way out either, because the area is completely surrounded by quicksand. Cait Sith does mention one special occasion where someone actually escaped, but he doesn't mention how it was accomplished.

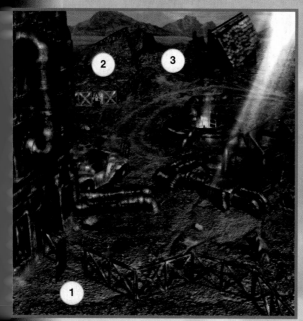

Barret is also with the team, but he's still in a bad mood and there are more dead bodies. Follow him off-screen, but watch your step around here—this place is filled with thieves and murderers.

BATTLE TIP: You'll fight a lot of Bandits in Corel Prison. They will often mug you and steal items. If you quickly kill the Bandit who steals your item, you'll get it back. However, if the Bandit gets away, your item is gone forever.

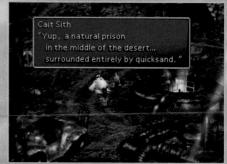

Cait Sith
"Yup, a natural prison
in the middle of the desert...
surrounded entirely by quicksand."

Barret
"Stay back!
This's something I gotta deal with."

Barret
"There's another...
another man that got a gun
grafted inta one of his arms.
It was four years ago..."

Follow Barret to the house located in the southeast. In this house, he explains to you what's happening and tells you more about Dyne. Dyne and Barret were best friends until the day North Corel burned to the ground. Barret and Dyne were

attacked by Scarlet on their return trip to North Corel. Both men lost the use of an arm during the attack and Dyne almost succumbed to what could have been his doom. But it looks like Dyne is back and Barret needs to find him.

First, head back to where you entered the prison, where you'll find another dead man. Go through the gate and then to the east to find Dyne.

This isn't a happy reunion of old friends. Dyne has never recovered from the destruction of North Corel. His only wish now is to destroy everything—including Barret and his daughter, Marlene.

BOSS FIGHT: DYNE

Barret fights this battle alone. Throughout most of the fight, you'll just continue to trade blows with Dyne while keeping up your health. Dyne's attacks build up Barret's Limit Meter quickly, so you'll have plenty of opportunities to hit Dyne.

Dyne has a magic attack called the S-Mine, but it's no stronger than his normal shot. The attack is extremely dangerous because he can use it immediately after using his normal attack. In effect, this attack causes about 300 points of damage. You should keep Barret's HPs around 300 to stay out of trouble.

89

WARNING! Dyne has a final attack called the Molotov Cocktail, which inflicts about 150 points of damage. He'll use it when you just barely "kill" him. However, if your last attack really hits him hard, you won't give him the chance. He also uses this attack when his HP gets low.

You receive a **Silver Armlet** for defeating this tough Boss.

Dyne is still alive after the fight; however, he's badly wounded. Barret tries to help his old friend, but Dyne has given up hope. As a gesture of goodwill, he gives Barret a pendant to give to Marlene, a keepsake of her mother, and then leaps to his death.

THE CHOCOBO RACE

ITEMS:

"Ranch" Materia **(A)**

In the morning, Cloud and the rest of the team pay a visit to Mr. Coates. He's reluctant to help the team at first, but Barret shows the pendant to Coates, who quickly changes his tune. If the team wants to get out of Corel Prison, they need to win a Chocobo Race.

Now it's time to meet Ester, Chocobo Racing Manager and all-around nice person. She offers to be Cloud's manager and says she'll lone him a decent Chocobo for the race. She takes you to the Jockey's Lounge where you

can talk with the other jockeys and grab the **"Ramuh" Materia (A)**. When the bells sound, follow the other jockeys out. Ester will give you some last-minute tips before the race begins, so pay attention.

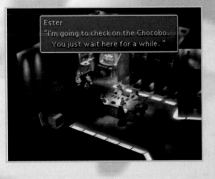

It's best to take Manual control of your Chocobo before the race even begins. At the start of the race, increase your Chocobo's speed so that there's a very *slow* drain on his stamina. This will give your Chocobo better speed than the other Chocobos and should enable you to get a small lead.

 TIP: Don't worry if a Chocobo goes flying past you. The jockeys are pushing their Chocobos too hard—they'll run out of steam before the race is over.

When you reach the "space theme" area, make your Chocobo sprint toward the finish line. If things go well, you should easily win the race. If not, keep trying until you do.

 TIP: You can slowly refill your Chocobo's stamina meter by holding R1 + R2 during the race. This enables you to push your Chocobo harder.

You're free from prison and Dio is very sorry about the mix-up. As an apology, he gives you a Buggy to help with your journey. He also tells you that Sephiroth is headed to Gongaga, a town located to the south.

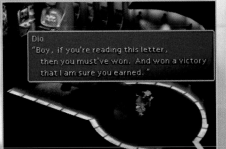

NOTE: You can cross the desert with the Buggy, but you can't return to Corel Prison.

TIP: You can return to the desert in the buggy; however, if you get lost, a Chocobo cart will help you out.

CHOCOBO CONTROLS

D-Pad	Move Left or Right
Select	Chooses Auto or Manual
●	Speed up
■	Slow down
▲	Sprint
Start	Ends race

BUGGY CONTROLS

D-Pad	Moves Buggy
●	Hop onto Buggy
■	Get out of Buggy

GONGAGA VILLAGE

GONGAGA VILLAGE

REE ITEMS:

"Titan" Materia **(A)**,
"Deathblow" Materia **(B)**,
X-Potion **(C)**, White
M-phone **(D)**

CCESSORY SHOP (E)

EM	COST
Headband	3000
Silver Glasses	3000
Star Pendant	4000
Talisman	4000
White Cape	5000
Fury Ring	5000
"Mystify"	6000
"Time"	6000
"Heal"	1500
"Transform"	5000

EAPON SHOP (F)

EM	COST
Hardedge	1500
Grand Glove	1200
Atomic Scissors	1400
Striking Staff	1300
Diamond Pin	1300
Boomerang	1400
mpaler	500
Shrivel	500
Molotov	400

EM SHOP (G)

EM	COST
Potion	50
Hi-Potion	300
Phoenix Down	300
Tent	500
Maiden's Kiss	150
Cornucopia	150
Soft	150
Hyper	100
Tranquilizer	100

EST (H)

nn	80

You'll know Gongaga Village when you see it because of the twisted mass of broken and burned metal in the middle of a jungle. You'll need to park the Buggy before entering the area.

NOTE: Have Aeris join your party if she isn't already in it and set her Limit Breaks to Level 1. You may want to spend some time in the area surrounding Gongaga Village building up her Limit Meter before you enter the jungle outside the town.

As soon as you enter the jungle, you'll find the Turks sharing some secrets. Reno and Rude attack the group, but Elena runs off to warn Tseng.

BOSS FIGHT: RENO AND RUDE

Reno and Rude tend to use a lot of magic in this battle. Having the Fire Ring equipped plus the **"Elemental-Fire" Materia** combination equipped in someone's armor will help you defend against their attacks.

 BATTLE TIP: Concentrate your initial attacks on Rude before going after Reno. Rude's the one performing all the healing in this battle.

Have Aeris use her Seal Evil Limit Break as soon as possible. It won't mute Rude or Reno, but it should paralyze them both,

which makes it easy to eliminate one or both of them. Winning the battle gets you an **X-Potion** and a Fairy Tale.

How did the Turks know about AVALANCHE's whereabouts? Maybe it's a spy. But there's no time to interrogate everyone, so follow Elena to the destroyed Mako Reactor. Scarlet and Tseng show up just after you arrive and they're looking for something called "Huge Materia," something for some kind of super weapon. This could be bad news. Check the reactor after they leave and you'll find the **"Titan" Materia (A)**, the junky Materia Scarlet referred to.

Return to the crossroads and take the second path to Gongaga Village.

 NOTE: There's a **"Deathblow" Materia (B)** on the path that leads back to the World Map.

Visit the hut on the south side of town. The people here ask if Cloud has ever met a man named Zack, who left Gongaga several years ago to join SOLDIER and hasn't been heard from since. Aeris recognizes the name as that of her first love, but even she hasn't seen him recently.

That's all you can do in Gongaga except for shopping. Go back to the Buggy and head for Cosmo Canyon.

 NOTE: There are no stairs in Gongaga Village, but there are "fireman's" poles. Don't miss the Weapon Shop located above the Accessory Shop.

COSMO CANYON

EST (A)

nn	100

ENERAL STORE (B)

EM	COST
Potion	50
Hi-Potion	300
Phoenix Down	300
Ether	1500
Tent	500
Maiden's Kiss	150
Cornucopia	150
Soft	150
Hyper	100
Tranquilizer	100

EAPON SHOP (C)

EM	COST
Butterfly Edge	2800
Tiger Fury	2500
Heavy Vulcan	2700
Prism Staff	2600
Silver Barrette	2500
Pinwheel	2600
Green M-phone	2400
Silver Armlet	1300

ATERIA SHOP (D)

EM	COST
MP Plus	8000
HP Plus	8000
Mystify	6000
Transform	5000

After leaving Gongaga, cross the river located southwest of the village and follow the path into the canyons. Here you'll find the town of Cosmo Canyon, which rests on the side of a plateau. This place is very distinguishable because of the planetarium located at the top. You can't miss it—the Buggy breaks down right in front of it!

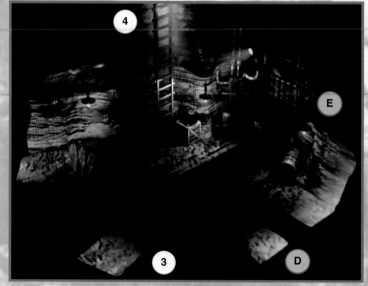

Cosmo Canyon, a community dedicated to the study of Planet Life and peace, is Red XIII's hometown. This is also the place Barret once promised to bring Biggs, Jessie, and Wedge after AVALANCHE had stopped Shinra's evil doings.

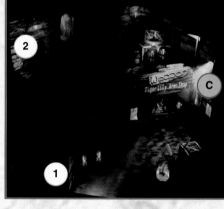

NOTE: When the Buggy breaks down, talk to the man in the middle of town who looks like a construction worker. Tell him you aren't here to study and he'll offer to fix the Buggy for you.

You discover something very big in Cosmo Canyon—Red XIII's real name is Nanaki. Follow Red XIII up the

stairs to the left to meet his grandpa, Bugenhagen, who lives in the planetarium at the top of Cosmo Canyon. Along the way, stop and talk to Barret, who shares a bit of AVALANCHE's history with you.

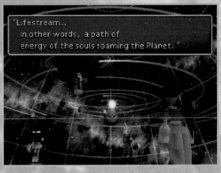

Bugenhagen is very much in tune with the planet and can even sense its despair. You'll get a chance to look at Bugenhagen's contraption, but you must find one other team member to join you. You can choose anyone in your party—with the exception of Red XIII. When you're all set, go back to Bugenhagen's.

Bugenhagen is already in his laboratory. Go inside and he'll teach you about the Lifestream and Shinra's destruction of the planet. When the lesson is over, talk to Bugenhagen one more time and then go to the center of Cosmo Canyon, where the rest of the team is resting around Cosmo Candle.

Make sure you talk to everyone on the team, but talk to Red XIII last. He talks a bit about his mother and father, which prompts Bugenhagen to appear. He asks you to create a party (which must include Cloud and Red XIII) and follow him to the locked door which you saw earlier. Bugenhagen opens a new path on your adventure by unlocking the door, which gives you access to the Cave of the Gi **(E)**.

GI CAVE

TEMS:

"Added Effect" Materia (A)
Black M-phone (B)
Ether (C)
Fairy Ring (D)
X-Potion (E)
Turbo Ether (F)
"Gravity" Materia

NOTE: You may want to equip your characters with items that prevent death. Most creatures in the Gi Cave can cast **Death Sentence.**

There are lots of holes in the walls of the first cave and inside each is a rock. Breaking a rock normally starts a fight, but one opens a secret door **(G)**. Check the map for its exact location.

GI SPECTOR

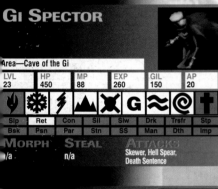

Area—Cave of the Gi					
LVL 23	HP 450	MP 88	EXP 260	GIL 150	AP 20

Slp	Ret	Con	Sil	Slw	Drk	Trsfr	Stp
Bsk	Psn	Par	Stn	SS	Man	Dth	Imp

MORPH	STEAL	ATTACKS
n/a	n/a	Skewer, Hell Spear, Death Sentence

HEG

Area—Cave of the Gi					
LVL 22	HP 400	MP 0	EXP 250	GIL 240	AP 20

Slp	Ret	Con	Sil	Slw	Drk	Trsfr	Stp
Bsk	Psn	Par	Stn	SS	Man	Dth	Imp

MORPH	STEAL	ATTACKS
n/a	n/a	Poison Fang, Holt Whip

SNEAKY STEP

Area—Cave of the GI					
LVL 21	HP 600	MP 65	EXP 270	GIL 330	AP 24

Slp	Ret	Con	Sil	Slw	Drk	Trsfr	Stp
Bsk	Psn	Par	Stn	SS	Man	Dth	Imp

MORPH	STEAL	ATTACKS
n/a	n/a	Triple Attack

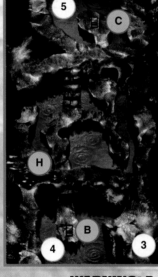

The next area is a small maze composed of several twisting paths. Walk down the stairs to collect several items or take the path on the bottom left to get the **"Added Effect" Materia** (you may remember this from the first map).

WARNING! Beware of the gold-colored liquid on the floor **(H)**. If you run on it, it will cause you to slide out of control and into a wall of spikes.

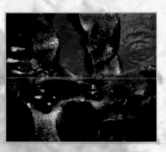

Now you have a decision to make. There are five tunnels and you need to decide which way to go. Here's the way things break down: the first tunnel connects to the fifth tunnel; the second and fourth tunnels take you to fights against creatures known as Stingers.

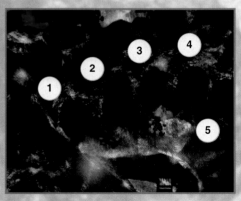

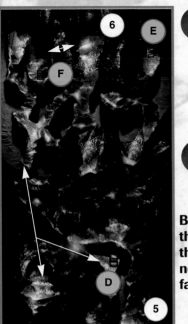

NOTE: There's one path that you must travel through—the second tunnel. You can skip the fourth path and avoid a tough fight, but keep in mind that skipping the fourth path means passing up an item.

NOTE: There are two secret passages in this chamber. Follow the arrows on the map to find the hidden chests.

Before you approach the troll-like face in the wall **(I)**, equip yourself with something that grants protection from fire. You'll need it because when you walk up to the face, it comes to life and attacks the party.

Boss Fight: Gi Nattak and Soul Fires

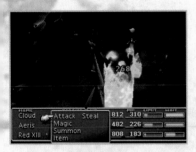

This boss can be a real pain, mainly because its Soul Fire henchmen have the ability to posses your characters. Once inside a character's body, it will occasionally cause fire damage. They can also heal themselves using their own Fire magic.

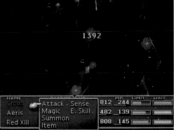

You can equip your team with gear that helps protect from fire to make this an easy fight. Gi Nattak's main weakness is Holy magic. This may seem odd, but the undead take damage from Cure spells—just avoid using Fire spells.

WARNING!
Gi Nattak can steal your MP and HP, so you may need to use several Ethers.

Also, make sure you use your **Summon Materia**, either **"Choco/Mog"** or **"Shiva."** Only use your normal attacks when you're out of MP. Defeating this Boss gets you a **Phoenix Down** and a **Wizer Staff.**

Follow Bugenhagen and the others out of the cave, and pick up the **"Gravity" Materia** on the way out.

Because of these actions, Red XIII finally sees his father's true fate—he was a hero after all. Now Red XIII can speak with pride when talking about his father. Bugenhagen asks Red XIII to continue on with the party so that they can make a difference. Red XIII meets up with you as you leave town.

Continue southwest out of Cosmo Canyon, and then head north along the coastline to reach your next destination, Nibelheim.

97

NIBELHEIM

ITEMS:

Luck Source (X2) **(A)**
Elixir **(B)**
Turbo Ether **(C)**
Platinum Fist **(D)**

GENERAL STORE **(B)**

ITEM	COST
Potion	50
Hi-Potion	300
Phoenix Down	300
Tent	500

REST **(A)**

Inn	100

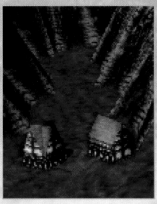

Nibelheim, Cloud and Tifa's hometown, is a small town that rests in the mountains. According to Cloud's memories, the town should be nothing but burnt earth, however, the town is just as it always was.

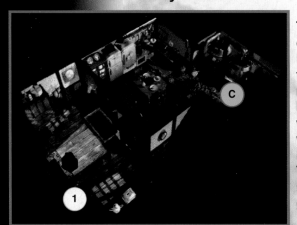

Talk about a cover-up. Everyone in the town insists that nothing ever happened. And who are the weird guys in the black capes? Talk to them and most of them will give you an item.

TIP: Check Tifa's house and you'll find the piano from Cloud's flashback. Remember the tune you played?

After checking out the town, return to Shinra Mansion. Two of the caped guys are out front, and one of them hints that Sephiroth is inside the mansion. Why would Sephiroth return to Nibelheim after all these years?

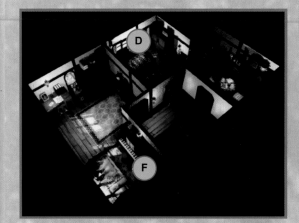

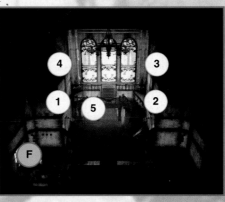

ITEMS:

Silver M-phone **(A)**
Enemy Launcher **(B)**
Magic Source **(C)**
Twin Viper **(D)**
"Odin" Materia **(E)**
Cosmo Memory **(F)**

The mansion is full of enemies this time around. Be careful and keep your hit points up.

Read the notes lying on the floor to the left of the entrance **(F)**. The first mentions someone trapped in the basement and the second mentions a safe. According to the note, you have 20 seconds to open the safe correctly. There are also hints on the paper for each of the dials. The hints are:

1. Look for the lid of the box with the most oxygen.

2. Behind the Ivory's short of tea and ray.

3. The creek in the floor near the chair on the second floor. Then to the left five steps, up nine steps, left two steps, and up six steps.

4. (missing)

You don't have to open the safe, but in case you're interested, here's what the code means when deciphered:

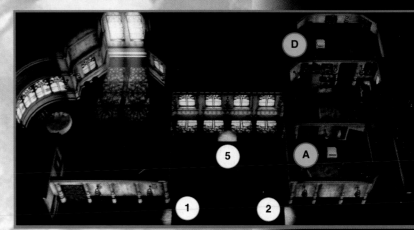

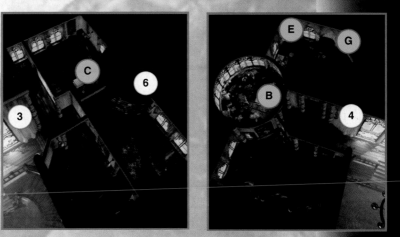

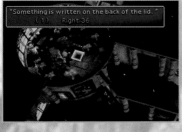

- The box with the most oxygen is the treasure chest upstairs in the atrium. Check the back of the lid.

- The Ivory's short of tea and ray must be the piano in the music room. Check the floor around the piano.

- There's a squeaky floorboard next to the chair in the upstairs bedroom. Follow the directions from that point.

- The last clue is written in invisible ink. While reading the clue sheet, try looking at the location where the Dial 4 clue should be.

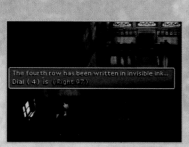

After checking everything, you should have the following combination:

Right 36, Left 10, Right 59, Right 97

Now is a good time to save your game. When you're ready, go upstairs and try to open the safe **(G)**. Turn the dial to the correct number, then press the ● button to enter it. As soon as the safe is open, you get attacked.

TIP: Don't go past any number while entering the combination or it won't work!

BOSS FIGHT: LOST NUMBER

This Boss can be tough, but here's an easy solution. Add Aeris to your party and set her Limit Breaks to Level 1. She can use Seal Evil against Lost Number and paralyze it for most of the battle. While it's paralyzed, have Cloud and your other party member pummel it with stong spells. You should be able to knock it down to half size before it recovers from the paralysis.

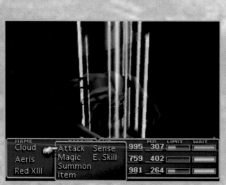

If the purple side dies, the red (magic) side will begin casting strong spells against the party. If the red side dies, the purple side will assault you with constant physical attacks. Fight the red side with your own physical attacks. The red side of Lost Number is very resistant to magic; fight the purple side with magic. Summon **"Choco/Mog"** and you might paralyze the monster again; if not, use Aeris' Seal Evil again as soon as her Limit Break is ready. For winning this battle, you get the Cosmo Memory, which is Red XIII's extreme Limit Break.

NOTE: Which sides lives and dies depends upon the last attack before the transformation. If the last hit is from a Spell, you'll face the red side; if the last attack is a physical blow, you'll face the purple side.

With the safe open, you can get the Basement Key and the **"Odin" Materia.**

Return to the basement area using the same path you used in Cloud's flashback at Kalm Inn. If you opened the safe, you can use the Basement Key to open the door located to the side of the library. This is where you'll meet a man named Vincent **(H)**. Talk to

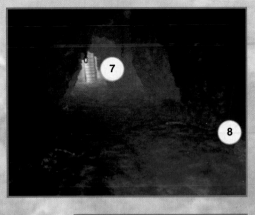

him about Sephiroth; he'll go back inside his coffin, but don't give up! Talk to him again and you'll get his name. He'll ask you about a lady named Lucricia, who he claims gave birth to Sephiroth. After getting this bit of info, you won't be able to get Vincent to open his coffin again.

Continue into the library. Sephiroth is inside and asks about the "Reunion." Cloud has no idea what Sephiroth is talking about, so Sephiroth invites Cloud to Mt. Nibel. Sephiroth then hits Cloud with a **"Destruct" Materia** and then leaves.

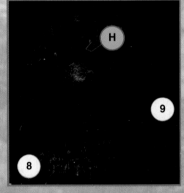

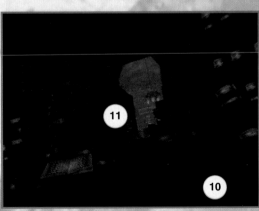

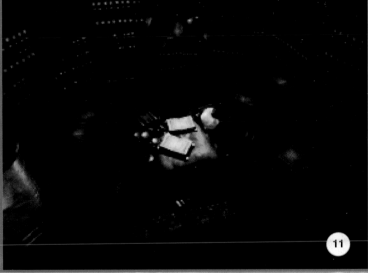

Return to Nibelheim and prepare for your journey over Mt. Nibel.

TIP: If you speak to Vincent before or after entering the library, he'll join your party as you leave.

Mt. Nibel

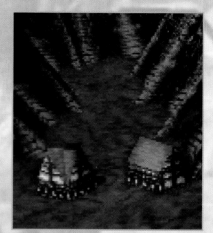

ITEMS:

- Rune Blade **(A)**
- Plus Barrette **(B)**
- Powersoul **(C)**
- Elixir **(D)**
- "Counter Attack" Materia **(E)**
- "Elemental" Materia **(F)**
- Sniper CR **(G)**
- "All" Materia **(H)**

To get to Mt. Nibel, take the path near the Shinra Mansion. Mt. Nibel is just a short walk away.

The first part of Mt. Nibel is fairly linear, although there are a couple of twisting paths off to the side where you can get items. The first path is obvious, but the second path is a little tough to see.

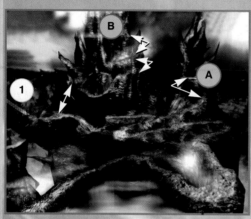

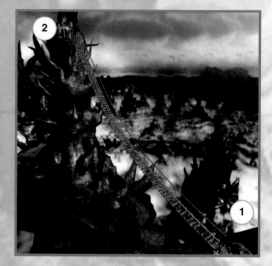

SONIC SPEED

Area—Nibel Mountains

LVL	HP	MP	EXP	GIL	AP
26	750	50	370	330	28

Slp	Ret	Con	Sil	Slw	Drk	Trsfr	Stp
Bsk	Psn	Par	Stn	SS	Man	Dth	Imp

MORPH	STEAL	ATTACKS
Speed Drink	Ether	Harrier, Swoop

DRAGON

Area—Nibel Mountains

LVL	HP	MP	EXP	GIL	AP
32	3500	250	900	1400	110

Slp	Ret	Con	Sil	Slw	Drk	Trsfr	Stp
Bsk	Psn	Par	Stn	SS	Man	Dth	Imp

MORPH	STEAL	ATTACKS
n/a	Gold Armlet	Dragon Fang, Flame Thrower

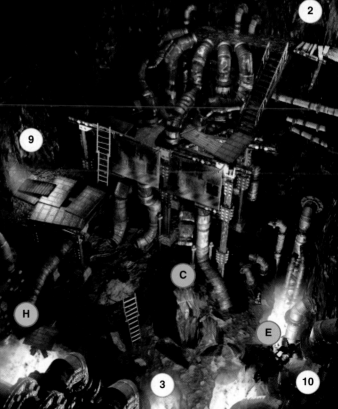

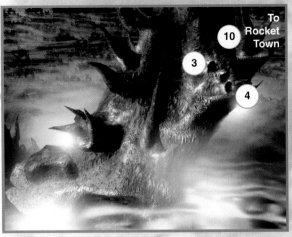

To
Rocket
Town

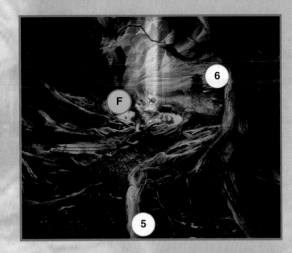

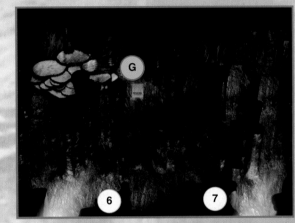

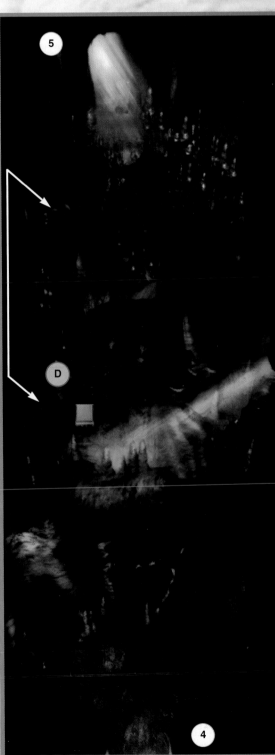

By riding the chutes after the bridge, you can grab several different items. Before you jump into a chute, climb down the ladder and push down the folding ladder so that you can climb back to the top. Don't touch the large creature at the bottom as you move about.

Chute #1 leads to the ground in front of the large scorpion-like creature.

Chute #2 leads to a small rock ledge that has a Powersoul that Tifa can use.

Chute #3 takes you down to the second level.

Chute #4 drops you off next to a chest containing an **"All" Materia**.

Chute #5 also leads to the second level.

When you have everything, take the southern path next to the large creature. This will take you to the area where Cloud fell during his flashback at Kalm.

 TIP: You can steal a **Gold Armlet** from Dragons, which is the best armor available at this point in the game.

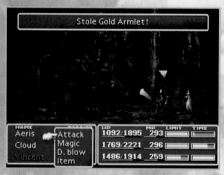

The cave below should look familiar to you, so hop down and go inside. You can get the chest by entering the top hole and following the hidden path marked on the map. Then continue until you see a fountain, but don't forget to grab the Materia next to it. At the fork in the path, go left and you'll see the Nibel Reactor just ahead. There's nothing to do at the plant, so use the door behind it to access yet another Boss.

Now would be a really good time to save your game. When you're ready, walk up and inspect the Boss to initiate combat.

Boss Fight: Materia Keeper

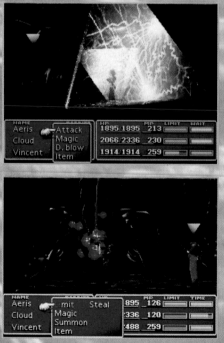

As you might expect, the Materia Keeper is one tough boss. Most of its attacks cause about 200 to 300 points of damage or more, and its Trine attack causes 500 points of damage to *each* of your characters. Fire spells heal the Materia Keeper and it's resistant to Gravity.

Use your Limit Breaks coupled with hard-hitting spells like **Bolt 2** and **Ice 2**, and then switch to your normal attacks when a character's magic gets low. Also, make sure you have your team ready to cast **Cure-All**. When the Materia Keeper's HP gets low, it'll start to heal itself with **Cure 2**. Fortunately, it only heals about 1,000 HP each time. When it's finally defeated, you'll receive a Jem Ring.

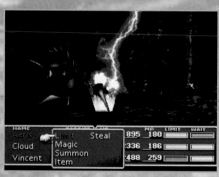

TIP: If you equip the Enemy-Skill Materia, the player can learn Trine.

The Materia Keeper drops a **"Counter Attack" Materia** on the ground, so pick it up and equip it right away. You may want to use a Tent after fighting the Materia Keeper, because your MP and HP will likely be low. With the path cleared, you can now leave Mt. Nibel.

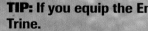

ROCKET TOWN

From Mt. Nibel follow the curve of the mountain range and eventually you'll see Rocket Town in the distance. Initially, this was earmarked as the sight for Shinra's space program, but something must have gone terribly wrong.

When you enter the town, hit the shops and pick up the latest Materia. Everyone keeps referring to the "Captain" as the man who speaks for the town. Maybe he's seen Sephiroth. Go to his house and check out back for him.

 NOTE: Talk to the old man outside the Item Shop, who asks you to look at the rocket with him. If you look at it, he'll give you the **Yoshiyuki**.

There's no Captain around, but there is a sweet little plane named *Tiny Bronco*. The Captain's assis-

tant, Shera, greets you and tells you to check the Rocket. She's also kind enough to inform you that President Rufus is headed to town, possibly to restart Shinra's space program.

If you climb to the top of the rocket, you'll find the Captain inside, whose real name is Cid. Cid is an ex-astronaut (well, almost) who had a failed launch and never made it into space. Today may be his lucky day; Rufus may reinvest in the space program. Anyway, Cid isn't about to let the team use the Tiny Bronco, so leave him alone and go back to his home.

Cid shows up later and lets Shera have it. What's the story there, eh? Shera will be happy to fill you in. The Shinra execs arrive shortly after Shera finishes her story.

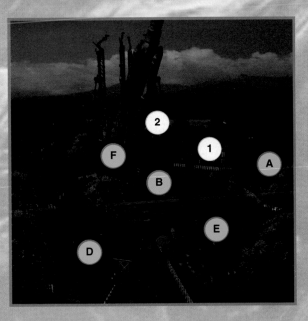

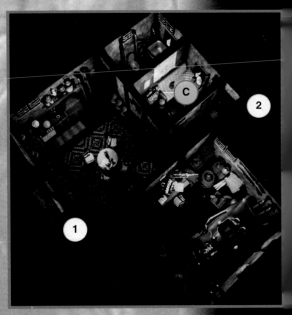

ITEMS:
- Power Source
- Yoshiyuki **(B)**
- Drill Arm **(C)**

WEAPON SHC
ITEM
- Shotgun
- Gold Armlet
- Power Wrist
- Protect Vest
- Earring
- Talisman

REST **(E)**
- Inn

ITEM SHOP (
ITEM
- Potion
- Hi-Potion
- Phoenix Down
- Ether
- Hyper
- Tranquilizer
- Tent
- "Barrier"
- "Exit"
- "Time"

Go outside and check on Cid again. Rufus has no intention of restarting the space program, but he does want to borrow the Tiny Bronco. Sephiroth is headed overseas and the Tiny Bronco's the best way to get across the ocean. Naturally, Cid's not too pleased with this request, but it looks like Palmer might try to steal the plane anyway. It's up to the team to stop him.

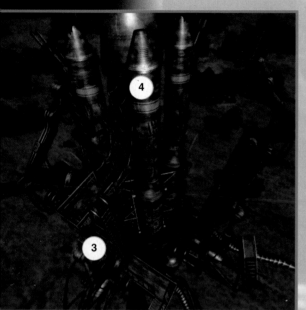

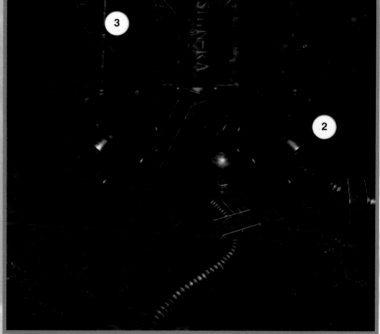

Boss Fight: Palmer

Palmer's not a tough opponent. Use your strongest spells against him and cast **Choco/Mog** or Aeris' Seal Evil to paralyze him. Then speed the team up with the **Haste** spell and keep pounding away. When executed correctly, Palmer will never get a shot off and you'll walk away with a new **Edincoat** and the Tiny Bronco.

If things don't go smoothly, prepare to face Palmer's Mako Gun. With this weapon, he can hit the team with several types of magic, including Fire, Ice, and Bolt.

There's no stopping the plane now that it's in motion. The team flies right through the middle of town and Cid quickly jumps on. Rufus isn't too happy about Cid's escape and his soldiers quickly shoot the Tiny Bronco out of the sky.

Although the plane crash-lands in the ocean, it's still salvageable as a boat in shallow water. With no place left to go and his dreams of outer space exploration shattered, Cid signs up with the team. Rufus was headed to the Temple of the Ancients, so maybe Sephiroth is there as well.

CONTROLLING THE TINY BRONCO

D-Pad	Move Tiny Bronco
Circle	Board Tiny Bronco
X	Get off Tiny Bronco

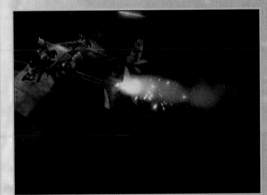

At this point, you can land on the island next to Yuffie's hometown of Wutai, or you can go back to the continent you just left and look for information on the Temple of the Ancients.

NOTE: You don't need to visit Wutai; it's just an optional part of the story. In effect, there's nothing in Wutai that needs to be done to complete the game, but you can pick up some valuable items there.

If you don't go to Wutai, skip the next portion of the walkthrough and go to the Weapon Seller, located east of Gongaga.

WUTAI

ITEMS:

- Dragoon Lance (A)
- Hairpin (B)
- Swift Bolt (C)
- Elixir (D)
- "MP Absorb" Materia (E)
- "HP Absorb" Materia (F)
- "Leviathan" Materia (G)
- "Steal as Well" Materia (H)
- Oritsuru (I)

ITEM SHOP (E)

ITEM	COST
Hi-Potion	300
Phoenix Down	300
Ether	1500
Hyper	100
Tranquilizer	100
Tent	500
Fire Veil	800
Swift Bolt	800
Choco Feather	10,000

WEAPON SHOP (J)

ITEM	COST
Murasame	6500
Diamond Knuckle	5800
Chainsaw	6300
Aurora Rod	5800
Gold Barrette	6000
Slash Lance	6500
Blue M-phone	5500
Razor Ring	6000
Shortbarrel	6400

REST (K)

Godo's House	Free

You'll have to leave the Tiny Bronco a good distance south of Wutai. There's shallow water to the north, but the Tiny Bronco can't get there. Park on the beach and then head north through the mountains.

You won't get far before Yuffie comes running and yelling at the top of her lungs. She's up to something, but is suddenly interrupted by a Shinra Attack Squad. These guys aren't too tough, but you'll soon notice something is missing...Your Materia is gone! By the time the battle is over, Yuffie is long gone and so is all your Materia. She must be headed to the only town on the island, Wutai. Head north and watch yourself—the trip won't be easy without your magic.

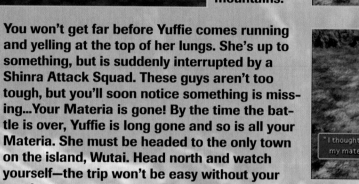

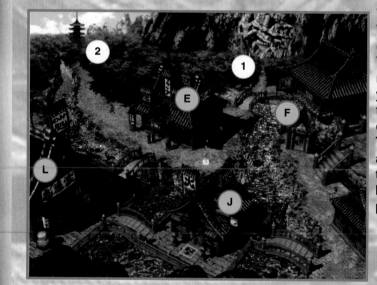

When you get to Wutai, you'll catch a quick glimpse of Yuffie, who quickly runs off. Looks like you're going to have to play a little game of hide-and-seek. Talk to the villagers and they'll point you toward Lord Godo's house in the northern part of Wutai.

FOULANDER

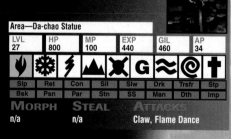

Area—Da-chao Statue					
LVL 27	HP 800	MP 100	EXP 440	GIL 460	AP 34

Slp	Ret	Con	Sil	Slw	Drk	Trsfr	Stp
Bsk	Psn	Par	Stn	SS	Man	Dth	Imp

MORPH	STEAL	ATTACKS
n/a	n/a	Claw, Flame Dance

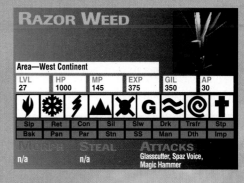

RAZOR WEED

Area—West Continent					
LVL 27	HP 1000	MP 145	EXP 375	GIL 350	AP 30

Slp	Ret	Con	Sil	Slw	Drk	Trsfr	Stp
Bsk	Psn	Par	Stn	SS	Man	Dth	Imp

MORPH	STEAL	ATTACKS
n/a	n/a	Glasscutter, Spaz Voice, Magic Hammer

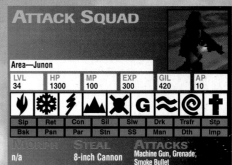

ATTACK SQUAD

Area—Junon					
LVL 34	HP 1300	MP 100	EXP 300	GIL 420	AP 10

Slp	Ret	Con	Sil	Slw	Drk	Trsfr	Stp
Bsk	Psn	Par	Stn	SS	Man	Dth	Imp

MORPH	STEAL	ATTACKS
n/a	8-inch Cannon	Machine Gun, Grenade, Smoke Bullet

GARUDA

Area—Da-chao Statue					
LVL 29	HP 1400	MP 200	EXP 520	GIL 520	AP 30

Slp	Ret	Con	Sil	Slw	Drk	Trsfr	Stp
Bsk	Psn	Par	Stn	SS	Man	Dth	Imp

MORPH	STEAL	ATTACKS
n/a	n/a	Rod, Ice2, Bolt2

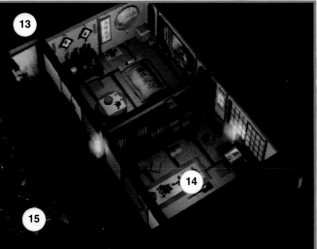

Godo is sleeping inside the house. After you talk to him several times, Yuffie will finally appear and sparks fly. Yuffie is Godo's daughter and apparently she's not too happy with her father's complacency. He chases her out of the room, which takes you back to square one.

NOTE: Visit the secret room in the bedroom adjacent to Godo's bedroom while you're in Godo's house. There's a fake wall that's clearly visible. Inside you'll find a Hairpin for Red XIII.

Return to the southern part of Wutai and search everywhere, even Turtle's Paradise and Da-chao. When you return from Da-chao, the boy outside the Item Shop says that he heard pounding from inside. Go in and investigate the treasure chest in the corner to find a **"MP Absorb"** Materia. Before you can put it into your pocket, Yuffie drops down and steals from you again. Well, at least you found her!

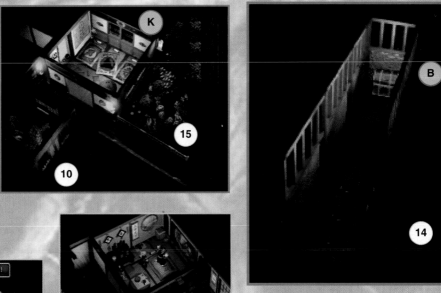

Go to the house near the entrance to Wutai to find Yuffie hiding behind the screen to the left of the entrance. Pull the screen back and she's off and running again.

Check over at the Turtle's Paradise. Notice the jar in front of the store? It sure is moving a lot. Now you've got her surrounded! Have Cloud

punch the jar several times to make Yuffie pop out. She realizes you've bested her and agrees to give you back your Materia.

Yuffie takes you to her basement and tells you to pull the left switch. In reality it doesn't matter which switch you pull, because it's a trap. As you might have guessed, Yuffie runs off again. Free your comrades and chase her down...again.

Head back to northern Wutai. You'll notice the gate to the left is now open. Walk up and ring the gong to open a secret door that leads to Yuffie's hideout. What's going on?

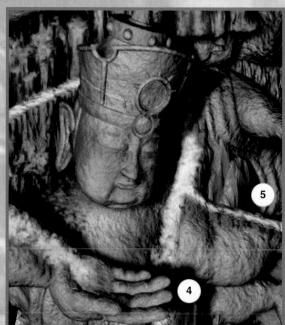

No, it can't be. Don Corneo is in Wutai and he's kidnapping Yuffie and Elena. Chase him and you'll be forced into combat against another one of Shinra's well trained Attack Squads.

Return to southern Wutai and you'll bump into the Turks. You won't have to fight Reno and Rude this time, but they do hint that Corneo is hiding on Da-chao. Run to the mountain and hunt him down.

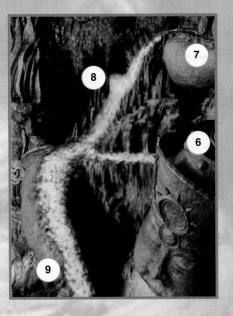

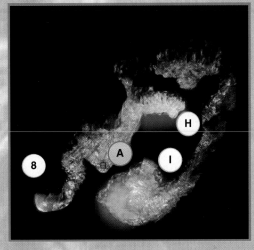

NOTE: You may want to buy a few Fire Vests from the Item Shop before moving on.

You'll find Corneo with Yuffie and Elena. They're both okay, but they're also strapped to the side of Da-chao.

BOSS FIGHT: RAPPS

This is a difficult fight because you're missing your Materia. Use your normal attacks and any magic items you have in your inventory. Your Limit Breaks will come in handy, but watch your health. If your character's levels are low, try the following party and strategy. Have Barret and Vincent join Cloud and take some time to get Barret and Vincent's Limit Breaks fully charged. When you enter the fight, have Barret use his Mind Blow attack to remove most of Rapps' MP. This keeps it from using the deadly Aero3 attack. Then have Vincent transform into any one of his beast forms. Also, move any items that enable you to cast a spell like Fire 3 or Bolt 3 to the front of your inventory. This should make the fight much easier.

Rapps can cause about 200-400 points of damage with its normal attack and the Scorpion Sting. Rapps also has an Aero3 attack that inflicts about 1,500 points of damage to a single character. This is usually more than enough to kill a member of your party and because you don't have magic, you'll need to use a lot of **Hi-Potions** and **Phoenix Downs**. Win the fight and you're given the Peace Ring.

Corneo isn't about to play fair, but the Turks save the day. The Turks leave without incident, but it's clear that there will be another battle someday.

With Yuffie back—and your Materia returned and out of order—you'll appear outside of Wutai. Don't go anywhere just yet, because you'll need rest and supplies. There's also one more thing to do in Wutai.

The local shops are friendlier now and you can climb the stairs in the Cat House **(F)**. Take a moment to rest and save your game, and then use the PHS to put Yuffie into your party. Equip her with your best Materia and return to the Pagoda of the Five Mighty Gods **(G)**.

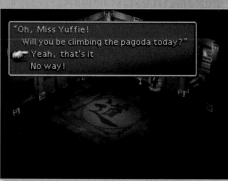

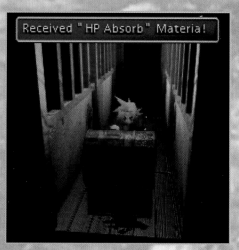

In the pagoda, Yuffie goes through a series of five trials. Each trial is a one-on-one fight against a formidable opponent. Re-equipping Yuffie for each fight makes her climb to the top much easier. Also, restore any lost HP or MP after each battle. Make it past the fifth Boss, and you'll receive the power of the Water God Leviathan.

BOSS FIGHT 1: GORKI

For this battle, equip Yuffie's armor with the **"Elemental-Gravity"** Materia combination, plus give her a **"Cure," "Barrier,"** and **"Counter Attack"** Materia. Gorki casts Demi 2 several times, but with an **"Elemental-Gravity"** Materia combination in your armor, you'll be just fine.

Cast Haste immediately and keep Yuffie's health up. Gorki will deplete its skill power quickly; the fight will then come down to who can hold out the longest. You receive an **X-Potion** for winning the battle.

BOSS FIGHT 2: SHAKE

Haste and **Barrier** are extremely important in this battle. Keep your HP up and watch for Shake's Rage Bomber attack. It can cause up to 600 points of damage, but Barrier helps cut the damage in half. Use **Choco/Mog** to paralyze Shake and the fight will be a breeze. The reward for this battle is a **Turbo Ether**.

BOSS FIGHT 3: CHEKHOV

This Boss isn't too difficult. Equip Yuffie with the Jem Ring before beginning this battle to keep Chekhov from using his Stare Down, which can paralyze Yuffie. Also, cast **Haste** and **Barrier** on Yuffie as soon as possible. Haste will enable you to take advantage of Chekhov's slow speed, while Barrier will cut its Absorb attack in half. An Ice Ring is your prize for winning this battle.

BOSS FIGHT 4: STANIV

In this fight, basically all Staniv does is hit you with its main weapon. (It has an attack called War Cry that causes Sadness, but it only affects your status.) Cast **Barrier** to cut its attacks down to roughly 150 points of damage, and then cast **Haste** on Yuffie. Sounds familiar, right? Just keep Yuffie's health up and keep recasting **Barrier** as it wears off. You can use spells, but it's not necessary. You receive an Elixir for defeating Staniv.

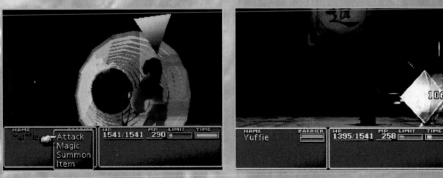

Boss Fight 5: Godo

It's easy to see why Godo sits in the fifth floor of the pagoda. This Boss has three faces, each with its own talents. The red face attacks with Beast Sword, which causes about 250-300 points of damage. It can also attack with **Trine**, which does close to 1,000 points of damage. The gold face casts

Sleepel or Mini and when Godo's HP gets low enough, Cure 2. The white face casts Drain, Bio 2, and Demi 3.

What's a low-level ninja to do? Start by equipping Yuffie with "Counterattack," "Heal," "Cure," "Time," and "Barrier"

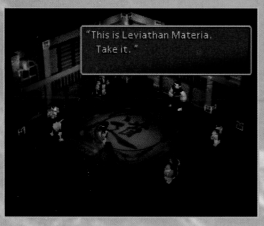

Materia. Then equip her weapon with the **"Added Effect-Poison" Materia** combination, which makes her attacks stronger, plus it poisons Godo. When the battle begins, cast **Haste** and **Barrier** and then concentrate on keeping Yuffie's health up. Use **Regen** immediately if you have it. From this point on, keep the **Barrier** up and keep Yuffie healed, and attack when you get a chance. Cast Slow on Godo to give yourself a speed advantage. If Yuffie's levels are really low, you may not be able to defeat Godo. If so, leave Wutai and come back later. Should you pull off a victory, you'll get the **"Leviathan" Materia** and Yuffie's ultimate Limit Break, All Creation.

There's nothing left to do in Wutai for now. Head back to the mainland and take the nearby river over to the Gongaga area.

NOTE: After acquiring the submarine, you should be able to get past Da-chao's fire cave. Check in the back of the book for more information.

114

THE CAT AND THE KEYSTONE

East of Gongaga Village is a Weapon Seller who lives in a house by himself. He can tell you a little about the Temple of the Ancients, but not much. The most important information he has is the fact that you need a Keystone to enter the Temple of Ancients. Unfortunately, he just sold the Keystone to Dio, the owner of the Gold Saucer.

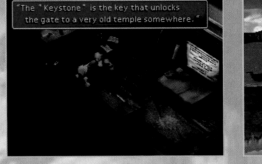

Head for North Corel and ride the Ropeway to the Gold Saucer. This time around you'll want to drop the 30,000 Gil for a lifetime pass to the park. You'll return here a lot if you decide to breed and race Chocobos.

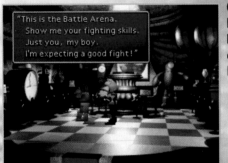

Go to the Battle Arena, check out Dio's show room and you'll find the Keystone, which is on display. When Dio shows up, Cloud asks to borrow the Keystone; however, Dio isn't going for it. There is another option: if you're willing to fight in the Battle Arena, Dio will give you the Keystone.

TIP: It doesn't matter how far you get in the Battle Arena, you just need to try. However, if you can defeat all eight opponents in the Battle Arena, you'll receive a Protect Vest and Choco Feather in addition to the Keystone.

After the battle Dio hands over the Keystone so you can be on your way. But wouldn't you know it, the Tram is out of order. It looks like you'll be spending the night. Fortunately, Cait Sith has connections and can get you into the Ghost Hotel.

In the middle of the night, Aeris comes and asks you to take her on a date. This is the perfect opportunity to tour the Gold Saucer and enjoy the rides for free. But first, you get invited to take part in the Gold Saucer's stage show.

NOTE: Aeris may not come to your room if you've treated her poorly. If this is the case, you may get a visit from another party member.

NOTE: Play along with the show if you'd like, but it's far more fun to mess it up.

115

After taking part in the show, it's time to venture to the Gondola ride. Look out the window when Aeris looks out to watch some really cool scenes.

After the ride, Cloud and Aeris bump into Cait Sith, who's attempting to steal the Keystone. Chase him to the arcade and then to the Chocobo Racing forum. The bad news is that you can't stop him before he gives the Keystone to Tseng of the Turks. So that's it! Cait Sith is the spy!

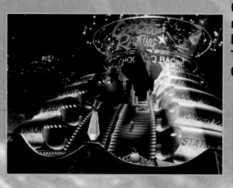

It looks like Cait Sith is staying with you regardless of your wishes. Fortunately, he knows where the Temple of the Ancients is, so hop in the Tiny Bronco and head out to sea.

NOTE: Check Cloud's dresser in the hotel and you'll receive an **Elixir**.

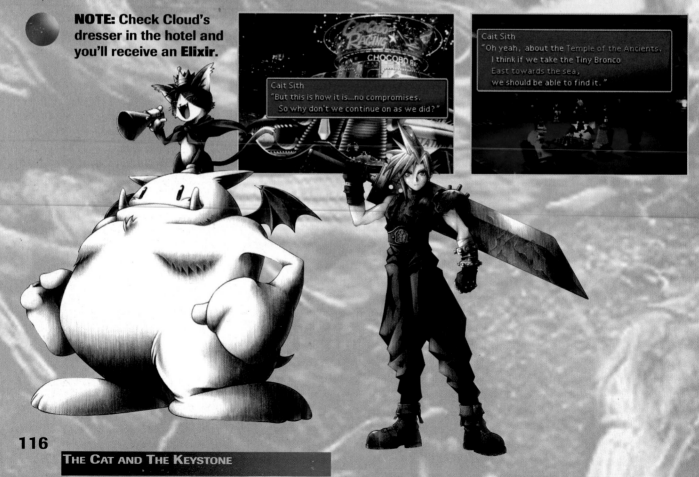

TEMPLE OF THE ANCIENTS

You can see the Temple of the Ancients from quite a distance. It looks like a huge ziggurat set in the middle of a jungle.

When you arrive, go to the top of the temple and search the man in black. He'll mention **Black Materia** and then vanish. Inside the temple, you'll find Tseng lying on the ground severely wounded. He turns over the Keystone and tells you to place it on the altar, which opens up the temple's inner-sanctum.

To Inner Sanctum

The next maze may look like an Escher painting, but it's really not that difficult to maneuver around it.

NOTE: You cannot walk on most of the area that you can see. Try to open the different doors and check the map's callouts to see where it will take you. Note that you can use vines as if they were ladders.

When you first enter the area, follow the purple guy. He'll let you rest in his chamber, which makes it easy to wander around until you've picked up everything.

There's a second Ancient in the southern part of the maze. When you get near him, he'll run into a nearby door, so follow him inside. There are huge "U"-shaped boulders rolling down the path between you and the Ancient. To get to the end of the path, stand so that the cut out part of the boulder lands where you're standing. This

ITEMS:
Trident **(A)**
Mind Source **(B)**
Silver Rifle **(C)**
Turbo Ether **(D)**
Rocket Punch **(E)**
"Luck Plus" Materia **(F)**
"Morph" Materia **(G)**
Nail Bat **(H)**
Work Glove **(I)**
Ribbon **(J)**
Princess Guard **(K)**
"Bahamut" Materia **(L)**
Trumpet Shell **(M)**
Megalixir **(N)**

ITEM SHOP (O)

ITEM	COST
Potion	50
Hi-Potion	300
Phoenix Down	300
Ether	1500
Hyper	100
Tranquilizer	100
Maiden's Kiss	150
Tent	500

KELZMELZER

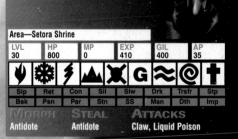

Area—Setora Shrine

LVL	HP	MP	EXP	GIL	AP
30	800	0	410	400	35

Slp	Ret	Con	Sil	Slw	Drk	Trsfr	Stp
Bsk	Psn	Par	Stn	SS	Man	Dth	Imp

MORPH	STEAL	ATTACKS
Antidote	Antidote	Claw, Liquid Poison

UNDER LIZARD

Area—Temple

LVL	HP	MP	EXP	GIL	AP
30	1400	140	440	0	45

Slp	Ret	Con	Sil	Slw	Drk	Trsfr	Stp
Bsk	Psn	Par	Stn	SS	Man	Dth	Imp

MORPH	STEAL
Remedy	Remedy

TOXIC FROG

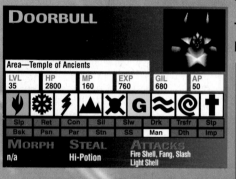

Area—Temple of Ancients

LVL	HP	MP	EXP	GIL	AP
26	500	100	420	260	30

Slp	Ret	Con	Sil	Slw	Drk	Trsfr	Stp
Bsk				SS			Imp

MORPH	STEAL	ATTACKS
Remedy	Impaler	Frog Jab, Frog Song, Poison

DOORBULL

Area—Temple of Ancients

LVL	HP	MP	EXP	GIL	AP
35	2800	160	760	680	50

Slp	Ret	Con	Sil	Slw	Drk	Trsfr	Stp
Bsk	Psn	Par	Stn	SS	Man	Dth	Imp

MORPH	STEAL	ATTACKS
n/a	Hi-Potion	Fire Shell, Fang, Slash, Light Shell

ANCIENT DRAGON

Area—Temple of Ancients

LVL	HP	MP	EXP	GIL	AP
34	2400	450	800	800	80

Slp	Ret	Con	Sil	Slw	Drk	Trsfr	Stp
Bsk	Psn	Par	Stn	SS	Man	Dth	Imp

MORPH	STEAL	ATTACKS
n/a	n/a	Horn, Southern Cross

8 EYE

Area—Temple of Ancients

LVL	HP	MP	EXP	GIL	AP
30	500	220	1000	720	100

Slp	Ret	Con	Sil	Slw	Drk	Trsfr	Stp
Bsk	Psn	Par	Stn	SS	Man	Dth	Imp

MORPH	STEAL	ATTACKS
n/a	n/a	Life Drain

JEMNEZMY

Area—Temple of Ancients

LVL	HP	MP	EXP	GIL	AP
24	800	80	510	400	50

Slp	Ret	Con	Sil	Slw	Drk	Trsfr	Stp
Bsk	Psn	Par	Stn	SS	Man	Dth	Imp

MORPH	STEAL	ATTACKS
n/a	n/a	Cold Breath, Fascination

will make the boulder pass harmlessly over you. Quickly get under the next boulder or run off to one of the sides to wait for a better opportunity. When you reach the end of the path, the trap will shut itself off and you'll return to the pool in the middle. In this area, you'll see a flashback of the Turks and Sephiroth from what must have been only a little while ago.

Cloud
"...Where is the room with the pictures on the walls?"

The next area is a large clock. There are twelve rooms surrounding the pit, each one marked with an hour number. Spin the hands of the clock so that the hour and minute hands form a bridge between your ledge and where you want to go.

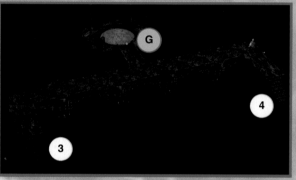

Pressing the ● button makes the hands go very fast. Pressing the ● button again causes the hands to slowly come to rest three spaces later. You can use this technique to quickly move time, or you can press the ▲ button to slowly move the clock backward or forward one space at a time.

TIP: While moving on the hands, beware of the second hand. If it hits you while you're moving, you'll get knocked off the clock and forced into a battle. However, you'll also get the **Nail Bat**.

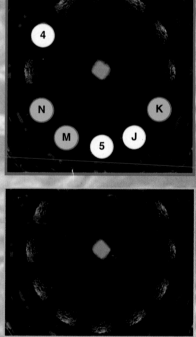

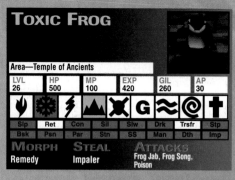

Room I:	Enemy encounter (Jemnezmy, Toxic Frog (x2))	Room VI:	Door maze
Room II:	Dead end	Room VII:	Trumpet Shell
Room III:	Enemy encounter (8 Eye (x2))	Room VIII:	Megalixir
Room IV:	Princess Guard	Room IX:	Dead end
Room V:	Ribbon	Room X:	To rolling boulder room
		Room XI:	Dead end
		Room XII:	Exit

As you enter this room, the guard runs away with the key to the next area. To catch him, you'll need to figure out his pattern. Each of the doors is somehow connected with another door on the map. Each time you enter a door, the guard comes out of a door and then enters a different one. You must figure out which door he will come out of next and enter that specific door to catch him.

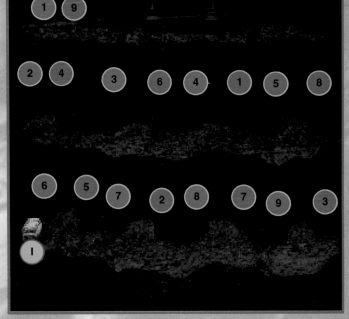

 TIP: You can jump down a level by pressing the ● button on the left side of the map; however, to get back up you must enter a door.

Find the door the guard went into on the map and check the number in red. Now locate that same number in blue elsewhere on the map. This is where the guard will come out.

After capturing the guard, he unlocks the door and gives you a chance to rest and save.

Just past the door you'll see the room from the earlier flashback. This is where you meet Sephiroth, who's busy absorbing the knowledge of the Ancients. He tells you about his master plan to become one with the planet. Sephiroth leaves and Cloud freaks out, but becomes fully aware of Sephiroth's evil plan in the process. As the team discusses the planet's fate, a Red Dragon attacks them.

Boss Fight: Red Dragon

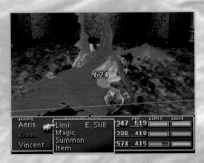

As the name *sort of* implies, the Red Dragon is a fire-based creature. Therefore, fire-based attacks will only heal it, plus it's immune to **Gravity** spells.

Start the battle by using **Bio 2** to poison it while casting **Barrier** and **Haste** on the entire team. This will cut down the dragon's bite from 700-800 points of damage to about 400.

Use **Regen** if you can and keep a close eye on your health. The **"Deathblow" Materia** is also a great way to deliver a punishing blow to the enemy. With this setup, it shouldn't be a long fight. You receive a Dragon Armlet for winning the battle.

119

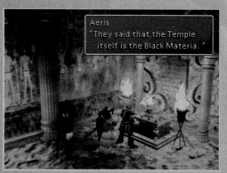

After collecting and equipping the **"Bahamut" Materia**, left behind by the Red Dragon, run to the right to find the **Black Materia** on an altar. There is a problem though: You can't take it out of the temple without killing one of your team members. Cait Sith happily volunteers to relinquish his stuffed body. Race back to the exit (12 in the clock room) to let Cait Sith inside. Is there something wrong with the exit room? It almost seems...alive!

Boss Fight: Demon's Gate

Quickly cast **Slow** on the Demon's Gate. This creature can attack quickly even when slowed, but at least its attacks will be more manageable. Also, cast **Barrier** and **Haste** on the entire party to help protect against the Gate's Demon Rush and avalanche attacks. This also enables the team to respond quickly to the Gate's actions. Having the **"Heal" Materia** will help counter the Petrif-Eye attack; otherwise, you'll need a few Softs.

Try to keep your HP around 1,000 and you'll be fine. The Gate is immune to both **Poison** and **Gravity** spells and is resistant to Earth. You receive the Gigas Armlet after defeating the Demon's Gate.

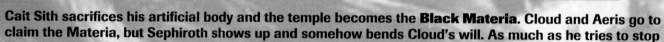

Cait Sith sacrifices his artificial body and the temple becomes the **Black Materia**. Cloud and Aeris go to claim the Materia, but Sephiroth shows up and somehow bends Cloud's will. As much as he tries to stop himself, Cloud hands the Materia over and then turns on his own team. This is quickly stopped, but what does it all mean? Why would Cloud do such a thing?

Cloud has a surreal dream of Aeris in the Sleeping Forest, which protects the City of Ancients. In the dream, she's going to try to stop Sephiroth on her own, but Sephiroth is on to her.

When Cloud awakens, Aeris has left the group and you're inside the Inn at Gongaga. Cloud quickly pulls himself together and the team leaves for the northern continent.

NOTE: The Tiny Bronco is parked right outside of Gongaga. Follow the coastline up to the large continent in the north.

BONE VILLAGE

Bone Village is an excavation site set on the edge of the Sleeping Forest. Talk to the people working the sight and they'll provide some valuable information regarding the area.

You'll need the Lunar Harp to get past the Sleeping Forest. To get the harp, you need to hire some workers to dig it up for you. Speak to the foreman and he'll ask you to place several workers, each of which costs 100 Gil (you can place 1 to 5 workers). These workers measure the tremors and point to the spot where they believe the harp is located. Try to pinpoint the location the workers are pointing at and have them dig in that spot. Don't place all the workers together or on the same level.

ITEMS:
Lunar Harp (A)
Mop
Buntline

ITEM SHOP

ITEM	COST
Diamond Bangle	3200
Rune Armlet	3700
Potion	50
Hi-Potion	300
Phoenix Down	300
Ether	1500
Hyper	100
Tranquilizer	100
Tent	500

Sleeping Forest

In the morning, the Lunar Harp is located in the chest near the front. If not, you'll need to try again.

NOTE: The Harp is on the highest tier near the bone tent. Set the workers in this area.

With the Harp in your possession, you're ready to enter the forest. You may want to stick around and dig for other useful items. Just remember that digging isn't free.

121

THE SLEEPING FOREST

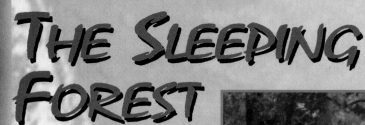

ITEMS:

"Kjata" Materia **(A)**
Water Ring **(B)**

With the Lunar Harp in hand, the Sleeping Forest greets you and lets you pass. There's a Red Materia that keeps appearing and disappearing in the trees. Grab it

Bone Village

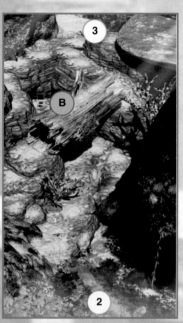

when it appears and you'll receive the **"Kjata" Materia.**

In the rocky area is a Water Ring. Pick it up and equip Cloud with it—it'll come in handy later.

You'll soon return to the World Map. Follow the canyon to the City of the Ancients.

The Sleeping Forest awoke...

City of the Ancients

Received "Kjata" Materia!

CITY OF THE ANCIENTS

There are three roads at the entrance to the city. Explore the two outside paths before venturing down the center.

Down the right path, you'll find a **Guard Source**, **"Enemy Skill" Materia**, and an **Elixir**. There's also a place to rest for free. Down the left path, you'll find a **Magic Source**, an **Aurora Armlet**, and a Save Point. Take a look around and settle in for the night.

Cloud awakens the team in the middle of the night, because he can hear Aeris' voice calling from the city. Take the center path back to find a huge shell house. Grab the **"Comet" Materia** from the top of the house before exploring the path in the middle.

ITEMS:
Guard Source **(A)**
"Enemy Skill" Materia **(B)**
Elixir **(C)**
Magic Source **(D)**
Aurora Armlet **(E)**
"Comet" Materia **(F)**

REST
Ancient Home   Free

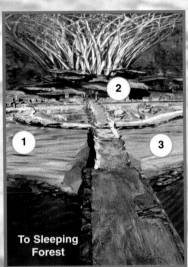

To Sleeping Forest

To Corel Valley Cave

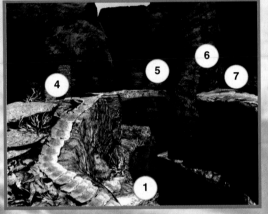

Cait Sith
"We're in luck. There's a bed in here."

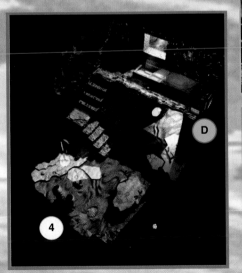

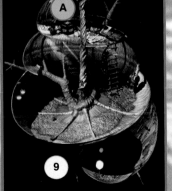

Below the house is a beautiful, crystalline city. Aeris is in the middle of the city, completely silent and locked in prayer. Cloud approaches her and immediately begins to freak out. There's nothing you can do here, because every action threatens Aeris' life. Sephiroth once again demonstrates his ability to manipulate Cloud. Your other party members can stop him from killing Aeris, but Sephiroth is more than willing to do his own dirty work. Aeris slumps to the floor and her **White Materia** falls to the waters below.

Now that Aeris is dead, Sephiroth flies away for the Promise Land, but he leaves another Jenova creature for Cloud to deal with.

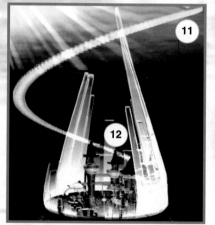

BOSS FIGHT: JENOVA-LIFE

Equip Cloud with the Water Ring because Jenova-LIFE's attacks are all water-based, which essentially makes Cloud invincible. Set up **MBarrier** to weaken its attacks against the rest of the party and cast **Haste** to speed up everyone else. While Cloud pounds away at Jenova-LIFE with his sword, have the rest of your team use **Quake 2** or **3** depending on your own experience.

WARNING! Jenova-LIFE will cast Reflect occasionally. If it does, cast **DeBarrier** to destroy its protection.

With **MBarrier** in effect, your **Cure** spells won't be as effective. You can cast **Regen** on the group for a more efficient healing process. Should your allies succumb to Jenova-LIFE's water attacks, wait until it runs out of skill power, then you can safely revive them without fear of losing them again. You receive a Wizard Bracelet after the battle.

NOTE: If you're wearing the **"Enemy Skill" Materia**, you can learn Jenova-LIFE's Aqualung attack.

With the threat destroyed and Sephiroth gone, our heroes pay their last respects to Aeris and set her body to rest. The team is now full of new purpose. What Sephiroth may claim to be his ultimate victory, may be his ultimate mistake.

125

CORRAL VALLEY CAVE

In the morning, the team heads for the Corral Valley Cave and Icicle Inn. The team hasn't had a rest since the Jenova-LIFE Boss fight, so use the beds in the next home for some rest. When you're ready, take the right path (the one Cloud envisions Sephiroth walking on) out of the area.

Climb the twisting "conch shell" stairs, and then walk around the outside of the shell to reach the high ledge. You can reach the chest in this area by simply walking to the left of the stairs and around the base of the shell.

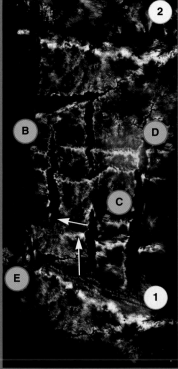

Scale the cracked cliffs by going inside the crack, and then push up or down as if climbing normally. When you reach a ledge, you're asked which direction you want to go. You may need to exit a crack and then re-enter it to go higher.

To City of the Ancients

TIP: Climb down the long ladder on the left side. At the bottom you'll find a **"MP"** Materia.

When you reach the World Map, head west, and then wrap around the mountains to the Icicle Inn.

EXP	GIL	AP
420	350	40

✖ G ≈ ◎ ✝

	Slw	Drk	Trsfr	Stp
	SS	Man	Dth	Imp

ATTACKS
Ice2, Dark Needle, Death Sentence

To Icicle Inn Area

ICICLE INN

As you explore Icicle Inn, you'll learn that Ifalno of the Cetra (Aeris' mother) lived here long ago, but it's rumored that the Shinra kidnapped her. Her home is still standing, so you can check out the recording equipment inside her house to learn more about Ifalno, Professor Gast, the Cetra, and Jenova.

You'll also learn that a man passed through the town earlier and headed for the Northern Limits. To reach the Northern Limits, you must pass through Great Glacier and scale the Gaea Cliffs.

ITEMS:
- Hero Drink **(A)**
- Vaccine **(A)**
- Turbo Ether **(B)**
- X-Potion **(C)**

WEAPON SHOP **(D)**

ITEM	COST
Organics	12000
Dragon Claw	10000
Microlaser	12000
Adaman Clip	11000
Hawkeye	12000
Red M-phone	11000
Mast Ax	13000
Lariat	12000
Tent	500
Hi-Potion	300

REST

Inn	200

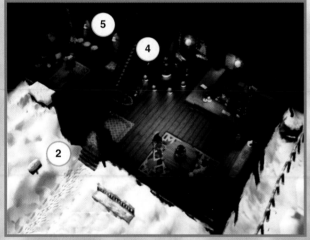

"Then, Ifalna, please tell us about the Cetra."

If you try to exit the town through the back, a local stops you. Tell him you're leaving and Elena suddenly appears, spouting something about how she's upset about Tseng. Dodge her punch by pressing to the left or right and she'll go rolling out of Icicle Inn.

NOTE: If Elena decks you, you'll awaken in Ifalno's house.

The remaining Shinra soldiers won't let anyone in or out of Icicle Inn until Rufus arrives. You can still get down to Great Glacier, but you'll need some supplies.

If you want to cross Great Glacier, you'll need a map... and there's only one map in town. This map is tacked to the wall at Mr. Holzoff's house. Mr. Holzoff isn't around, so he won't mind if you borrow the Glacier Map **(F)** and the supplies from the back room.

How does one get down to Great Glacier? Snowboarding seems to be the big rage around here, so maybe Cloud can borrow one. Check with the family who lives in the center home **(G)**. You can borrow the boy's snowboard since he won't be using it anytime soon.

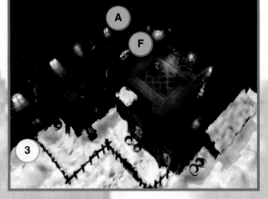

SNOWBOARD CONTROLS

D-Pad Up	Kick off when stopped
D-Pad Left	Move left
D-Pad Right	Move right
D-Pad Down	Brake
D-Pad Left + R1	Edge left
D-Pad Right + R2	Edge right
■	Brake
X	Jump

NOTE: Before entering Great Glacier, equip your party with armor and accessories that defend against Ice attacks.

The steep hill behind Icicle Inn is a monster snowboarding course. You need to fly through tight turns and dodge obstacles on your way down the course. Most of the time, you can make the turns by just using the D-Pad, but sharper curves require sharper turns. Prepare to use the Edge Left or Right command a lot. This will help you make those tough turns, which in turn makes you a master snowboarder. If you need to slow down, use the breaks to get past some of the obstacles and curves.

The course splits twice near the bottom. Check out the Great Glacier maps to see where each path takes you.

Left, Left = 1
Left, Right = 2
Right, Left = 3
Right, Right = 4

GREAT GLACIER

Great Glacier can be a confusing place at times, because there are lots of little side paths that lead to larger areas. The larger areas are all visible on the map, but it's sometimes difficult to tell just where you are.

 TIP: Just because you're moving east and west on a side path doesn't mean you're not also going north and south. Keep this in mind to avoid getting lost.

The first thing you need to do is determine where you landed and locate that spot on the map. Your main goal is getting to Gaea Cliffs, the red check mark on the Glacier Map. However, there are other things to do and see here.

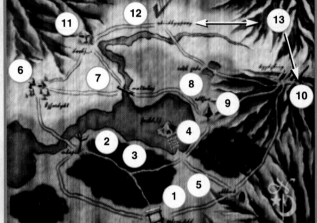

 WARNING! You can only spend so much time in the cold before passing out. If you pass out, you'll get rescued and taken to Mr. Holzoff's house at the base of the Gaea Cliffs.

Take some time to explore some of the following areas as indicated on the maps:

1. **Entrance to Great Glacier and one of the snowboard landing zones. Can return to Icicle Inn from here. You land here if you go left and then right.**

2. **Nothing to do here.**

3. **Snowboard landing area if you choose to go left twice.**

4. **Cross the ice flow to reach a small cave and a Safety Bit. You can only step on the large ice blocks, so be careful. When you step on a block, all adjacent small blocks switch to large blocks and all large blocks switch to small blocks. If you get trapped on a block, you're forced to try again.**

5. **There's a cave here that serves as an exit from Great Glacier. Take the slide to go to the base of the hill below Icicle Inn. Snowboard landing area if you go right twice.**

6. **There's an Elixir in a cave here.**

7. **Nothing to do here.**

8. **The Hot Springs are here. Touch the water (G) and then visit the Snow woman (see #13 below).**

9. **Snowboard landing area if you choose to go right and then left.**

10. **Nothing to do here.**

11. **Nothing to do here.**

12. **Area is difficult to navigate because of winds. Place flags using the ● button to create landmarks. Place them close together so you can see two at the same time. (Use them as reference points.) "All" Materia is in a hut in the center of the area. Go north from here to reach the Gaea Cliffs.**

13. **The Snow woman's cave is here. The area is accessbile only from Area 12. Talk to her after touching the Hot Springs and she attacks. Defeat her to get the "Alexander" Materia.**

129

EMS:
Mind Source (**A**)
Poison (**B**)
Safety Bit (**C**)
Elixir (**D**)
"All" Materia (**E**)
"Alexander" Materia (**F**)

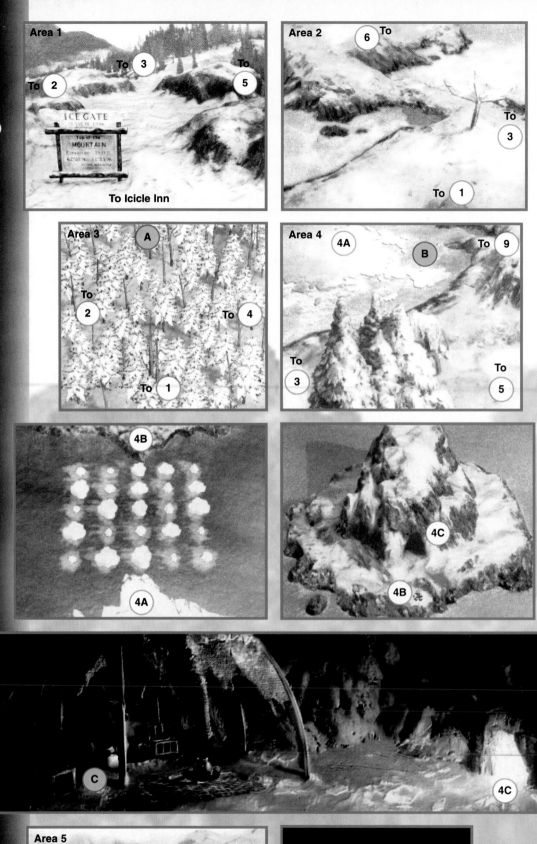

5B

Area 6
To 11
To 11
6B
6A
To 7
To 2

6B
D
6A

Area 9
To 7
To 10
To 4

Area 7
To 6
To 9

Area 8
12
To
G
To 10

Area 11
To 13
To 6

Area 10
To 8
To 9
To 8 From 13
To 5

Area 12
To 12
E

Area 13
To 12
13A
To 10

13A
F

ITEMS:
- Javelin **(B)**
- Elixir **(C)**
- Fire Armlet **(D)**
- Last Elixir (Megalixir) **(E)**
- Speed Source **(F)**
- Enhance Sword **(G)**

If you pass out on your first trip to Great Glacier, which is likely to happen, you'll wind up in Mr. Holzoff's **(A)** house at the base of the Gaea Cliffs. Listen to his story and heed his advice.

"You collapsed at the Great Glacier. It's a miracle you're all right."

TIP: Once you visit Mr. Holzoff, you can always return to his house to rest and save.

MALBORO

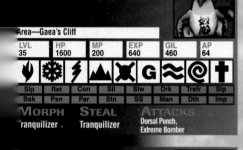

Area—Gaea's Cliff

LVL	HP	MP	EXP	GIL	AP
44	4400	900	1000	100	100

Slp	Ret	Con	Sil	Slw	Drk	Trsfr	Stp
Bsk	Psn	Par	Stn	SS	Man	Dth	Imp

MORPH	STEAL	ATTACKS
n/a	M-Tentacles	Frozen Beam, Bad Breath, Bio2

HEADBOMBER

Area—Gaea's Cliff

LVL	HP	MP	EXP	GIL	AP
35	1600	200	640	460	64

Slp	Ret	Con	Sil	Slw	Drk	Trsfr	Stp
Bsk	Psn	Par	Stn	SS	Man	Dth	Imp

MORPH	STEAL	ATTACKS
Tranquilizer	Tranquilizer	Dorsal Punch, Extreme Bomber

ZOLKALTER

Area—Gaea's Cliff

LVL	HP	MP	EXP	GIL	AP
30	950	90	700	700	60

Slp	Ret	Con	Sil	Slw	Drk	Trsfr	Stp
Bsk	Psn	Par	Stn	SS	Man	Dth	Imp

MORPH	STEAL	ATTACKS
Antidote	n/a	Bite, Toxic Barf

STILVA

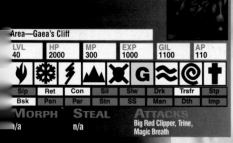

Area—Gaea's Cliff

LVL	HP	MP	EXP	GIL	AP
40	2000	300	1000	1100	110

Slp	Ret	Con	Sil	Slw	Drk	Trsfr	Stp
Bsk	Psn	Par	Stn	SS	Man	Dth	Imp

MORPH	STEAL	ATTACKS
n/a	n/a	Big Red Clipper, Trine, Magic Breath

When climbing the cliffs, you'll move between ledges. At each ledge, you need to raise Cloud's body temperature by repeatedly tapping the ■ button. You must do this at every ledge to keep Cloud's body temperature around 37 degrees. If his body temperature falls below 26 degrees, Cloud passes out and awakens in Mr. Holzoff's house.

To Great Glacier

After the first set of cliffs, you'll reach a small cave. Take the left path after the first door, and then follow the trail to a small cliff with an ice boulder resting on the edge. Push the boulder off the edge to destroy the barricade that blocks the lower trail. Now return to where you veered off and continue to the next set of cliffs.

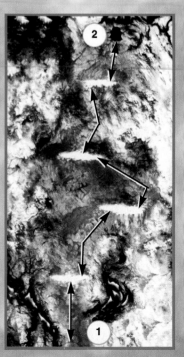

In the next cave there's a door and a chest you can't seem to reach. For now, head right and follow the trail to a room full of huge icicles. As you walk along the edge, you'll enter four battles. In each battle, there's a huge Icicle in the back row of the enemy ranks. Attack the Icicle until it breaks, then jump down to the room below after breaking all four Icicles. Now you can reach the door and chest that were previously inaccessible.

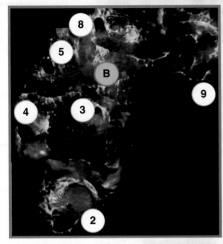

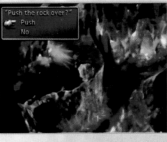

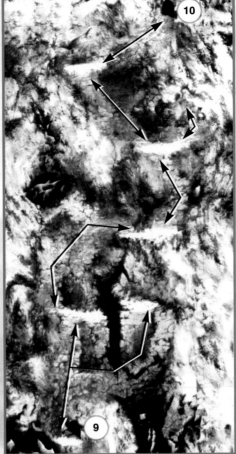

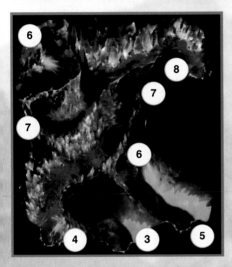

There's a Save Point just inside the next cave, so save your game and dip your hands in the adjacent pool (**H**) if your HP and MP are low. Also, equip everyone with items that absorb or protect against both **Fire** and **Ice** spells. Just down the path, the party encounters a huge beast blocking an icy hall.

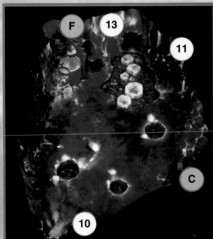

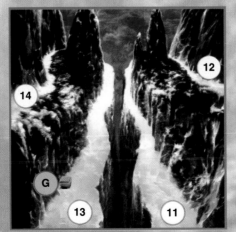

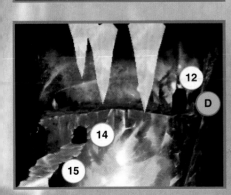

133

BOSS FIGHT: SCHIZO

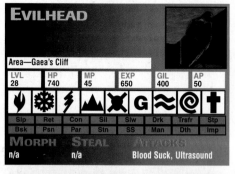

EVILHEAD

Area—Gaea's Cliff

LVL	HP	MP	EXP	GIL	AP
28	740	45	650	400	50

Slp	Ret	Con	Sil	Slw	Drk	Trsfr	Stp
Bsk	Psn	Par	Stn	SS	Man	Dth	Imp

MORPH	STEAL	ATTACKS
n/a	n/a	Blood Suck, Ultrasound

Schizo's right side is fire-based and its left side is ice-based, so casting **Fire** on the right side or **Ice** on the left side heals that side. To make matters worse, both sides of Schizo are invulnerable to **Gravity**. As you might expect, Schizo's right side attacks with Fire Breath and its left side attacks with Ice Breath, but both sides can also cast Quake 3 on the entire party.

ICICLE

Area—Gaea's Cliff

LVL	HP	MP	EXP	GIL	AP
30	3000	300	500	0	0

Slp	Ret	Con	Sil	Slw	Drk	Trsfr	Stp
Bsk	Psn	Par	Stn	SS	Man	Dth	Imp

MORPH	STEAL	ATTACKS
n/a	n/a	Icicle Drop

Start the battle by casting **MBarrier** and **Regen** on the team. Then have one of your characters cast **Ice 3** on Schizo's right side, while another character hits the left side with **Fire 3**. This should make short work of Schizo. Note that both heads get a final attack that causes up to 1,000 points of damage. The team receives a **Dragon Fang** for taking care of Schizo.

You've reached the summit! Climb the last cliff outside and see what Sephiroth is up to.

To Crater

18

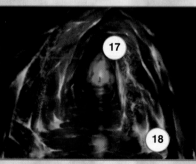

17

18

16   H   17

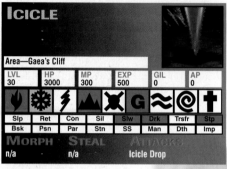

As you move deeper into the crater, you'll find Sephiroth's unwilling followers making their way to the center.

 TIP: If you encounter a fallen follower, check him and he may transform into an item. Also, keep an eye out for the Save Point and the **"Neo Bahamut"** Materia.

"...b, back...to...Sep... ...i...roth..."

You may want (or need) to use a Tent to get some rest. Also, take a moment to equip anything that absorbs or protects against **Fire** spells.

GRENADE
Uses Bomb Blast after getting hit twice.

Area—Whirlwind Maze						
LVL 32	HP 2000	MP 0	EXP 900	GIL 400	AP 100

🔥	❄	⚡	⛰	✖	G	≈	◎	✝

Slp	Ret	Con	Sil	Slw	Drk	Trsfr	Stp
Bsk	Psn	Par	Stn	SS	Man	Dth	Imp

MORPH	STEAL	ATTACKS
n/a	Right Arm	Bomb Blast, Bodyblow

ITEMS:
"Neo Bahamut" Materia **(A)**
Hi-Potion **(B)**, Ether **(B)**
Kaiser Knuckle **(C)**
"MP Turbo" Materia **(D)**
Poison Ring **(E)**

To Gaea Cliffs

Shinra soon shows up with the whole gang: Rufus, Scarlet, Heidegger, and even Hojo. Ignore them for now, and keep moving toward the center.

The wind is whipping around the crater, causing large barrier walls to form. Don't cross the barriers until the wind calms down a bit or you'll get shoved back and forced into a fight. Later barriers will have green waves rushing through them. These waves never dissipate and must be avoided in the same manner.

WIND WING

Area—Whirlwind Maze						
LVL 36	HP 1900	MP 350	EXP 800	GIL 500	AP 60

🔥	❄	⚡	⛰	✖	G	≈	◎	✝

Slp	Ret	Con	Sil	Slw	Drk	Trsfr	Stp
Bsk	Psn	Par	Stn	SS	Man	Dth	Imp

MORPH	STEAL	ATTACKS
Phoenix Down	Hi-Potion	Tailbeat, Sham Seal, Aero3, White Wind

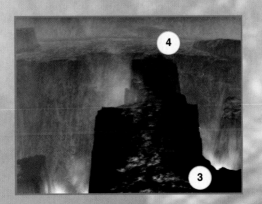

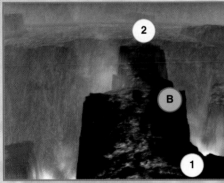

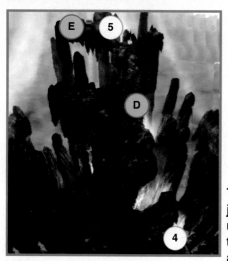

Tifa
"We need to cross
when the wind is calm,
or we'll get swept off!"

The team bumps into Sephiroth **(D)** just as he's killing a few shrouded figures. He disappears for a moment, but then launches a sneak attack from above.

Boss Fight: Jenova-DEATH

Jenova–DEATH attacks with two types of fire magic: Red Light and Tropic Wind. (It can also cast Silence, but rarely does.) So, equipping your team with armor and accessories that protect against Fire makes this a short fight.

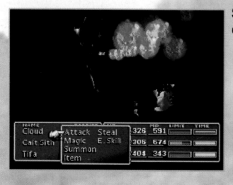

Start the battle by setting up **MBarrier** and casting **Haste** and **Regen** on the entire party. Then have someone cast **Slow** on Jenova-DEATH, which gives you a slight advantage from the start. Normal attacks cause a decent amount of damage as do Level 3 magic attacks. Also, keep the **Esuna** spell ready if Jenova-DEATH casts Silence on the team. Defeat Jenova-DEATH and you'll receive a **Reflect Ring**.

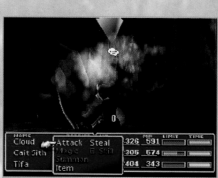

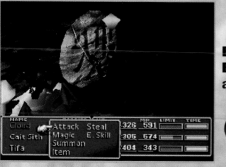

Sephiroth is deep within the crater, but Cloud now has the **Black Materia** under his control although he can't use it yet. Give the **Black Materia** to one of your party members (actually your choices are pretty limited) and move on.

TIP: You'll find an **"MP Turbo" Materia (D)** and a Save Point just ahead. Consider using another Tent if the Jenova-DEATH battle left the team hurting.

The wind barriers get even trickier at this point. Now you need to dodge the green waves and bolts of lightning. Time your moves carefully.

As the team draws closer to Sephiroth, they begin to see things and places like Nibelheim. Here you'll see the same scene you saw in the Kalm Inn, but things are slightly different. Cloud is nowhere to be found. Cloud writes the illusions off as a prank, but Tifa seems to be a bit more disturbed by the images. Sephiroth claims that Cloud was created by Hojo just like the others and that he too is a Jenova-filled puppet. Cloud realizes the folly in his memory, but seems to recover before it can destroy him.

The Shinra execs have arrived at the center of the crater just in time to see the WEAPONS awake from their long slumber. At the same time, whoever is carrying the **Black Materia** gets a mysterious visit from Tifa, who says to bring the **Black Materia** to the center of the crater. This same character then runs off, which enables you to see that it was actually Sephiroth—not Tifa—all along.

The team joins the Shinra execs in the middle of the crater and the character who's carrying the Black Materia shows up shortly thereafter. Cloud takes the **Black Materia** and delivers it to Sephiroth. At this point, all hell breaks loose and the WEAPONs are awakened.

THE EXECUTION

Seven days later, Tifa awakens and finds herself locked in a Shinra lab with Barret. She also learns that the crater is now encased in a protective barrier and the WEAPONS are wreaking havoc everywhere. Sephiroth managed to summon Meteor and it now hangs in space like a huge time bomb waiting to destroy everything.

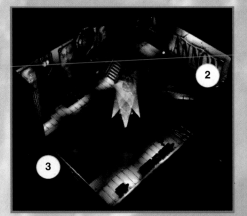

To make matters worse, Rufus has decided to publicly execute Barret and Tifa. The world needs a scapegoat and who better to take the fall than AVALANCHE?

Barret and Tifa are led to a gas chamber so their deaths can be broadcast to the entire world. Tifa is set to go first, so she's strapped into a gas chamber and left to die, but the guard drops his key next to Tifa's chair.

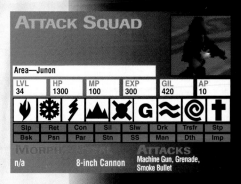

ATTACK SQUAD

Area—Junon

LVL	HP	MP	EXP	GIL	AP
34	1300	100	300	420	10

🔥	❄	⚡	⛰	✖	G	≈	◎	✝

Slp	Ret	Con	Sil	Slw	Drk	Trsfr	Stp
Bsk	Psn	Par	Stn	SS	Man	Dth	Imp

MORPH	STEAL	ATTACKS
n/a	8-inch Cannon	Machine Gun, Grenade, Smoke Bullet

SOLDIER: 2ND

Area—Junon

LVL	HP	MP	EXP	GIL	AP
5	4000	340	1000	750	85

🔥	❄	⚡	⛰	✖	G	≈	◎	✝

Slp	Ret	Con	Sil	Slw	Drk	Trsfr	Stp
Bsk	Psn	Par	Stn	SS	Man	Dth	Imp

MORPH	STEAL	ATTACKS
n/a	Remedy	Fight, Sword of Doom

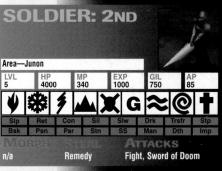

139

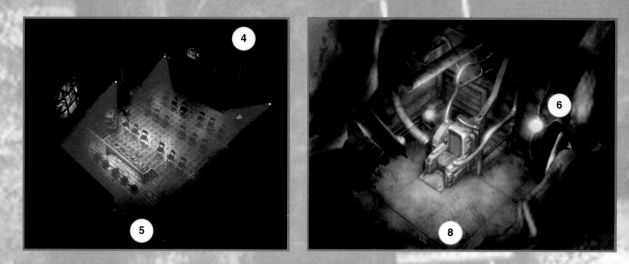

Before the switch can be pulled, Klaxons begin to blare as WEAPON approaches Junon. During the confusion, Cait Sith reveals himself and frees Barret. The two must now stop the gas chamber, but the door won't open.

To Airport

Talk to Cait Sith and then look for the gas chamber's control room. Scarlet locks the press room, so Cait Sith suggests you run to the airport, which is to the right. They bump into Yuffie next, who's disguised as a reporter. Now you'll have a full party for the trip to the Airport.

NOTE: If you haven't used Cait Sith or Yuffie much up to this point, equip them before going too far.

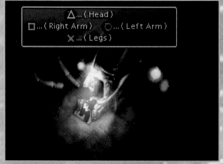

With the confusion created by WEAPON's attack, Tifa gets a chance to save her own life. You must maneuver her head, arms, and legs to reach the key and unlock her restraints. Use Tifa's legs twice to pull the key over to her, and then press the ▲ button to make her sit up in the chair. Now use her legs and head simultaneously to get the key into her mouth. Unlock her left arm by pressing the ● and ▲ buttons together, and then use her left arm a second time to grab the key and unlock her right restraint. Now flip the switch to the left of the chair to shut off the gas. Tifa can't open the door to the chamber from the inside, but she's about to get a little help.

141

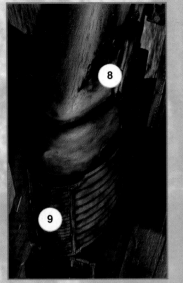

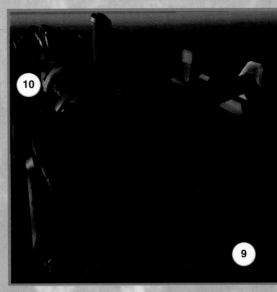

After WEAPON cuts a hole in the chamber wall, climb through the hole and scale down the front of the building. Run down the gun to the end of the barrel, where you'll meet up with Scarlet and engage in a slapping match, which Tifa wins easily. Sprint toward the end of the cannon as soon as you hear Barret's call.

Looks like the team has a new vehicle...the Highwind.

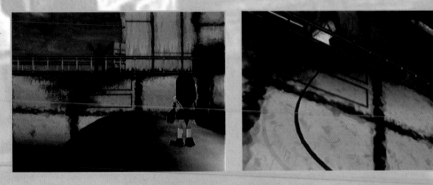

Highwind Controls

●	Move forward
X	Lands
▲	Switch to inside of Highwind
D-Pad Up	Lower altitude
D-Pad Down	Raise altitude
D-Pad Left	Turn left
D-Pad Right	Turn right
L1	Sharp turn left
R1	Sharp turn right
Select	Toggle map
Start	Toggle map

NOTE: The Highwind can fly anywhere, but can only land on smooth, grassy terrain. In some cases, you may have to land far from your target and hike the rest of the way.

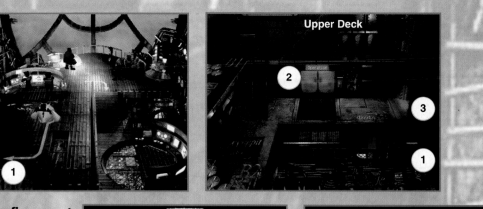

The team's next mission is to figure out what happened to Cloud. Talk to everyone onboard the ship and then make your way down to the Operations Room so you can create your new party. Now you can fly the airship to the northern continent.

NOTE: The Highwind has everything the team needs— with the exception of shops. If you need to save or rest, go to the Highwinds Operations Room and speak with the man there.

THE SEARCH FOR CLOUD

Fly to Icicle Inn and talk to the people there. Several mention Mideel Island to the south and a good doctor who lives there. This is your clue to Cloud's whereabouts—hop back in the Highwind and head to Mideel.

While exploring the island, you'll find a lonely dog in the middle of town. As Tifa stops to pet the pup, she over-hears two people talking about a "pokey-headed" guy washing up on shore. Sure enough, it's Cloud...but something is wrong.

He's been exposed to an extreme amount of Mako energy and has contracted Mako poisoning. Tifa stays with Cloud for the moment, while the rest of the team looks for a way to stop Meteor.

With the rest of the team back on the airship, Cait Sith shares some information. Shinra is continuing to collect **Huge Materia** for their Super Weapon. They've already raided the Nibelheim Reactor and are preparing to collect from the Corel and Fort Condor Reactors.

Have Cid create a new team of three and head for North Corel.

MIDEEL

ITEMS:
- Elixir **(A)**
- "Contain" Materia

ITEM SHOP (B)

ITEM	COST
Hi-Potion	300
Phoenix Down	300
Ether	1500
Hyper	100
Tranquilizer	100
Remedy	1000
Tent	500

WEAPON SHOP (C)

ITEM	COST
Crystal Sword	18000
Crystal Glove	16000
A-M Cannon	18000
Crystal Comb	17000
Crystal Cross	18000
Crystal M-phone	18000
Partisan	19000
Winchester	18000
Crystal Bangle	4800
Wizard Bracelet	12000

ACCESSORY SHOP (D)

ITEM	COST
Amulet	10000
Fire Ring	8000
Ice Ring	8000
Bolt Ring	8000
Fairy Ring	7000
Jem Ring	7500
White Cape	5000

You may want to shop a little before leaving Mideel. There's plenty to buy here and the jungle is a great place to bump up your experience points.

When you speak to the White Chocobo, he acts a little standoffish. But if you have Samolen (Mimett) Greens in your inventory, the little guy will warm up to you in no time. If you're willing to hand over one Samolen (Mimett) Green, you can tickle the Chocobo behind the ear and he'll drop a **"Contain"** Materia. This can only be done after Mideel has been destroyed.

MATERIA SHOP (E)

ITEM	COST
HP Plus	8000
MP Plus	8000
Transform	5000
Gravity	8000
Destruct	9000

REST (F)

Clinic Nurse	Free

RUNAWAY TRAIN

When the team reaches North Corel, head down the tracks to the Corel Reactor. They reach it just in time to watch Shinra drive away with the **Huge Materia** in the back of a train. Fortunately for the team, Cid can drive anything, so they steal a train and chase the Shinra train.

To catch up to the Shinra train, you can alternate the levers left (D-Pad Up) and right (▲) to speed up the train and align it with the enemy train. Try to get a slow rhythm going, and then build up your speed.

NOTE: Remember, you only have 10 minutes to catch the enemy train, board it, and then reach the cabin and stop it before it crashes into North Corel.

An enemy, each one tougher than the last, protects each train car. It's important that you make quick work of them so that you have plenty of time left when you reach the engine.

Car #1: Gas Ducter

Easy fight; hit it hard with anything but **Bio.**

Car #2: Gas Ducter (x2)

Same as first one, but twice as tough.

Car #3: Wolfmeister

Susceptible to water; use the enemy skill **Aqualung** or the summon Materia **"Leviathan."** You can poison it, but it may not help much.

Car #4: Eagle Gun

Use **Bolt** spells against it; avoid casting **Earth** or **Water** spells on it.

Engine: Attack Squad

This thing isn't tough. Hurry through the conversation before the fight. There's no time to waste!

Now you must stop the train. Move both levers down and then up, alternating back and forth until the train stops.

With the train stopped, Corel is saved and you've received your first piece of **Huge Materia.** As a debt of gratitude, the people of North Corel give you the **"Ultima" Materia.** Now hop back in the Highwind and head for Mt. Condor.

NOTE: If you fail to save North Corel, you not only lose the **Huge Materia** but you'll have to pay 50,000 Gil for the **"Ultima" Materia!**

145

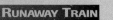

Return to Fort Condor

This is the final battle at Fort Condor. You'll face tougher odds than ever before, so you'll need to take lots of money. This will help you buy enough troops to put up a strong fight.

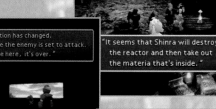

Place lots of troops along the mountainside, and focus on placing Fighters and Attackers down low backed up by Shooters, Defenders, and Repairers. You may want to place Stoners, Tristoners, and Catapults at the top of the three paths to block the enemy advance if they get past your front line. Lastly, place a few Defenders around the hut as backups. They can move in and attack or fill holes as needed. If the enemies make it to the shed, you're forced to fight the Enemy Commander.

After the battle, the Condor is killed but the baby Condor lives. Check outside and you'll find the **"Phoenix" Materia** next to the nest. Talk to the old man downstairs and he'll hand over the **Huge Materia**.

Cid tells you to go see Cloud, so hop in the Highwind and return to Mideel.

146

CLOUD'S COMA

When you visit Cloud in the clinic, you find out that there's no change in his condition and Tifa seems to have giving up hope. Around this time, the town begins to shake. Run outside and you'll find one of the WEAPONs attacking the town.

BOSS FIGHT: ULTIMATE WEAPON

You just need to survive this fight. Ultimate WEAPON will attack with several powerful spells that can cause about 1,500 points of damage to each character simultaneously.

Cast **MBarrier** immediately to soften the blow, and keep everyone healed. Use each team member's Limit Breaks, because they'll be built up after one or two turns. These should cause enough damage to make Ultimate WEAPON fly off.

Ultimate WEAPON may be gone, but the threat is far from over. The Lifestream bursts through and destroys Mideel. Tifa tries to get Cloud out, but they both drop into the middle of the Lifestream.

Tifa awakens to find herself in a seemingly empty void. Voices from the dark question her actions and challenge her to confess; she's quickly overcome with emotion and sinks into the darkness.

When she awakens she's in a surreal world with not one, but three, Clouds. His conscious hangs overhead as if watching and waiting for answers. Which Cloud should you talk to first? Start with the one at the top **(A)**.

147

This is Nibelheim just as it was five years ago. Again we see Sephiroth's entrance and, again, Cloud follows him—but this time Tifa intervenes. Cloud wasn't the one with Sephiroth—it was the boy that Sephiroth showed Cloud back at the Crater.

Next, speak to the Cloud on the left (B). Nibelheim appears again, but this time it's a reenactment of the night at the well. Nothing has changed as Cloud and Tifa remember it, but it's still not enough to prove who Cloud is.

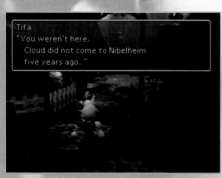

Tifa asks Cloud to think of a memory about her, one she wouldn't know. Cloud complies by admitting that he wanted to join SOLDIER to draw Tifa's attention.

He takes her to the point in time where Tifa's mother died, a time when Tifa was so wrapped up in her emotions that she failed to notice Cloud. There was an accident and Cloud was blamed for hurting Tifa.

After that incident, Cloud began to look for a way to make Tifa notice him and strength seemed like the answer. He would become like Sephiroth. Tifa remembers this, enabling Cloud to come one step closer to being whole again.

They return to Nibelheim and go to the Mako Reactor some five years ago. Sephiroth wounds Tifa and then Zack (this must be the Zack from Gongaga Village) enters the scene. Sephiroth defeats Zack, but Cloud grabs his sword and sneaks up on Sephiroth as he's reaching for Jenova.

148

Zack
"Cloud...
  Kill Sephiroth..."

Cloud was in soldier garb the entire time, hiding behind a mask. He bested Sephiroth and saved Tifa and Zack's lives.

With the truth now uncovered, Cloud is whole again. His consciousness pulls together and they leave the Lifestream.

"Let's go back, Cloud.
  Back to everyone......"

The team is reunited but there are two more **Huge Materia** to collect. Take the Highwind to Junon, because the team must locate the underwater facility before Shinra can move the Materia.

NOTE: With the Highwind in your possesion, you can breed Chocobos at the Chocobo Farm you visited earlier in the game. Chocobo breeding is time consuming and expensive, but it enables you to acquire some of the most powerful Materia and items in the game. For more information on Chocobos, refer to the section "Choco Bill's Complete Guide to Chocobos."

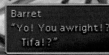

Barret
"Yo! You awright!?
  Tifa!?"

149

DESTROYED MIDEEL

A)

	COST
	50
n	300
	80
	500

SHOP (B)

	COST
	10000
	8000
	8000
	8000
	7000
	7500
	5000

OP (C)

	COST
	600
	600
	600
	750

Things look pretty bad in Mideel. The entire town was swallowed up by the Lifestream and only the people remain. At first, you'll notice that the shops don't have much merchandise, with the exception of the Accessories Shop. However, if you go to the west side of town, Cloud can hop the rocks to a hidden area in which the doctor, nurse, and the crazed consumer are all trapped. The nurse will still restore your lost HP and MP as she did when the clinic was above ground. However, the most notable change is that the crazed consumer is now selling everything he purchased before the town went under.

CRAZED CONSUMER (WEAPONS) (D)

ITEM	COST
Crystal Sword	18000
Crystal Glove	16000
A-M Cannon	18000
Crystal Comb	17000
Crystal Cross	18000
Crystal M-phone	18000
Partisan	19000
Winchester	18000
Crystal Bangle	4800
Wizard Bracelet	12000

CRAZED CONSUMER (MATERIA) (D)

ITEM	COST
HP Plus	8000
MP Plus	8000
Transform	5000
Gravity	8000
Destruct	9000

REST (E)

ITEM	COST
Clinic Nurse	Free

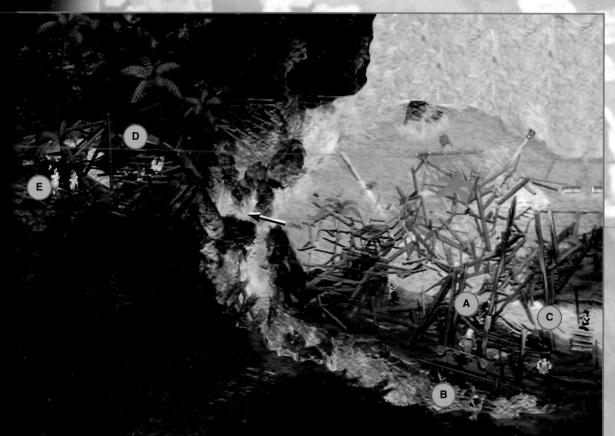

THE UNDERWATER REACTOR

When you reach Junon Village, you have to ride the elevator up to Junon for 10 Gil. (This should give you a good idea of just how little Shinra's troops get paid.) There's no need for a disguise this time around; just head down to the main street and follow it to the sector that splits the left and right sections of town.

ITEMS:

Battle Trumpet **(A)**
Scimitar **(B)**
Leviathan Scales **(C)**

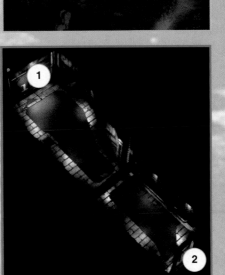

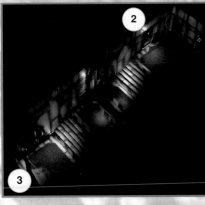

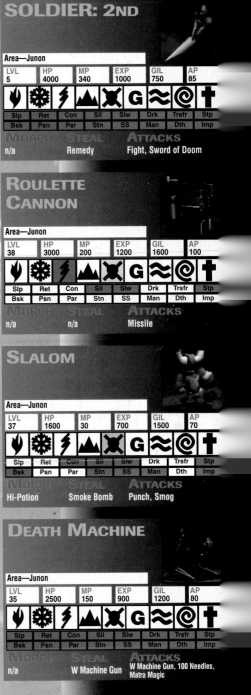

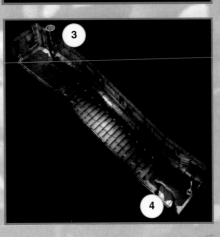

SOLDIER: 2ND

Area—Junon

LVL	HP	MP	EXP	GIL	AP
5	4000	340	1000	750	85

Slp	Ret	Con	Sil	Slw	Drk	Trsfr	Stp
Bsk	Psn	Par	Stn	SS	Man	Dth	Imp

MORPH	STEAL	ATTACKS
n/a	Remedy	Fight, Sword of Doom

ROULETTE CANNON

Area—Junon

LVL	HP	MP	EXP	GIL	AP
38	3000	200	1200	1600	100

Slp	Ret	Con	Sil	Slw	Drk	Trsfr	Stp
Bsk	Psn	Par	Stn	SS	Man	Dth	Imp

MORPH	STEAL	ATTACKS
n/a	n/a	Missile

SLALOM

Area—Junon

LVL	HP	MP	EXP	GIL	AP
37	1600	30	700	1500	70

Slp	Ret	Con	Sil	Slw	Drk	Trsfr	Stp
Bsk	Psn	Par	Stn	SS	Man	Dth	Imp

MORPH	STEAL	ATTACKS
Hi-Potion	Smoke Bomb	Punch, Smog

DEATH MACHINE

Area—Junon

LVL	HP	MP	EXP	GIL	AP
35	2500	150	900	1200	80

Slp	Ret	Con	Sil	Slw	Drk	Trsfr	Stp
Bsk	Psn	Par	Stn	SS	Man	Dth	Imp

MORPH	STEAL	ATTACKS
n/a	W Machine Gun	W Machine Gun, 100 Needles, Matra Magic

151

SUBMARINE CREW

Area—Junon					
LVL 32	HP 1500	MP 85	EXP 850	GIL 500	AP 80

Slp	Ret	Con	Sil	Slw	Drk	Trsfr	Stp
Bsk	Psn	Par	Stn	SS	Man	Dth	Imp

MORPH	STEAL	ATTACKS
n/a	8-inch Cannon	Machine Gun, Hand Grenade

GHOST SHIP

Area—Water Tunnel					
LVL 44	HP 6600	MP 100	EXP 1600	GIL 2000	AP 60

Slp	Ret	Con	Sil	Slw	Drk	Trsfr	Stp
Bsk	Psn	Par	Stn	SS	Man	Dth	Imp

MORPH	STEAL	ATTACKS
Guide Book	Phoenix Down	CentoElmos Fire, Slap, Goannai

HARD ATTACKER

Area—Underwater Reactor					
LVL 32	HP 2500	MP 150	EXP 750	GIL 600	AP 58

Slp	Ret	Con	Sil	Slw	Drk	Trsfr	Stp
Bsk	Psn	Par	Stn	SS	Man	Dth	Imp

MORPH	STEAL	ATTACKS
n/a	n/a	Bodyblow, Oil

GUARDIAN

Area—Underwater Reactor					
LVL 40	HP 4000	MP 340	EXP 940	GIL 500	AP 60

Slp	Ret	Con	Sil	Slw	Drk	Trsfr	Stp
Bsk	Psn	Par	Stn	SS	Man	Dth	Imp

MORPH	STEAL	ATTACKS
n/a	n/a	Jumping Blow, Rocket Punch, W Rocket Punch

UNDERWATER MP

Area—Underwater Reactor					
LVL 34	HP 1000	MP 100	EXP 820	GIL 600	AP 80

Slp	Ret	Con	Sil	Slw	Drk	Trsfr	Stp
Bsk	Psn	Par	Stn	SS	Man	Dth	Imp

MORPH	STEAL	ATTACKS
n/a	Shinra Alpha	Machine Gun, Hand Grenade

NOTE: Your characters will pause in the middle of the street. Cloud mentions that something seems to be missing. What is it? The Junon cannon!

"How 'bout, whoever stays alive, gets to take her out?"

This area should look familiar from your first visit to Junon. Follow the group of soldiers to the Underwater Reactor elevator and ride it down to the ocean floor. Unfortunately, there are two soldiers on the elevator who attack you to show off for the elevator operator. You'll run into a lot of these guys as you make your way to the reactor.

NOTE: There's an alarm in the hall before the elevator. Cloud can trip the alarm, but it doesn't effect the game in any way.

"OK! Back to work!! Back to work!!"

When you reach the ocean floor, enter the plant and take the elevator down. Follow the walkway to the reactor's core, but watch for Shinra patrols.

"You, you're Cloud!!"

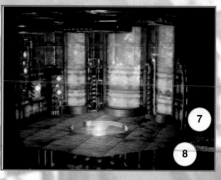

The team arrives a little too late. Shinra has the Huge Materia, but they haven't loaded it onto a submarine yet. Run to the submarine bay and try to intercept.

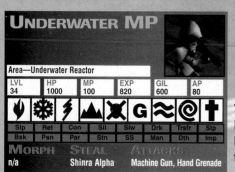

SENIOR GRUNT

Area—Underwater Reactor					
LVL	HP	MP	EXP	GIL	AP
35	2600	245	930	800	90

Slp	Ret	Con	Sil	Slw	Drk	Trsfr	Stp
Bsk	Psn	Par	Stn	SS	Dth	Imp	

MORPH	STEAL	ATTACKS
n/a	n/a	Handclaw, Harrier Beam, Water Wave

Wouldn't you know it? Reno is here and he's brought along a nasty surprise.

GUN CARRIER

Area—Underwater Reactor					
LVL	HP	MP	EXP	GIL	AP
39	3400	240	860	1600	75

Slp	Ret	Con	Sil	Slw	Drk	Trsfr	Stp
Bsk	Psn	Par	Stn	SS	Man	Dth	Imp

MORPH	STEAL	ATTACKS
n/a	n/a	Normal Shell, Bodyblow

Cait Sith
"There's the submarine dock just ahead of us."

153

BOSS FIGHT: CARRY ARMOR

The Carry Armor isn't too difficult to defeat. You can take advantage of its weakness to Bolt spells if you come equipped with **"Lightning"** and **"Ramuh"** Materia.

At the start, set up **MBarrier** and cast **Haste** and **Regen** on the entire party. Don't waste time trying to cast effects like **Slow** or **Stop** on the Carry Armor, because it's immune to any kind of negative status. Use **Bolt** and **Ramuh** to deal some serious damage, while concentrating your attacks on the left and right arms. With the arms and legs out of the way, it's left with the center torso and the Lapis Laser attack. The **MBarrier** should cut the Lapis Laser's damage down from about 1,500 to 750. Just keep casting **MBarrier** as it runs out.

During the battle, the Carry Armor may pick up one of your characters. He/she cannot participate in the battle and the time bar on any status effects will be locked in place until the character is freed. After the character has been grabbed, there are only two ways to recover him/her. The first is to kill and then resurrect the character once the Carry Armor has dropped the lifeless body. This isn't difficult to do since any attacks against the Carry Armor will also cause damage to any captured heroes. You can also release a captured character by destroying the arm that holds the character. If the Carry Armor can capture two of your characters and kill the third, the battle is lost and the game is over. You receive the **God's Hand** for winning the battle.

Because of the distraction caused by the Carry Armor, the submarine gets away. But don't worry—the team can just hijack the other enemy sub and chase down the runaway. Before boarding the enemy sub, grab the chests scattered across the docks.

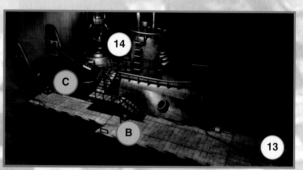

 NOTE: Be absolutely sure you get the Leviathan Scales before leaving. You'll need them to put out the flames in the fire cave at Wutai.

The submarine crew isn't about to give up their ship easily. Fight your way onboard and take over the controls. Your friends from the parade are manning the control center, but you don't have to kill them—it's your decision.

 TIP: You can steal a decent piece of armor called the Shinra Alpha from the captain if you decide to kill the crew.

THE SUBMARINE BATTLE

SUBMARINE MINI-GAME CONTROLS

BUTTON	WHAT IT DOES
D-Pad Up	Descend
D-Pad Down	Ascend
D-Pad Right	Turn right
D-Pad Left	Turn left
▲	Speed up
■	Fire torpedo
[X]	Slow down
R1	Sonar

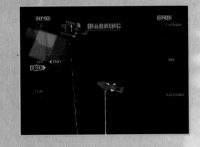

Now that you have a sub, you can chase down the enemy sub that's carrying the **Huge Materia**—but there's a catch: You must do this in 10 minutes or less.

Try to stay behind the RED enemy sub, because it's the one that's carrying the **Huge Materia**. It isn't necessary to destroy the Yellow subs, but they'll be trying their hardest to sink you.

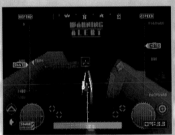

TIP: You can shoot as many as four torpedoes at a time. Try to lock onto your target and unload the whole group, which is normally enough to take out a Yellow sub.

If the enemy gets a lock on you, speed up and dive deep. This will normally shake the torpedoes off your tail.

Mines are the small polygons on top of the square columns. You can pass through the columns without taking damage, just don't go too high.

TIP: Don't worry too much about mines. Unless you're at full speed, you'll have plenty of time to react and adjust your course. Be careful when you enter the sonar screen, that you don't accidentally run into a nearby mine.

Use your sonar often to prepare you for what lies ahead. Plus, you can use sonar to help relocate the RED submarine if you lose track of it.

When you win the battle, you receive the Shinra Sub as a vehicle for the rest of the game. Although the submarine has limited range and can't pass through shallow water, you can use it to check out the ocean floor and any underwater caves. You can dock at the small, rocky notches around the coast (like the one next to Junon).

155

Cloud
"Junon Airport...
We should make it if we hurry."

SUBMARINE WORLD MAP CONTROLS

BUTTON	WHAT IT DOES
D-Pad Up	Move forward/reverse direction
D-Pad Down	Reverse direction/move forward
D-Pad Left	Turn left
D-Pad Right	Turn right
●	Board sub/move forward
[X]	Exit sub/dive/surface
L1	Turn left
R1	Turn right

The team picks up a radio signal declaring that Shinra is about to ship out another **Huge Materia** from the Junon Airport. Park the sub and get up there quickly.

The team arrives just in time to see the Materia leave by way of plane. The team needs to intercept the **Huge Materia** at Rocket Town. Get back to the Highwind and get moving!

Cloud
"Rocket Town, of course."

THE FIRST MAN IN SPACE

When the team arrives at Rocket Town, they find Shinra busy at work repairing the rocket and preparing for launch. After forcing your way past the guards, you'll meet up with Rude again.

NOTE: If Cid isn't in your party, you're forced to take him along at this point. Make sure you equip him adequately for the next battle.

"Don't let them get any further!
Everyone, ATTACK---!"

Cid
"If you're gonna kick those *#$% Shinra
out of my rocket,
then take me with you!"

BOSS FIGHT: RUDE AND ATTACK SQUAD

Start the battle by getting rid of the *Attack Squad* guys, or they will try to put your team to sleep. Rude isn't too tough—he uses **Bolt 2** and his normal attack causes about 300 to 500 points of damage. His Guard Spark attack can cause about 1000 points of damage and Rude can use it as many as three times in a row. An Mbarrier will cut the damage down to 250-500 points.

When Rude's health begins to get low, he starts casting **Cure 2** on himself. If you have **Reflect**, cast it on him and the **Cure** spell will heal your team instead.

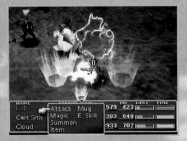

NOTE: It's not a bad idea to equip everyone with armor that protects or absorbs lightning, but it's not essential to winning the battle.

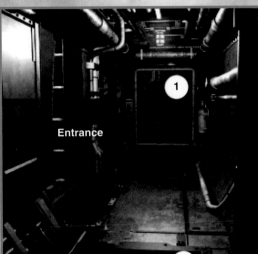

Entrance

Upon entering the cockpit, the team finds that the rocket is nearly ready to launch. This seems to quickly change Cid's mind about Shinra's plans to blow up Meteor. He decides that he should pilot the rocket into space—and no one's going to convince him otherwise.

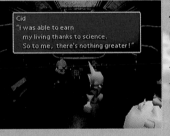

The rocket launches without a hitch and the crash course with Meteor is locked in. Cid returns to his senses and points you toward the **Huge Materia** chamber.

The **Huge Materia** is locked into the rocket's core. You can decipher the lock, but the team only has three minutes to do so. Listen to Cid's clues and you can figure it out. When you succeed, you can take the **Huge Materia** with you. If not, it remains locked in the ship's belly with no chance of getting it back.

NOTE: If you fail, you may want to return to a saved game and try the combination again.

157

TIP: If you give up or you don't want to risk losing the Materia, the lock's combination is: ●, ■, [X], [X].

With or without the **Huge Materia**, it's time to bail out. Head down to the engine room where the escape pod is waiting.

The team escapes, but not without incident. Cid has renewed respect for Shera's work, thanks to a faulty oxygen tank. From the escape pod, the team witnesses the collision between the rocket and Meteor. It's damaged, but Meteor quickly begins to pull itself together. This is not good.

Escape Pod

158

THE ANCIENT MACHINE

Return to Bugenhagen's laboratory in Cosmo Canyon to discuss how to overcome Meteor and Sephiroth. However, this proves uneventful until Bugenhagen suggests that you return to the Ancient City. Before you can do this, though, you'll need to store the **Huge Materia** in Bugenhagen's lab. This may seem odd, but it does have a purpose. Before you leave, take a close look at the blue **Huge Materia** and you'll receive the **"Bahamut ZERO"** **Materia**.

Hop back into the Highwind and make your way to the Ancient City. Once there, take the left path to the back. Bugenhagen explains the use of the **White Materia** and finds clues to locate a hidden Key. The Key is hidden in a place "even sunlight can't reach," which suggests a cave of some sort.

Hop back into the Highwind and head for the coast. You've searched nearly every cave in the outer world, so it's time to explore underwater.

Take the submarine down and head to the south. The Shinra sub you wrecked earlier is lying on the bottom here. Inspect the wreckage, and you'll find the last of the **Huge Materia**.

WARNING! There's a huge creature roaming around this area. It's one of the new WEAPONs that were added to the American version of *Final Fantasy VII*. Avoid it for now, because it's ultra-powerful and *WILL* make mincemeat out of your team until your character's levels and Materia are maxed out. If the WEAPON is blocking something you need, surface and then dive again. This moves the WEAPON to another location.

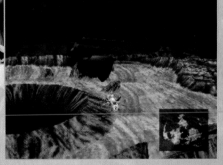

Now head north and hug the west wall until you come to a side passage. In the back, you'll find a wrecked plane that you can inspect, although it's not necessary. (Refer to the "Wrecked Plane" section of this book for more details.)

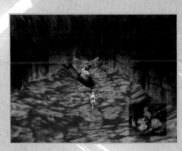

159

Go back to the main area and continue north. After passing through a narrow passage, take a hard left and follow the canal to an underwater cave. Surface when you reach the end of the cave and you'll appear in the middle of a lake. Park the submarine along the rock wall and use the PHS to place Vincent into your party (if he isn't already with you). Enter the waterfall to learn more about Vincent's past.

TIP: Visit this spot again during Disk 3 and you'll receive Vincent's ultimate weapon and Limit Break.

After the story, dive again and go back toward the main underwater passage. Instead of going south, continue to the north until you find another underwater cave. Follow it until you see the Key of the Ancients. Take the key back to Bugenhagen at the Ancient City.

When Bugenhagen uses the Key in the ancient device, you learn that Aeris has already prayed for Holy; however, Sephiroth's presence keeps Holy from moving. If Sephiroth isn't eliminated, Holy will be unable to stop Meteor from destroying the planet.

As the team leaves the Ancient City, Cait Sith reports that the Junon cannon has been found. Shinra has attached it to the Mako Reactors at Midgar and plans to use it to destroy Sephiroth. The team had better return to Midgar—and fast!

WEAPON ATTACKS

When the team reaches the Highwind, the entire area starts to quake. Another WEAPON is on the move and it's headed straight for Midgar. Fly back to Midgar and land the Highwind near the northern coastline. Find a good spot on the beach and wait for it to arrive.

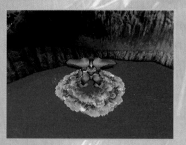

BOSS FIGHT: DIAMOND WEAPON

Diamond WEAPON is one tough customer, but the team should be more than a match for it. Start the fight by casting **MBarrier** on the entire team, and then cast **Regen** and **Haste**. You may also want to cast **Barrier** to reduce the damage from Diamond WEAPON's physical attacks.

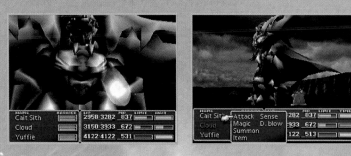

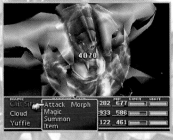

Attack Diamond WEAPON with your most powerful spells and summons. **Ultima**, **Comet**, and **Knights of the Round** work really well. Diamond WEAPON can't be harmed by physical attacks, so stick to magic unless you're trying to mug the beast. Beware when Diamond WEAPON begins to count down, because this means it's preparing for its super attack. The Diamond Flash does about 1500 to 3000 points of damage to each character and mutes those who survive, which makes it difficult to quickly heal your team. You may want to equip a team member with the Ribbon accessory to protect him/her from the Mute effect. That way, when the countdown reaches "1," you can hold off on that character's action until after the Diamond Flash connects. This enables you to quickly cast **Cure 3** and save anyone else from getting picked off by one of Diamond WEAPON's weaker attacks.

After the battle, Diamond WEAPON is stunned but is still moving toward Midgar. Shinra's Cannon, Sister Ray, is up and running and prepared to fire—but so is WEAPON. The blast from the Sister Ray cuts through WEAPON and destroys Sephiroth's barrier, but not until WEAPON has already fired upon Midgar.

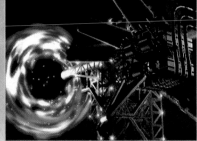

Hop in the Highwind and head north. Sure enough, there's nothing stopping the team from entering the crater. However, Cait Sith alerts the team that the Sister Ray is overloading and preparing to fire a second shot at the crater. Hojo has taken control of the cannon and there's nothing that Shinra can do to stop him.

Head to Midgar but fly over it instead of landing. The team dons parachutes and enters Midgar commando style.

Reeve
"Hojo, STOP!
The cannon, no,
Midgar itself is in danger!"

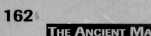

RETURN TO MIDGAR

Follow Cait Sith into the back alleys and then underground. There are lots of items to get in this area, but you must go out of your way to collect them.

NOTE: Collect the items at the end of the ramp to the right of the entry, and the item up the large ladder near the back of the second platform. You can't go back for them after the floor breaks.

Cait Sith
"Please!
Hurry and come to the Mako Cannon!"

Start

Follow the steps and ladder down to the lower level. Head right and the floor will drop out from under the team. Climb the red pipes and take the chute down. Follow the stairs up to the Save Point and the next area.

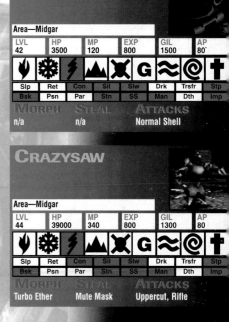

BEHEMOTH

Area—Midgar					
LVL 45	HP 7000	MP 400	EXP 1500	GIL 2200	AP 100

Slp	Ret	Con	Sil	Slw	Drk	Trsfr	Stp
Bsk	Psn	Par	Stn	SS	Man	Dth	Imp

MORPH	STEAL	ATTACKS
n/a	Phoenix Down	Claw, Horn Lift

CROMWELL

Area—Midgar					
LVL 42	HP 3500	MP 120	EXP 800	GIL 1500	AP 80`

Slp	Ret	Con	Sil	Slw	Drk	Trsfr	Stp
Bsk	Psn	Par	Stn	SS	Man	Dth	Imp

MORPH	STEAL	ATTACKS
n/a	n/a	Normal Shell

CRAZYSAW

Area—Midgar					
LVL 44	HP 39000	MP 340	EXP 800	GIL 1300	AP 80

Slp	Ret	Con	Sil	Slw	Drk	Trsfr	Stp
Bsk	Psn	Par	Stn	SS	Man	Dth	Imp

MORPH	STEAL	ATTACKS
Turbo Ether	Mute Mask	Uppercut, Rifle

ITEMS:
(1st area) Elixir **(A)**
Megalixir **(B)**
Aegis Armlet **(C)**
Starlight Phone **(D)**
Elixir **(E)**
Max Ray **(F)**
(Tunnels) Power Source
Guard Source
Mind Source
Magic Source
"W-Item" Materia
(Shinra HQ) Pile Banger
Master Fist
Glow Lance
HP Shout
(Sister Ray)
Elixir **(G)**
Mystile **(H)**
Missing Score **(I)**

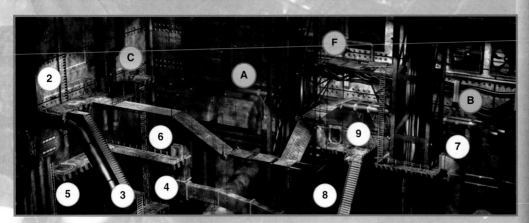

163

This takes the team to the train tunnels. The Sister Ray is to the north, but there are items that can be collected to the south. The choice is yours whether or not to take the risk of going south.

When you proceed northward, the team bumps into the Turks again but this time all three of them are together. You're given the option of not fighting them this time around.

Received "W-Item"!

Elena
"What are you doing! Let's go!"
Okay, let's end this
No, let's not go

9

Dead End
(Extra Items)

Shinra H.Q.

11

10

MANHOLE

Area—Midgar

LVL	HP	MP	EXP	GIL	AP
35	2500	110	900	3000	80

🔥	❄	⚡	⛰	✖	G	≈	◎	✝

Slp	Ret	Con	Sil	Slw	Drk	Trsfr	Stp
Bsk	Psn	Par	Stn	SS	Man	Dth	Imp

MORPH	STEAL	ATTACKS
n/a	n/a	Throw

CRAZYSAW

Area—Midgar

LVL	HP	MP	EXP	GIL	AP
44	39000	340	800	1300	80

🔥	❄	⚡	⛰	✖	G	≈	◎	✝

Slp	Ret	Con	Sil	Slw	Drk	Trsfr	Stp
Bsk	Psn	Par	Stn	SS	Man	Dth	Imp

MORPH	STEAL	ATTACKS
Turbo Ether	Mute Mask	Uppercut, Rifle

SHADOW MAKER

Area—Midgar

LVL	HP	MP	EXP	GIL	AP
42	2000	120	500	500	25

🔥	❄	⚡	⛰	✖	G	≈	◎	✝

Slp	Ret	Con	Sil	Slw	Drk	Trsfr	Stp
Bsk	Psn	Par	Stn	SS	Man	Dth	Imp

MORPH	STEAL	ATTACKS
n/a	Graviball	Slow

GROSSPANZER

Area—Midgar

LVL	HP	MP	EXP	GIL	AP
46	4600	200	800	2100	80

🔥	❄	⚡	⛰	✖	G	≈	◎	✝

Slp	Ret	Con	Sil	Slw	Drk	Trsfr	Stp
Bsk	Psn	Par	Stn	SS	Man	Dth	Imp

MORPH	STEAL	ATTACKS
n/a	n/a	Midgar, Missile, Machine Guns, Ram

BOSS FIGHT: RENO, RUDE, & ELENA

This is a tough fight. Cast **Wall** (or **Barrier** and **MBarrier**), **Regen**, and **Haste** on your party immediately. Then use attacks that damage all three Turks at once. Summon spells work really well in the fight, as does **Bio** to poison the entire group.

TIP: Each of the Turks is carrying a special item. Be sure to take them.

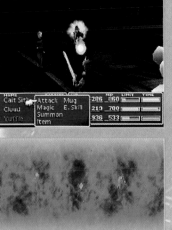

Watch out for Elena and Rude. Elena casts **Confusion** and uses a Fire attack that damages the whole group. Rude uses his fist, but can inflict critical hits that cause as much as 4000 points of damage. Reno is always a threat, but for some reason doesn't seem to play a major part in this battle.

NOTE: If you fight, you may want to return to the Save Point and use a Tent to heal your wounds.

Continue north and take the first left to reach the cannon; or, you can take the second left, which

takes you to Shinra Headquarters. This path enables you to get Cait Sith's ultimate weapon (Floor 64), the Glow Lance (Floor 63), and two weapons from the gift shop, but you can't go any higher than the 65th floor.

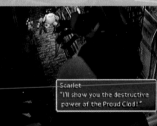

Choosing the left path places the team at the base of the Sister Ray, directly in the path of Heidegger and Scarlet's new toy.

Boss Fight: Proud Clod

The Proud Clod is composed of two parts: armor and body. Your first target should be the armor (the lower target). After destroying this, you'll cause more damage to the body. The Proud Clod has more attacks than you can imagine. The most powerful ones are its side guns (500 to 1500) and the Beam Cannon (1000 to 1500 vs. everyone). And watch out for the Rainbow Ray—it doesn't cause any damage, but it does cast **Reflect** on one of your characters. If this happens, use **DeBarrier** to eliminate the spell so you can heal and protect that character normally.

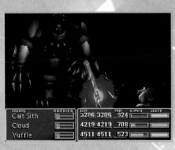

165

You can normally set up with **Wall**, **Regen**, and **Haste** and then use attacks against Proud Clod that will damage both sections. **Slash-All** works well as do most summon spells. In the end the battle is likely to become a slugfest. Of course, you could just cast **Knights of the Round** once and call it a day. You receive the **Ragnarok** for winning the battle.

Continue onward and scale the stairs to reach the Sister Ray. Check all the chests on the way up. Barret's ultimate weapon, the Missing Score, is in one of them.

 NOTE: The Missing Score won't be there unless Barret is in your party.

At the top, the party finds Hojo busy overloading the Sister Ray. He's not about to give in, but he's more than happy to show off his Jenova powers.

Boss #1: Hojo

This can be the quickest of the three fights. Concentrate your attacks on Hojo and leave his Capsule companions alone, because they'll regenerate if you kill them. Cast **Haste** on the entire party and use **Deathblow** and strong magic attacks to knock out this Boss.

166

Boss #2: Helletic Hojo

Take out the right arm immediately. Its hit points are lower than the rest of Hojo's body. Hojo may later regenerate this arm, but it's what causes most of the damage. Helletic Hojo can also cast **Sleepel** and **Confu** on one of the party members, but it's not much of a threat. After the right arm is destroyed, focus on the torso section. You can kill Helletic Hojo without ever attacking the left arm.

Boss #3: Lifeform-Hojo

This Hojo form has super-fast attacks that cause close to 500 points of damage each and a negative status. Its Combo attack launches several of these punches against one or more opponents. If it attacks a character equipped with a **"Counter Attack" Materia**, each punch can be countered. Hojo uses a lot of status effects and spells that can hit the entire party at once. Keep **Esuna** ready or you may find your entire party poisoned, silenced, slowed, or put to sleep. You may want to set up **Wall** and **Regen** at this point in the fight, but **Regen** is really too slow to be of much help. This is also the best time to use your strongest spells and summons. **Gravity** is the only thing that doesn't affect Hojo. You'll pick up a **Power Source** for winning this battle.

Shinra is defeated and nothing is left to stop the team from taking on Sephiroth.

 WARNING! After entering the North Cave, it becomes difficult to leave. The path to Sephiroth is extremely long and tough. If you haven't collected everyone's ultimate weapons and Limit Breaks, tried Chocobo breeding, or collected the ultimate summon (Knights of the Round), you should reenter the Highwind and do so now.

Many of these side quests will lead you to high-powered items and Materia. These things can make a huge difference in the battles to come. Of course, this is all optional, but the Final Fantasy series is all about fun and discovery. I strongly urge you to *at least* create a save game outside of the North Cave so that you can later return and try all the things you may have missed. But most of all, just have fun.

The Final Confrontation

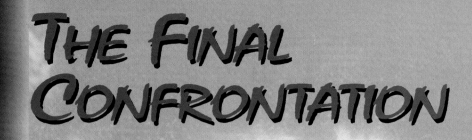

ITEMS:

- Save Crystal **(A)**
- Guard Source (x3)**(B)**
- Mind Source (x2) **(C)**
- Magic Source **(D)**
- Elixir **(E)**
- "HP Absorb" Materia **(F)**
- Power Source (x2) **(G)**
- Hero Drink **(H)**
- Megalixir **(I)**

At the start you'll notice a cave, which is your way back to the Highwind just in case you need to return for anything. Also, notice the first chest, because inside is a very important item—the Save Crystal.

⬤ **WARNING!** There are no Save Points within the Crater, but the Save Crystal enables you to create a single Save Point anywhere you like. Keep this with you until otherwise noted. Creating the Save Point too far out can be very frustrating.

⬤ **NOTE:** Nearly every creature in the Crater has the ability to instantly kill your characters. Take lots of **Phoenix Downs** and **Ethers**.

Start

1

DARK DRAGON

Area—The Crater

LVL	HP	MP	EXP	GIL	AP
57	14000	600	5000	2500	350

🔥	❄️	⚡	⛰️	✖️	Ⓖ	≈	◎	✝

Slp	Ret	Con	Sil	Slw	Drk	Trsfr	Stp
Bsk	Psn	Par	Stn	SS	Man	Dth	Imp

MORPH	STEAL	ATTACKS
n/a	Dragon Armlet	Laser, Dragon Force, Claw, Bite

GARGOYLE
Temporarily stone

Area—The Crater

LVL	HP	MP	EXP	GIL	AP
43	2000	200	800	2500	80

🔥	❄️	⚡	⛰️	✖️	Ⓖ	≈	◎	✝

Slp	Ret	Con	Sil	Slw	Drk	Trsfr	Stp
Bsk	Psn	Par	Stn	SS	Man	Dth	Imp

MORPH	STEAL	ATTACKS
n/a	n/a	Petrify, Bite, L4 Death

PARASITE

Area—The Crater

LVL	HP	MP	EXP	GIL	AP
51	6000	300	1100	1000	100

🔥	❄️	⚡	⛰️	✖️	Ⓖ	≈	◎	✝

Slp	Ret	Con	Sil	Slw	Drk	Trsfr	Stp
Bsk	Psn	Par	Stn	SS	Man	Dth	Imp

MORPH	STEAL	ATTACKS
Remedy	Remedy	Head Attack, L5 Death, Magical Breath, Para Tail

Ready to go? Follow the twisting path into the crater. At the cliffs, take the right path down, and then climb back up the left. This enables you to collect the various items located along the path in the most efficient manner.

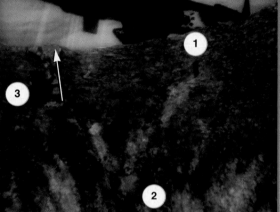

1

3

2

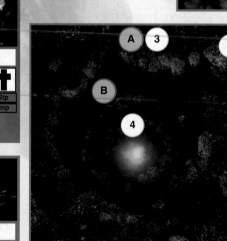

A 3

2

B

4

G → F 4

E

B

D

C

5

When you first enter the next area, go to the left and explore the cave. You'll need to return to the top and take the right path to actually access to the next area.

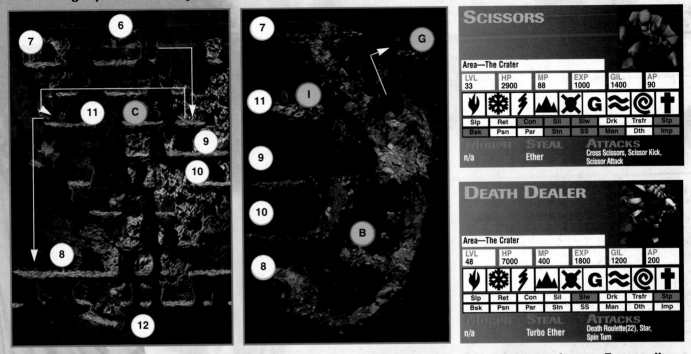

SCISSORS

Area—The Crater

LVL	HP	MP	EXP	GIL	AP
33	2900	88	1000	1400	90

Slp	Ret	Con	Sil	Slw	Drk	Trsfr	Stp
Bsk	Psn	Par	Stn	SS	Man	Dth	Imp

MORPH	STEAL	ATTACKS
n/a	Ether	Cross Scissors, Scissor Kick, Scissor Attack

DEATH DEALER

Area—The Crater

LVL	HP	MP	EXP	GIL	AP
48	7000	400	1800	1200	200

Slp	Ret	Con	Sil	Slw	Drk	Trsfr	Stp
Bsk	Psn	Par	Stn	SS	Man	Dth	Imp

MORPH	STEAL	ATTACKS
n/a	Turbo Ether	Death Roulette(22), Star, Spin Turn

You meet up with the rest of the group here and get the chance to split the entire party in two. Eventually, you'll want to explore both sides, but for now go to the right. This is a decent spot for the Save Point, but you may prefer something closer to Sephiroth.

NOTE: Be careful which way you send your characters. Only those sent down the same path with Cloud will be able to join him until you reach the Crater's center.

Received "HP Absorb" Materia!

Cloud
"The road splits into two. We'll split into two groups."

169

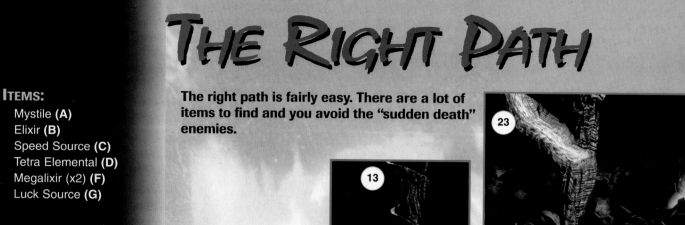

THE RIGHT PATH

ITEMS:

Mystile **(A)**
Elixir **(B)**
Speed Source **(C)**
Tetra Elemental **(D)**
Megalixir (x2) **(F)**
Luck Source **(G)**

The right path is fairly easy. There are a lot of items to find and you avoid the "sudden death" enemies.

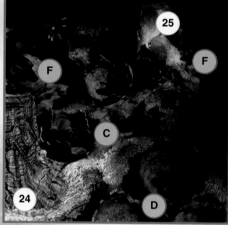

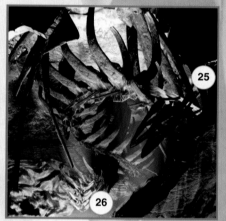

MALBORO

Area—The Crater					
LVL 44	HP 4400	MP 900	EXP 1000	GIL 100	AP 100

Slp	Ret	Con	Sil	Slw	Drk	Trsfr	Stp
Bsk	Psn	Par	Stn	SS	Man	Dth	Imp

MORPH	STEAL	ATTACKS
n/a	M-Tentacles	Frozen Beam, Bad Breath, Bio2

DRAGON ZOMBIE

Area—The Crater					
LVL 54	HP 13000	MP 400	EXP 4000	GIL 2800	AP 300

Slp	Ret	Con	Sil	Slw	Drk	Trsfr	Stp
Bsk	Psn	Par	Stn	SS	Man	Dth	Imp

MORPH	STEAL	ATTACKS
n/a	Cauldron	Poison Bite, Body Tail, Pandora's Box

THE LEFT PATH

ITEMS:

Turbo Ether (x2) **(A)**
Speed Source **(B)**
"Mega-All" Materia **(C)**
X-Potion (x2) **(D)**
Vaccine **(E)**

The left path is actually two paths. The first takes you through some very natural-looking terrain; the second is a series of rocky ledges. Each path has great items, so make sure you explore them both.

To get the **"Mega-All" Materia** near the bottom of the rocky path, press the ● button just as Cloud lands on the step next to it. If not, he jumps right past it.

Remedy **(F)**
Elixir **(G)**
Remedy **(H)**
Magic Source **(I)**,
Vaccine **(J)**
"Shield" Materia **(K)**
Imperial Guard **(L)**
Hero Medicine **(M)**
"Counter" Materia **(N)**
"W-Magic" Materia **(O)**

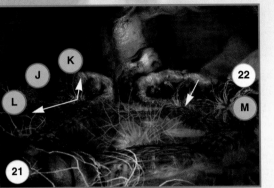

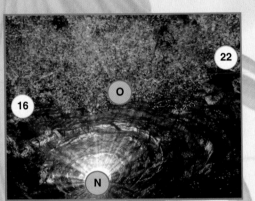

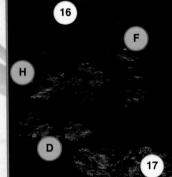

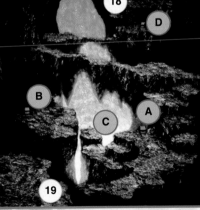

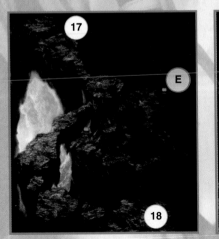

BEHEMOTH

Area—Midgar					
LVL 45	HP 7000	MP 400	EXP 1500	GIL 2200	AP 100

Slp	Ret	Con	Sil	Slw	Drk	Trsfr	Stp
Bsk	Psn	Par	Stn	SS	Man	Dth	Imp

MORPH	STEAL	ATTACKS
n/a	Phoenix Down	Claw, Horn Lift

MASTER TONBERRY

Area—The Crater					
LVL 40	HP 8000	MP 200	EXP 6000	GIL 6800	AP 200

Slp	Ret	Con	Sil	Slw	Drk	Trsfr	Stp
Bsk	Psn	Par	Stn	SS	Man	Dth	Imp

MORPH	STEAL	ATTACKS
n/a	Elixir	Everyone's Grudge

ALLEMANGE

Area—The Crater					
LVL 48	HP 8000	MP 200	EXP 1300	GIL 1360	AP 100

Slp	Ret	Con	Sil	Slw	Drk	Trsfr	Stp
Bsk	Psn	Par	Stn	SS	Man	Dth	Imp

MORPH	STEAL	ATTACKS
n/a	Eye Drop	Claw, L4 Death, L3 Flare

CHRISTOPHER

Area—The Crater					
LVL 34	HP 6000	MP 200	EXP 1300	GIL 800	AP 80

Slp	Ret	Con	Sil	Slw	Drk	Trsfr	Stp
Bsk	Psn	Par	Stn	SS	Man	Dth	Imp

MORPH	STEAL	ATTACKS
n/a	Earth Drum	Stardust March, High/Low Suite

When you reach the bottom of North Cave, talk to everyone on your team. They'll all hand over items they've located on their way to the bottom. This is also a great place to put the Save Crystal **(P)**. When you're ready, head down the center path.

GIGHEE

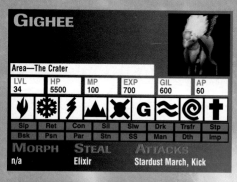

Area—The Crater

LVL	HP	MP	EXP	GIL	AP
34	5500	100	700	600	60

Slp	Ret	Con	Sil	Slw	Drk	Trsfr	Stp
Bsk	Psn	Par	Stn	SS	Man	Dth	Imp

MORPH	STEAL	ATTACKS
n/a	Elixir	Stardust March, Kick

ALLEMANGE

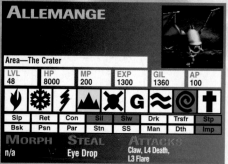

Area—The Crater

LVL	HP	MP	EXP	GIL	AP
48	8000	200	1300	1360	100

Slp	Ret	Con	Sil	Slw	Drk	Trsfr	Stp
Bsk	Psn	Par	Stn	SS	Man	Dth	Imp

MORPH	STEAL	ATTACKS
n/a	Eye Drop	Claw, L4 Death, L3 Flare

MAGIC POT

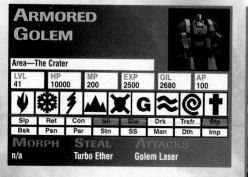

Area—The Crater

LVL	HP	MP	EXP	GIL	AP
41	4096	128	8000	8500	1000

Slp	Ret	Con	Sil	Slw	Drk	Trsfr	Stp
Bsk	Psn	Par	Stn	SS	Man	Dth	Imp

MORPH	STEAL	ATTACKS
n/a	n/a	Bad Mouth

ARMORED GOLEM

Area—The Crater

LVL	HP	MP	EXP	GIL	AP
41	10000	200	2500	2680	100

Slp	Ret	Con	Sil	Slw	Drk	Trsfr	Stp
Bsk	Psn	Par	Stn	SS	Man	Dth	Imp

MORPH	STEAL	ATTACKS
n/a	Turbo Ether	Golem Laser

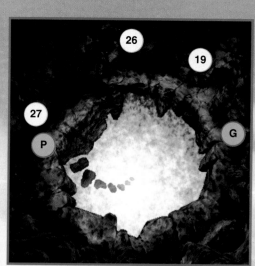

As you progress toward the center of the planet, you're forced to fight several battles against Iron Men and Dragon Zombies. Both of these enemies could pass as Bosses in their own right, so take the necessary precautions.

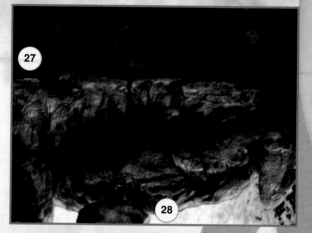

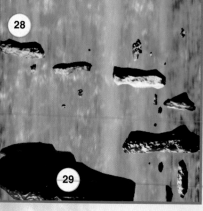

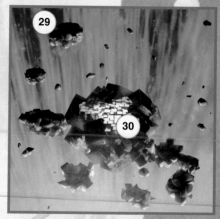

 WARNING! There's no turning back at this point. Be absolutely sure you're ready to advance.

At the very center, you'll come face-to-face with Jenova.

BOSS FIGHT: JENOVA-SYNTHESIS

Jenova-SYNTHESIS is three parts torso, and two parts arms. It's important that you enter this fight with **Slash-All** or attacks that can damage all three parts at one time. Doing so enables you to knock out the weaker arms quickly. When the arms fall, focus on the torso. Begin the fight by setting up the usual defense of **Wall**, **Regen**, and **Haste**. This makes it easy to keep your HP up and provides solid protection from Jenova's attacks. Watch out for Jenova's final countdown. After a count of five, it attacks the party with Ultima causing lots of damage.

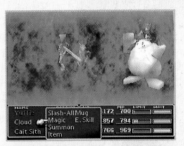

After defeating Jenova-SYNTHESIS, the team is dropped deeper into the planet's core. They arrive at a bizarre structure that is pulsing with the Lifestream power.

NOTE: The final battle takes place in this same area.

Depending on how your fight against Jenova went, you'll be prompted to split your party into one, two, or three groups. One group is the easiest configuration and three is the most challenging. No matter how many groups you make, the first group will face Sephiroth in the final battle. However, the second and/or third group must still be well equipped. The game ends if you lose any of the three groups during the fight against Bizarro-Sephiroth.

BOSS FIGHT: BIZARRO-SEPHIROTH

TIP: For a quick win, use **Knights of the Round** to hit all the parts of Sephiroth's body for 70,000 points of damage.

The basic idea behind this fight is pretty simple. There are five parts to Bizarro-Sephiroth: the head (A), Torso (B), Core (C), Left Magic (D), and Right Magic (E). The Head, Left Magic and Right Magic are all easily destroyed, but Sephiroth can quickly regenerate them. The torso is tougher and is healed each turn by the core. This is what keeps Bizarro-Sephiroth going. If the torso goes, the whole creature dies. The core is incredibly strong and cannot be damaged until its defenses are removed. Once the Core is destroyed, the torso is easily conquered.

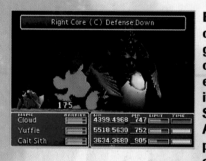

Bizarro-Sephiroth attacks with several types of magic. Be sure to keep Wall up and use a generous amount of Cure spells. The team can also be hit with some pretty nasty status effects, so equip your characters with any items that protect against negative statuses. Sephiroth's strongest attack is the Fallen Angel, which reduces each of the affected party member's life to one point. This is easily countered with **Regen** and **Cure 3**, but can be deadly to a poorly equipped team. The core can also blast the team with a powerful attack that not only does a solid amount of damage, but causes several negative status effects including confusion, poison, and slow.

In the single team fight, you'll want to concentrate on Sephiroth's Left and Right Magics (D & E). Once these are destroyed, the Core's (C) defense drops. Destroy the Core, then attack the Torso section (B) to finish off Bizarro-Sephiroth.

When using two teams, have the first team eliminate the Left Magic and the Head, then switch to the right team when given the chance. When the right team destroys the Right Magic and Head (it may be necessary to destroy the Left Magic as well), the Core's right defense drops. Have the right team destroy the right side of the core, then switch back to the left team. The Core's left defense should now be down. Attack the left core until it is destroyed, then focus your attention on the Torso.

NOTE: Each time you switch to a new team, it's as if they haven't yet fought. They can use the maximum limit of any summons or all spells they're equipped with, even if they already used the maximum amount earlier in the battle.

In a three-team situation, you'll begin the fight in front of Bizarro-Sephiroth. Switch to the left team as soon as the middle team destroys a piece of Sephiroth. Follow the instructions for a two-team battle until you've destroyed both sides of the Core. Immediately switch back to the middle team and have them finish off Sephiroth by taking out the Core and then the Torso.

174

Boss Fight: Safer Sephiroth

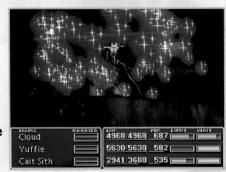

Your first priority should be setting up **Wall** and casting **Regen** and **Haste** on the party. Also, heal anyone who may have been seriously injured in the last battle and restore MP to those who may have exhausted their supply. Sephiroth has several powerful attacks. The Pale Horse does a small amount of damage and hits the effected party member with every status effect in the book. Be sure you have Esuna or a Remedy handy to counter this attack. The Shadow Flare hits a single character for nearly 7000 points of damage. Unless your levels are high or you're packing a couple of "HP Plus" Materia, this is something to worry about. There's not much you can do about the attack, but hope that **Wall** is there to absorb some of the damage. Deen is a fairly weak attack that does about 1000 to 1500 points of damage, but in a battle like this you can't take anything for granted. Then there's Sephiroth's summon spell, the Super Nova. This lengthy summon engulfs the party in a blast of cosmic proportions and typically does about 3000 to 5000 points of damage. Be sure you have a **Cure 3** ready after this one.

Keep **Wall** up throughout the battle and quickly remove any negative statuses Sephiroth might use on the party. Use **DeBarrier** to remove Sephiroth's barrier and to strengthen your attacks. Always try to use attacks that hit more than once, Limit Breaks, 2x Cut, Comet 2...anything. If you can keep your characters alive and move quickly, Sephiroth shouldn't be too tough to beat.

With Sephiroth defeated Holy is free to counter Meteor's power, but did the team work fast enough? Is the threat really removed? Well...I'm not about to spoil the ending for you, so defeat Safer-Sephiroth and find out for yourself!

175

FINDING YUFFIE

While roaming around a forest, you may run into a strange little girl named Yuffie Kisaragi. Yuffie is a female ninja and a Materia hunter.

Finding Yuffie isn't always easy. You have to walk or drive around any forest area until you encounter her. Yuffie appears just like any other enemy creature, but she has the temporary name "Mystery Ninja." She's a tough fighter, but you should be able to defeat her without much trouble. Equip yourself so you're well protected against fire.

After defeating Yuffie, you'll go to a small map that has a save point. Yuffie is lying down here, but she's fine. Examine her and you'll start a long dialogue.

 TIP: If you want to figure this out on your own, you can't take your eyes off Yuffie. She's a thief and can't be trusted.

WARNING! If that morsel of info isn't enough, then read on. However, you must be warned that the following information gives *everything* away.

First, don't use the Save Point. Doing so means you must take your eyes off Yuffie and when you return to the main screen she'll be gone—along with some of your Gil. Second, don't insult Yuffie's abilities. She's a ninja and very proud of her skills. Third, don't do anything that might result in your losing sight of Yuffie.

Examine Yuffie and she'll challenge you to another fight.

Yuffie: "You spikey-headed jerk! One more time, let's go one more time!"
Answer: Not Interested.

Now she's feeling cocky, so she taunts you. Talk to her again.

Yuffie: "You're pretty scared of me, huh!?"
Answer: ......petrified.

She'll start to leave, but turns back to yell:

Yuffie: "I'm really gonna leave! REALLY!"
Answer: Wait a second!

She seems to be getting the picture.

Yuffie: "You want me to go with you?"
Answer: ......That's right.

Yuffie: "All right! I'll go with you!"
Answer: ......Let's hurry on.

You've done it! From this point forward, Yuffie Kisaragi will be under you command.

FINDING VINCENT

Vincent is locked away in the Shinra Mansion's basement. The door to his room is locked, but the key is easily obtained...sort of. Unlock the safe on the top floor of Shinra Mansion and fight the Boss, Lost Number. After winning the battle, you'll find the Basement Key in the safe. Unlock the door and talk to Vincent, who's resting in the center coffin. Tell him about Sephiroth and he'll return to sleep. Wake him again and get him to tell you his name. He'll go back to sleep again, but on your way out of Shinra Mansion, he'll stop you and join the team.

Key to the City

It's possible to get back into Midgar without using a parachute. Visit the Number 7 gate late in the game and you'll find a man outside who can't seem to find

this key. He mentions that he might have dropped it at an excavation site. Well, there's only one excavation sight around and it's in Bone Village.

Talk to the site foreman at Bone Village and tell him you're looking for "Normal Treasure." Place your hired hands around the top area and set off the blast. They should all point to the location of the "Key to Sector 5." Now you can enter Midgar anytime you want.

Why not visit the Weapon Shop in Wall Market one more time. The owner has another special item for sale, but the price is fairly steep (129,000 Gil to be exact). However, it's a one-of-a-kind item called the **Sneak Glove**, which makes it easier to steal from enemies.

The Backroom

The general store in *Cosmo Canyon* has a back room that's roped off when the team first arrives. Check back again later and the rope has been removed. Now the team can access the hidden back room and collect an **Elixir**, **Magic Source**, and the **"Full Cure" Materia**.

Lucrecia's Cave

After acquiring the submarine or a Gold Chocobo, you can reach Lucrecia's Cave, which is located behind a waterfall in a lagoon in the Nibel area. To reach it by submarine, you must come through an underwater cave just east of the lagoon and park against the rocky ledge left of the waterfall. The Gold Chocobo can simply ride over the mountains, but you must dismount it near the ledge.

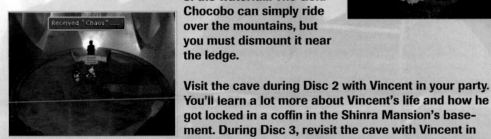

Visit the cave during Disc 2 with Vincent in your party. You'll learn a lot more about Vincent's life and how he got locked in a coffin in the Shinra Mansion's basement. During Disc 3, revisit the cave with Vincent in your party to find his ultimate weapon, Death Penalty, and his Chaos Limit Break.

Sleeping Old Man

Directly east of Junon is a small cave that is only accessible by using the Highwind or riding on a Blue/Gold Chocobo. Inside is a sleeping man who mumbles out your statistics when you speak to him. For example, he can tell you how many times you've fought and how many times you've escaped from battle. He also hints at the concept of "Master Materia."

The sleeping man gives you an item under the following circumstance: *You must talk to him when the last two digits of the number of battles you've fought match.* For instance, speaking to him after fighting 588 times may get you a **Bolt Ring**. You can only do this once.

177

However, there is one very special item you should look for — Mythril. Speak to the man when the last two digits match, and he may give you a piece of Mythril. You can then exchange this item with the weapon seller east of Gongaga Village for Aeris' Great Gospel Limit Break.

WEAPON SELLER

East of Gongaga Village is a weapon seller who normally has nothing for sale. However, there are two times when you can acquire items or information from him. The first occurs while looking for the Keystone, which he sold to Dio, the owner of the Gold Saucer. The second time occurs after collecting a piece of Mythril from the sleeping man. In exchange for the Mythril, he lets you open one of his two boxes. The large box next to the bed contains a normal item, but the small box upstairs contains Aeris' Great Gospel Limit Break. You can always rest here for free.

CRASHED GELNIKA

Monsters: Unknown 2, Unknown, Serpent, Unknown 3

ITEMS: Heaven's Cloud **(A)**, Escort Guard **(B)**, Conformer **(C)**, "Double Cut" Materia **(D)**, Megalixir (x2) **(E)**, Spirit Lance **(F)**, Outsider **(G)**, Highwind **(H)**, "Hades" Materia **(I)**

The Gelnika is in the alcove underwater and directly west of the underwater Mako Reactor. This is an optional area, but there are some great items here.

 WARNING! Be careful when approaching the Gelnika. The Emerald WEAPON is sometimes in front of the Gelnika. If the Emerald WEAPON is there, resurface and dive again—it should have moved on.

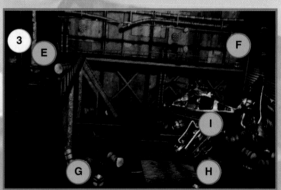

The Gelnika is a very dangerous place, so make sure you save upon entering the ship. There are no monsters in the entrance area, but the rest of the ship is crawling with all kinds of bizarre creatures.

As you first enter, take the first door on Cloud's right, which is the generator room. Most of the items in this room are on the lower floor, some of which are hidden. Don't miss the **Conformer** or the **"Double Cut" Materia.**

In the hall before the cargo bay, the team may bump into Reno and Rude of the Turks, depending on when you do this quest. If you've already had your final battle with the Turks while stopping the Sister Ray, then Reno and Rude won't be around. Otherwise, a fight will ensue.

The cargo bay has two more "must-have" items. One is Cid's Highwind Limit Break and the other is the **"Hades" Materia.** It's a long walk to both items and Shinra's freakish beasts are out for blood.

You may want to save before leaving the Gelnika. If Emerald WEAPON is sitting in front of the Gelnika when you exit, you might accidentally initiate combat.

178

Tropical Getaway

At Costa del Sol there's a real estate agent selling President Shinra's vacation home for the not so low price of 300,000 Gil. There's not much you can do with the place except take the party and rest. There are some items in the basement, but you can grab those without purchasing the home.

Turtle's Paradise Flyers

Turtle's Paradise in Wutai is having a special contest. They've placed six flyers around the planet, each with an advertisement for the restaurant. The restaurant owner is offering a prize to anyone who can locate all six flyers. Where do you look?

Flyer #1

The first flyer is in the heart of the Sector 5 Slum. Look inside the house on the east side of town. You'll find the flyer tacked to the wall in the boy's room upstairs.

Flyer #4

The fourth flyer is attached to the Tiger Lily Arms Shop in Cosmo Canyon. The shop is along the path that leads to Bugenhagen's house.

Flyer #2

This is the tough one. You MUST find this flyer on one of your two trips to Shinra HQ. If you don't, you can't win the contest. The flyer is stuck to the bulletin board at the back of the lobby's first level.

Flyer #5

Go to the inn and check out the wall next to the innkeeper's desk.

Flyer #3

Check out the Ghost Hotel at the Gold Saucer to find the third flyer. It's inside the hotel's lobby next to the Item Shop's entrance.

Flyer #6

This one's easy. It's actually right next to Turtle's Paradise in Yuffie's basement. Check the banner on the wall outside the trap room.

I know what you're thinking, that better be one heck of a prize. Well it's no Ultima Weapon, but I don't think you'll be disappointed. Talk to the owner of Turtle's Paradise, he's one of the guys behind the bar, and he'll give you a Power Source, Guard Source, Magic Source, Mind Source, Speed Source, Luck Source, and a Megalixir.

All Lucky 7's

Any character whose hit points are reduced to 7777 after an attack gets the All Lucky 7's effect. The character goes into a mad rage and begins attacking the enemy non-stop, landing a hit for 7777 points of damage each time.

To get this you must first get your character's HP over 7777. This means the All Lucky 7's effect can only happen to high-level characters or those equipped with several

179

Points are 7777, that character's HP is reduced to 1. So you can't carry the All Lucky 7's effect over to another battle.

 NOTE: It may be possible to keep this effect if you can find a way to equip your character with Materia that alters the character's HP level so that it's exactly 7777. So far I haven't found a way to do it, but that doesn't mean it isn't possible.

Special Cinema

After Cloud finds himself, visit the basement at Shinra Mansion again (in Nibelheim). Upon entering the library area, you'll flash to a special cinema that explains how Cloud ended up back at Midgar with Zack's sword in his hand and decided to become a mercenary.

Chocobo Breeding and Racing

Chocobos are fun-loving creatures that are often kept as pets and used as transportation. After acquiring the Highwind, you can raise your own Chocobos at Choco Bill's Chocobo Ranch near the Mythril Mine. Raising Chocobos isn't cheap. You'll need to buy stables from Choco Bill at 10,000 Gil a piece and you'll end up spending a small fortune on Greens and Nuts. It's also quite time consuming due to the cost and time it takes to train and breed Chocobos.

Getting Started

Purchase several stalls from Choco Bill (no less than three), and then begin hunting for a Chocobo. As you probably know by now, Chocobos can be found anywhere there are Chocobo tracks on the landscape. What you may not know is that each area yields Chocobos of different qualities. To breed the best, you need to find the best. Here's a quick list of the various areas and the type of Chocobos you can find in each:

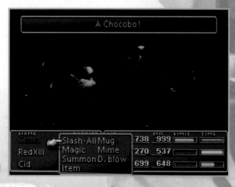

Area	Classes
Chocobo Ranch Area	Poor, Weak
Junon Area	Fair, Poor
Gold Saucer Area	Good, Average
Rocket Town Area	Mediocre
Wutai Area	Average, Fair
Icicle Inn Area	Wonderful, Weak
Mideel Area	Great, Fair

You can capture four Chocobos at a time, but then you'll need to return to the Chocobo Ranch to choose who the keepers are. Choco Billy will always give you his recommendation. Follow the list below to help you determine what type of Chocobo you have by interpreting Choco Billy's comments.

CHOCOBO TYPES	CHOCO BILLY'S ASSESSMENTS
Wonderful	"This…is a wonderful Chocobo!"
Great	"This is a great Chocobo."
Good	"Mmm, this seems like a good Chocobo."
Fair	"Mmm, this one's not bad."
Average	"This is a pretty average Chocobo."
Mediocre	"This Chocobo's so-so."
Poor	"This one doesn't seem to be very good."
Weak	"I really can't recommend this one."

Once you have a selection of quality Chocobos, you'll want to feed and train them. Chocobos eat Greens, which can be found in the wild or purchased from Choco Billy and the Chocobo Sage. Greens raise one or several of a Chocobo's stats. These stats include:

Speed	Makes Chocobo run faster
Intelligence	Chocobo paces itself better
Stamina	Can push Chocobo harder for longer
Attitude	Chocobo behaves better

Higher quality Greens provide more of an increase than cheaper Greens, but they cost more. You can expect to feed some Chocobos as much as 500,000 Gil worth of Greens. Check out the various Greens and what they do:

GREEN	LOCATION	PRICE	+SPEED	+INTELLECT	+STAMINA
Gysahl	Bill's	100	No	No	Yes
Krakka	Bill's	250	No	Yes	No
Tantal	Bill's	400	Yes	Yes	Yes
Pahsana	Bill's	800	No	Yes	No
Curiel	Bill's	1000	Yes	No	Yes
Mimett	Bill's	1500	Yes	No	Yes
Reagen	Sage's	3000	Yes	No	Yes
Sylkis	Sage's	5000	Yes	Yes	Yes

If you feed your Chocobo a Green and it fails to raise its statistics, you've maxed out the statistics that particular Green effects. You can also use Greens to make a Chocobo stay around longer during a battle. The better the Green, the longer it captures the Chocobo's attention.

Chocobos also eat nuts, but only when they're breeding. You should never need to purchase a nut. This is mainly because the only nuts you should ever need are the Zeio Nut and the Carob Nut, both of which are used to breed special Chocobos, but neither of which can be purchased.

After maxing out your Chocobos stats, you should race them before trying to breed them. Racing Chocobos and increasing their classes helps to ensure that the Chocobos' offspring will be champion material. Two *S Class* Chocobos will have a much better chance of breeding a special Chocobo than two *C Class* Chocobos.

Once you have a male and a female Chocobo that have been properly trained, you're ready to create a special Chocobo.

SPECIAL CHOCOBOS

At one time, there were two now extinct types of Chocobo roaming the planet: The **Mountain-Chocobo** and the **River-Chocobo**. The Mountain-Chocobo was a green tinted bird with the ability to cross mountains. The River-Chocobo

was a blue bird that could cross any shallow body of water. Remember that there are some parts of this planet that just can't be reached by conventional means. On the other hand, the right kind of Chocobo can cross anything. These two would sure come in handy, but no one seems to know how these two were bred.

There's a guy named Chocobo Sage, who no one has seen in years. It was thought that he either moved to some far-off land or just plain disappeared. However, it's known that he lives on the northern continent deep within the mountains. You can ask him for some Reagen Greens, but you'll need an airship to reach his cabin. You can also ask him about breeding Mountain- or River-Chocobos. He may even be able to tell you about the Black Chocobo. Make sure you revisit him from time to time. When you do find him, let Choco Bill's daughter, Chole, know and she'll keep track of any information he may give you.

NOTE: Chocobo Sage's pet Chocobo has the "Enemy Skill" Materia. Check out its stall when you get there.

If you need the real scoop right away, here's what you need to know:

To get a Mountain- (Green) or River- (Blue) Chocobo you need to mate a Great or a Good Chocobo using the Carob Nut. You can't buy the Carob Nut in a store; instead you'll need to steal it from the ferocious Vlakorados that roam the woods near Bone Village. You can also increase your chances of breeding a special Chocobo if the parents are both S Class racers.

The Mountain-and-River (Black) Chocobo is created when a Mountain- (Green) and River- (Blue) Chocobo mate using a Carob Nut. Again it's not absolute, but you can increase your chances of obtaining a Black Chocobo by training the mother and father hard.

Once you have a Black Chocobo, you can attempt to breed the ultimate Chocobo. These Gold Chocobos can go absolutely anywhere. They can even reach that mysterious island northeast of the Chocobo Ranch. Have the Black Chocobo mate with a Wonderful Chocobo and feed them a Zeio Nut. These nuts are the rarest of all the nuts. They can only be found on a small island northeast of Chocobo Ranch. Note, however, that there are creatures in the woods known as Goblins. You should be able to steal the Zeio Nut from them during a battle.

The Materia Caves

After you've bred some special Chocobos, you can reach the secret Materia Caves scattered across the world. Each one contains a special Materia you won't find anywhere else in the world. Check the map in the back of the book for each cave's exact location.

Materia Cave #1—Knights of the Round

This cave can only be reached with a Gold Chocobo, but once you have the Knights of the Round Materia you'll know why.

Materia Cave #2—Quadra Magic

You'll need your airship and a Blue Chocobo to reach this cave.

Materia Cave #3—HP <—> MP

You can reach this cave with a Green or a Blue Chocobo.

Materia Cave #4—Mimic

Reaching this cave requires the use of a Green Chocobo.

Chocobo Sage

In the mountains deep within the arctic continent, you'll find a small house with a strange man named Chocobo Sage. He has advice on how to raise the Green, Blue, Black, and Gold Chocobos. You can also pick up an "Enemy Skill" Materia just for stopping by and speaking with his pet Chocobo.

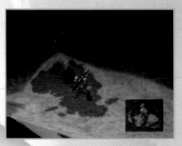

There's also stuff to buy at the Chocobo Sage's house. Here you'll find the coveted Sylkis Greens as well as several other Chocobo related items. Porov Nut *2000;* Pram Nut *1500;* Sylkis Greens *5000;* Reagan Greens *3000.*

The Chocobo Sage's house can only be reached by airship or on the back of a Chocobo with mountain crossing abilities. If you have trouble finding it, it's directly west of the **Corral Valley Cave's** west exit.

Ancient Forest

The Ancient Forest is just east of Cosmo Canyon. You can't reach it until you either defeat Ultimate WEAPON, or you've bred a Gold Chocobo. The earlier you can get here, the more worthwhile the items are. For instance, Cloud can obtain his Apocalypse sword here, but if he already has his ultimate weapon, the Ultima Weapon, he's already defeated the Ultimate WEAPON.

The Ancient Forest is one huge puzzle where you must figure out how to use the frogs, insects, and other items to get through the path. You can pick up frogs and insects and move them to various locations. Placing them in the right spot initiates an interaction with something. Insects can be used to close pitcher flowers and to lure out frogs. Frogs can shut pitcher flowers, and then launch you to new areas as they bust out.

Insects

When placed in a pitcher flower, the flower shuts and creates a step or bridge. The flower reopens after digesting the insect; the insect will no longer appear in that area. Insects can also be sacrificed to lure a frog out of a hollow tree. When a flower or a frog eats an insect, it won't reappear until you leave and reenter the area.

Frogs

You can place frogs in pitcher flowers just like insects, but the flowers can't digest frogs. After a few seconds inside a flower, the captured frog bursts out. If Cloud is standing on the flower when the frog breaks free, he gets catapulted to areas he may not normally be able to reach.

Beehives

Throwing a beehive into a mutant flytrap is the only way to get the flytrap to shut its jaws. Unlike frogs and insects, beehives remain inside flytraps until you leave the area.

Pitcher Flower

Pitcher flowers can capture insects and frogs inside their petals. While holding a victim, the flower's lid creates a step or bridge that Cloud can use to reach far-off areas. Insects are eventually digested and removed from the area, but frogs jump out of the flower after a few seconds.

Mutant Flytrap

These snapping flowers can injure Cloud and his companions. Most of the time, you can work your way around or over a flytrap, but sometimes you'll need a beehive to shut it's yap.

Stamen

The springy, pink stamen can be used to fling Cloud to a different area or a higher ledge. They're often the best way over an obstacle.

Hollow Trees

By placing an insect in front of a hollow tree, you can lure out a frog. Each tree only contains one frog.

Area 1:

Monsters: Diablo, Rifsak, Epilonis

ITEMS: Spring Gun Clip **(A)**, Supershot ST **(B)**

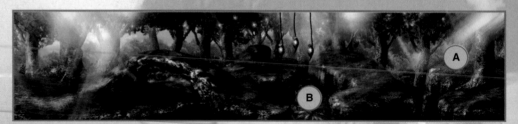

Pick up the three insects near the start and move them all to the area near the pitcher flowers. After you gather them, place each one in a pitcher flower to make a bridge to the other side. You must place one insect in the pitcher flower and then stand on the closed pitcher flower to place the next insect. To get the item from the mutant flytrap, approach it from the right and barely step on it. You should be able to pick up the Supershot ST without alarming the flytrap.

Area 2:

ITEMS: "Slash-All" Materia **(C)**, Minerva Band **(D)**

Pick up an insect and then jump to the high ledge. Lay the insect down on the left so that it jumps into the pitcher flower. If a frog eats the insect, place the frog into the pitcher flower and use the flower bridge to reach the opposite side.

Once across, pick up the nearby frog and put it in the left pitcher flower. Then stand on top of the flower until the frog pops out. The resulting force throws Cloud onto the high ledge to the left, where he can pick up a large beehive. Take the beehive and set it just left of the mutant flytrap, which should cause it to pop right into the middle of the flytrap causing it to shut. You can now grab the **"Slash-All" Materia** on the right side of the flytrap. Pick the frog back up and put it in the right pitcher flower, and then have Cloud stand on the flower until he's thrown to the right.

Area 3:

ITEMS: "Typoon" Materia (**E**)

Pick up the two insects and put them in the pitcher flowers so Cloud can reach the springy stamen. This puts him deep in the forest's canopy. Follow the limbs up and all the way to the right to find the **"Typoon" Materia.**

Go back all the way to the left and climb down the limb to Area 2 and to the item that was inaccessible before, the Minerva Band. To return to Area 3, you need to hop down and use the frog trick again.

Make your way back to the treetops and go about halfway to the right. Walk behind the broken limb just before the three springy stamens and you'll find a path that leads back down to Area 3.

Place an insect in the open pitcher flower to reach the beehive. Put the beehive in the mutant flytrap the same way you did in Area 2 and then use the second insect to reach the left area again. Grab an insect and put it in front of the hollow tree to lure out a frog. Leave the frog for a moment and go grab the other insect in this area. Put that insect in the pitcher flower to the right, and then grab the frog and hop back to the right side.

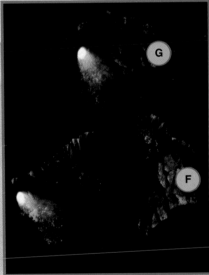

Run to the right and set the frog down near the rightmost pitcher flower so that it jumps inside. Stand on the flower until the frog bursts out so that Cloud is thrown to the cave on the right.

Area 4:

ITEMS: Apocalypse (**F**), Elixir (**G**)
There are no puzzles inside the cave, just a couple of easy-to-get items. Exit the top of the cave to leave the forest.

ULTIMATE WEAPONS

Each character has a weapon that is considered his/her ultimate weapon. These weapons often have strange characteristics that enable them to pack an extremely strong punch, but Materia typically can't grow while placed in an ultimate weapon. Therefore, it's kind of a double-edged sword—you'll want to use them, but only with Materia that's been mastered.

Cloud: *Ultima Weapon*

Cloud can obtain his ultimate weapon, the Ultima Weapon, by destroying Ultimate WEAPON. Confused? On Disc 3 you can find Ultimate WEAPON, hovering over a lake in the eastern continent.

Barret: *Missing Score*

Barret's ultimate weapon, the Missing Score, can be found on the steps that lead up to the Sister Ray just before the team encounters Hojo.

Tifa: *Premium Heart*

After getting the "Key to Sector 5," you can return to Wall Market and check the broken vending machine again. It's fixed, sort of. It dispenses Tifa's ultimate weapon, the Premium Heart, and then breaks down again.

Aeris: *Princess Guard*

While wandering around the Temple of the Ancients, you'll find Aeris' ultimate weapon, the Princess Guard, just off the clock room. It's at the end of the IV hallway.

Red XIII: *Limited Moon*

After taking Bugenhagen to the Ancient City, return to Cosmo Canyon with Red XIII in your party. He finds Bugenhagen in pretty bad shape, but Red XIII walks away with his ultimate weapon, the Limited Moon.

Cait Sith: *HP Shout*

During the team's second raid on Shinra's Headquarters, you can pick up Cait Sith's ultimate weapon, the HP Shout, from a locker in the health spa located on the 64th floor. The locker is on the left side of the third row.

Yuffie: *Conformer*

When you have the submarine, locate the crashed Gelnika just off the coast by the Gold Saucer. Inside the generator room is Yuffie's ultimate weapon, the Conformer.

Cid: *Venus Gospel*

After the rocket in Rocket Town has been launched, talk to the old man outside the Item Shop. He's the one who's been so obsessed with the rocket. If you speak with him several times, he'll eventually give you Cid's ultimate weapon, the Venus Gospel.

Vincent: *Death Penalty*

After acquiring the submarine or a Gold Chocobo, you can reach Lucrecia's Cave, located behind a waterfall in a lagoon in the Nibel area. Visit the cave with Vincent in your party during Disc 2. Then during Disc 3, revisit the cave with Vincent in your party to get his ultimate weapon, Death Penalty.

LEVEL 4 LIMIT BREAKS

Cloud: *Omnislash*

Fight in the Battle Arena at Gold Saucer until you get at least 32,000 battle points. The points can then be exchanged at the Battle Arena for the Omnislash Limit Break.

Barret: *Catastrophe*

Revisit North Corel once Meteor has been summoned and speak to the lady in the middle house on the west side of town. She'll give Cloud the Catastrophe for Barret's Limit Break.

Tifa: *Final Heaven*

After reaching Nibelheim, take Tifa to her house and play the song from Cloud's flashback at the Kalm Inn. The song is: **Do-Re-Mi-Ti-La Do-Re-Mi-So-Fa-Do-Re-Do, or X, ■, ▲, R1/L1+▲, R1/L1+■, X, ■, ▲, R1/L1+X, ●, X, ■, X.** When finished with the tune, press Start and Tifa will say she has the sheet music for that song. Inside the sheet music she finds a note and her Final Heaven Limit Break.

This trick can be performed during Disc 2 and Disc 3.

Aeris: *Great Gospel*

Speak with the sleeping old man near Junon when you've fought a number of battles where the last two digits of the number are the same. He'll give you a piece of Mythril that can be exchanged for Aeris' Great Gospel Limit Break, which is in the small box.

Red XIII: *Cosmo Memory*

To get Red XIII's Cosmo Memory Limit Break, you must defeat the Lost Number Boss in Shinra Mansion. This requires opening the safe on the second floor of the house.

Yuffie: *All Creation*

Yuffie receives her All Creation Limit Break for defeating Godo, her father, at the top of the Pagoda of the Five Mighty Gods.

Cid: *Highwind*

After getting the submarine, locate the crashed Gelnika off the shore of the Gold Saucer. Inside the cargo bay, you'll find Cid's Highwind Limit Break.

Vincent: *Chaos*

After acquiring the submarine or a Gold Chocobo, you can reach Lucrecia's Cave, which is located behind a waterfall at a lagoon in the Nibel area. Visit the cave with Vincent in your party during Disc 2. Then during Disc 3, revisit the cave with Vincent in your party and you'll get his Chaos Limit Break.

ULTIMATE WEAPON

During Disc 3, you can chase down Ultimate WEAPON. Defeating it means you get Cloud's ultimate weapon and you'll gain access to the Ancient Forest near Cosmo Canyon.

Ultimate WEAPON will be hovering over the lake near Junon. Fly up to it to enter combat. Fight it as you've fought most bosses up to this point. Put up a Wall or MBarrier and keep the party healed. Then pummel the creature with your strongest spells, summons, and attacks. After taking a few thousand points of damage, Ultimate WEAPON will fly off just as it did in Mideel.

Chase the beast with the Highwind and stay on its tail until it hovers over another location. Its favorite spots seem to be Nibelheim, Midgar, Mideel, and Cosmo Canyon. As soon as it stops, enter combat again. You can ram it with the Highwind without taking damage. In fact, it causes the Ultimate WEAPON to find a new target more rapidly.

Ultimate WEAPON can't heal itself after a battle and will eventually head for Cosmo Canyon, its final resting place. Defeat it there and it plummets to the planet, destroying a large portion of the canyon. For defeating it you receive the Ultima Weapon, Cloud's ultimate weapon, and you can now reach the Ancient Forest through the destroyed area.

THE AMERICAN CREATURES

The two creatures added to the American version of *Final Fantasy VII* are quite possibly the game's greatest challenge. Those players with enough guts and power to destroy the two new weapons will receive two very valuable prizes.

187

EMERALD WEAPON

The first of the new creatures roams the ocean floor and makes its first appearance when the team acquires the submarine. You'll want to avoid this creature early on, since your party simply won't have any chance of destroying it.

Later acquiring the Final Attack, Knights of the Round, Mime, W-Summon, and Mega All Materias you can put up a decent fight.

So how tough is Emerald WEAPON? Its basic attack does about 7000 points of damage, so it can immediately knock out a character. Once its smaller lasers open, it can hit the party with eight consecutive attacks. Four of the attacks do about 3000 to 4000 points of damage. The other four drain about 300 to 500 MP with each hit. To make matters worse, it can also hit the team with its super weapon that does 9999 points of damage to each character. As far as HP goes, the weapon has well over 500,000 hit points and you've only got twenty minutes to destroy the creature.

First, collect the Underwater Materia before you head into this battle. Having it equipped eliminates the 20 minute time limit and makes the fight much easier. You'll need a lot of HP and MP to put up a decent fight. Mastered Materia are a must. You'll want to use each of your Materia as much as possible. Try using W-Summon to cast two Knights of the Round and have each of the members of your party equipped with Mime. If they can mime the summons, you can cast an endless chain of Knights of the Round until the creature dies. Also, equip as many characters as possible with the Final Attack—Revive Materia combination. This will help if the creature uses its ultimate attack or just gets a lucky shot. Have lots of Turbo Ether on hand, since Emerald Weapon can drain your MP quickly. If you win the battle you'll receive the Earth Harp. On its own it's not much, but it can be traded in at Kalm for some incredible prizes (Check the Kalm Traveler section).

RUBY WEAPON

Ruby WEAPON appears once Ultimate WEAPON has been destroyed. You'll find it peaking out of the sand surrounding the Gold Saucer. To initiate combat fly into its head and it will surface.

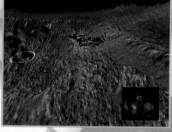

Unless the WEAPON's claws are buried in the sand, its torso is invulnerable. Attacking it at such a time will prompt Ruby WEAPON to use its quicksand attack that instantly eliminates a member of the party. Typically Ruby WEAPON will use this attack twice, cutting your party down to one. This, of course, makes the battle a lot tougher. Once Ruby WEAPON buries its claws, attack the torso at full force—Quad Magic and Bahumat ZERO works pretty well, but Knights of the Round typically prompts Ruby WEAPON to retaliate with Ultima. Be sure you equip you characters with the Final Attack—Revive combination or you won't stand a chance.

For winning the battle you receive the Desert Rose. It may not seem like much at first, but it can be traded in at Kalm for a cool prize (Check the Kalm Traveler section).

KALM TRAVELER

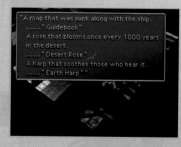

Check the top floor of the rightmost building in Kalm. There you'll find a man who's completely content with the world. However, once Meteor is summoned and the Weapons are attacking, the man will become discontented. At this time he'll begin searching for three items: the Guide Book, Earth Harp, and Desert Rose. Bringing him any one of these items will prompt him to reward the party.

The Guide Book is located in the Underwater Reactor, but it's not in a treasure chest. You'll have to Morph a creature called the Ghost Ship to pick up the item. It can usually be found in the tunnels along the ocean floor. Take the item back to the traveler and he'll give you the Underwater Materia. This item eliminates the 20 minute timer in the fight against the Emerald WEAPON.

The Earth Harp and the Desert Rose are prizes for defeating the two new weapons. You'll receive the Earth Harp if you can defeat the Emerald WEAPON. If you best the Ruby WEAPON you'll receive the Desert Rose. Take the items back to the traveler and he'll give you the Master Summon, Master Magic, and Master Command Materia. In exchange for the Desert Rose, the traveler will give you a Gold Chocobo.

MASTER MATERIA

If you master all of the Materia in a single group, revisit Bugenhagen's planetarium and examine the Huge Materia that matches the category you've mastered. Doing so will get you the Master Materia for that group. Master Materia basically equip you with all—or almost all—of the spells, summons, commands, or effects from that group. For instance, the Master Summon Materia equips you with every summon spell and enables you to use each of them an unlimited number of times, providing that you have the MP to do so.

DA-CHAO FIRE CAVE

There's a small fire cave carved into the side of Da-chao at Wutai. The fires inside block anyone from reaching the end of the cave, but they can be put out with the right item. During the raid on Shinra's Underwater Reactor, Cloud can pick up the "Leviathan Scales" from a treasure chest on the dock. The scales hold Leviathan's power of water and will put out any flame they come in contact with. Use "Leviathan Scales" on each of the fires in the Da-chao cave to find the Oritsuru Weapon (A) for Yuffie and the "Steal as Well" Materia (B).

GOLD SAUCER; BATTLE ARENA

At the Battle Arena, one member of your party can participate in a series of battles to win Battle Points that can be exchanged for valuable prizes. The cost is 10 GP (not Gil) and there's very little risk.

The basic premise is simple. The chosen fighter can fight up to eight random encounters of increasing difficulty. Any damage or negative effects from a previous fight are carried over to the next fight. After any win, the player may choose to continue or stop. If the player stops, he/she receives any Battle Points collected up to that point. Should the player choose to go on, your fighter is hit with a random effect, chosen via a one-reel slot machine.

NOTE: Fighters aren't actually killed in the Battle Arena. Even if they're defeated, they leave the arena with exactly the same amount of HP and MP with which they entered.

Before giving it a try, equip some of the following Materia and equipment. Equip a powerful weapon with plenty of Materia slots and choose armor that drains or blocks magic effects (the Tetra Elemental is particularly effective). The Ribbon is the must-have accessory for the Battle Arena. It can stop any negative effects monsters might try to lay on your fighter. It can even prevent some of the slots effects like Poison, Frog, and Mini.

Equip Materia slots with the essentials, including Restore, Time, Barrier, and Counter. Counter Attack and Counter come in handy, as do Deathblow and Mega All. These enable you to inflict as much damage as possible with every attack. The more Counter Attack Materia you equip, the more times your fighter can take advantage of an enemy's attack. Also, equip the Added Effect—Contain combination to your weapon. This will Stone a lot of your enemies before the battle gets underway. The Final Attack—Revive combination will save you if the enemy manages to overcome your fighter. Also, drop any "All" Materia that aren't combined with an attack Materia. It won't do any good to have a spell like Cure—All when there's only one person in the battle.

The Slots effects can make or break any battle. Most aren't too serious, but a couple can really hamper your progress. In some ways, the worst effects are the most beneficial because they bump up your battle points. Here's a quick glimpse at all the effects and what they do.

All Materia Broken
All the Materia you have is disabled, but your HP rises quickly.

Command Materia Broken
All Command (yellow) Materia is disabled and all extra commands are lost.

Independent Materia Broken
All Independent (purple) Materia is disabled.

Support Materia Broken
All Support (blue) Materia is disabled.

Summon Materia Broken
All Summon (red) Materia is disabled.

Magic Materia Broken
All Magic (green) Materia is disabled.

Mini
Fighter is shrunk at the beginning of the next battle.

Frog
Fighter is transformed into a frog at the beginning of the next battle.

Poison
Fighter is poisoned at the beginning of the next battle.

Speed
Fighter's speed is reduced to half of current speed.

Sword Broken
Fighter's sword is broken, base strength is used to determine damage done.

Armor Broken
Fighter's armor is broken; base defense is used to determine resistance to attacks.

Accessory Broken
Fighter's accessory is broken and its effect is lost.

Item Command Sealed
Fighter can no longer use items during battle.

HP
Fighter's maximum HP cut in half.

MP
Fighter's maximum MP cut in half.

HP & MP
Fighter's maximum HP and MP cut in half.

Zero MP
Fighter's current MP reduced to zero.

10 Levels Down
The fighter's level is reduced by 10, which causes a loss in statistics.

5 Levels Down
The fighter's level is reduced by five, which causes a loss in statistics.

Time x30 Damage
Fighter loses HP equal to the time in the fighter's time bar at the end of the last battle times thirty; doesn't kill the fighter.

Cure
Fighter is fully cured at the beginning of the next battle.

Lucky 7
Fighter receives no handicap.

The maximum amount of BP you can have at any one time is 64,000, which is enough to exchange for the best item. Spend any points you collect *before* you leave the Battle Arena or you'll lose them all. You can exchange for the following items: Remedy *100*; "Enemy Lure" Materia *250*; Right Arm *500*; "Pre-Emptive" Materia *1000*; Regan Greens *2000*; "Speed Plus" Materia *4000*; Stardust *8000*; Championship Belt *16,000*; Omnislash *32,000*; "W-Summon" Materia *64,000*

After collecting 64,000 Battle Points, you're offered the chance to compete in the special battles. However, you must have also purchased the Omnislash and the W-Summon Materia. This is a tougher fight, but there are different prizes to win. The prizes include: Gambler, Masamune Blade, Combat Diary, and Autograph

CHOCOBO RACING

There are lots of great items to obtain at the Chocobo Races. Most of them are only available to those lucky enough to pick a winner in an S-class race. This class isn't available to just anyone; you won't get the chance to try it until you've become a full-blown Chocobo jockey.

Picking a winner isn't easy. You must factor in each Chocobo's top speed, stamina, attitude, and the skill of the jockey. Stamina seems to be the most important attribute, but a poor jockey can run even the best Chocobo into the ground. You should wait until you actually participate in Chocobo races before trying to get the really good items. Otherwise, you'll end up spending a lot of Gil that could instead be used to breed your own championship-quality Chocobo.

SPEED ARENA

A game of fast reflexes—shoot the various moving targets to gain points. Collect 3000 or more points for a prize. Do extremely well and you'll receive the Parasol. Keep your laser power up. Don't press the "shoot" button too long—it makes it weak. Use short multiple blasts, or in gamer terms, just tap it really fast. Of course, you can use a turbo controller to really crank up your score.

Targets range in value from 30 to 70 points. There is one very special target that is worth 1000 points. The item is the large UFO near the end of the course. Just keep the crosshairs on the UFO and keep your laser power up. You can pick up 200 points in the desert by shooting the yellow boulder on top of the canyon wall.

Here are the targets and their approximate point value listed in the order of appearance: Ghost *40*; Cactus *30-50*; Blue Plane *50-60*; Jet Plane *50-60*; Yellow Boulder *200*; Yellow Ship *60*; Star *40*; Icicle *40-50*; Spiny Ball *70*; Balloon *30*; Big Balloon *70*; Lil' UFO *60*; Rocket *50*; Lava Rock *70*; Chopper *40-50*; Big UFO *1000*; Zeppelin Engine *????*; Paddle Wheel *1*

WONDER SQUARE

There are lots of games to play at Wonder Square. Some are versions of the mini-games you play while working your way through FF7, but most are totally unique.

ARM WRESTLING MEGA SUMO—Cost: 100 Gil; Difficulty Levels: 2

Arm wrestle one of two opponents to win a small amount of Gil. The Sumo Wrestler is easier than the Wrestler, but both opponents are fairly easy to defeat. Quickly tap the ● button until you pin your opponent's arm. You get 1 Gil for defeating the Sumo; 2 Gil for defeating the Wrestler.

SUPER DUNK—Cost: 200 Gil; Difficulty Levels: None

Hold the ● button for less than a second to charge your shot, and then release. When charged correctly, you'll score a basket and get to shoot again. If you miss, the game ends and you receive 1 Gil for each basket scored. You get to continue shooting until you miss, so the amount of Gil you receive depends upon your own abilities. If you score 10 in a row, you'll get the opportunity to play Double Chance. If you make the shot, you'll double your GP, but if you miss, your GP drops back down to 1 and your game ends.

WONDER CATCHER—Cost: 100 Gil; Difficulty Levels: None

This is the simplest game at Wonder Square. Deposit 100 Gil and you'll either receive a small amount of GP, a Potion, or nothing. This is the biggest waste of Gil in the arcade.

3D BATTLER—Cost: 200 Gil; Difficulty Levels: Increasing

This fighting game plays a lot like "paper, rock, scissors." You pick an attack and your opponent picks an attack. If the attacks are the same, no one takes damage. If one player's attack beats the other's attack, the losing player takes a hit. The first person to deliver 10 successful hits to his opponent wins. The attacks are:

    ▲ = Upper body attack; Beats Low, Loses to Mid, Ties Upper

    ■ = Mid portion attack; Beats High, Loses to Low, Ties Mid

    X = Lower portion attack; Beats Mid, Loses to High, Ties Low

FORTUNE TELLING—Cost: 50 Gil; Difficulty Levels:

N/A

Okay, this isn't really a game. But for 50 Gil, you get a small glimpse into the future. Don't play this several times on the same visit, because your fortune won't change until you leave that section of Wonder Square.

MOG HOUSE—Cost: 100 Gil; Difficulty Levels: N/A

To help Mog fly, you give him Kupo nuts. If you don't feed him enough, he won't have the strength to fly; if you feed him too many, he'll fall on his little Mog bottom. So how many is just enough? Follow Mog's reactions. If he's still hungry, he'll make a little grumbling noise and rub his tummy. If he's had enough, he'll squeak and jump into the air. Stop feeding him at this point and he should fly without any trouble. To make it easier, feed him five the first time and three the second time.

Bonus! After defeating Mog House talk to the guy behind you. In appreciation of your fine puzzle-solving skills, he gives you 30 GP. Not too shabby!

G BIKE—Cost: 200 Gil; Difficulty Levels: N/A

You can access this game the first time you enter the Gold Saucer. Enemy bikers chase a little blue truck. You must protect the truck by knocking enemy bikers down. There are two types of Bikers: Red and Orange. The Orange Bikers are decent riders, but they tend to dive right in without thinking. The Red Bikers pose a much larger threat. Instead of coming towards you, they run from you. The real danger here is that the Red Bikers tend to draw you away from the truck, which enables the other Bikers to cause some damage while your attention is diverted.

Stay close to or behind the truck and hit the enemy bikers as they approach. If one gets past, don't go after him *unless* he attacks the truck. If he backs off, don't chase him—make him come to you. It's possible to push over enemy Bikers with your hog, but it's much slower than using your sword. You can also topple enemy Bikers using the "domino effect." If you knock over a Biker in front of another enemy, it causes them to collide. Bikes are worth 500 points each, but each time the enemy hits the truck, you lose 25 points. If you do well you'll receive a small amount of Gil, but if you do really well you'll receive a decent amount of Gil and an item.

SNOW GAME—Cost: 200 Gil; Difficulty Levels: 3

There are three snowboarding courses Beginner, Expert, and Crazy. The challenge increases by adding additional obstacles, increasing the speed, and tightening the turns. Throughout the course, there are balloons (Red balloons are worth one point, Blue are worth three, and Green are worth five).

You get technique points according to how well you perform. If you make it through the course without hitting a wall you receive a perfect score. Not all things deduct points; for example, you can hit a Mog while it's on its sled and not lose points, but if you hit it after it's fallen off its sled, you lose one point. Do well on a course and you'll pick up a little GP and an item.

TIP: Find a yellow ballon at the beginning of the course and you'll enter Time Attack Mode. Set the record, and then try to top your score as you race the Mog ghost.

TORPEDO ATTACK—Cost: 200 Gil; Difficulty Levels: 5

This game isn't available until after you've stolen your own submarine and fought with a Shinra submarine. Before the game begins, you're given five choices. You can either reenact the battle at the underwater Mako Reactor or you can choose from four original levels. The levels get progressively harder by increasing either the amount of enemy subs or the ability and toughness of the enemy commanders. The amount of GP you receive is the same regardless of the difficulty level.

During a battle, you can shoot as many as four torpedoes at a time. Try to lock onto your target and unload the whole group, which is normally enough to take out an enemy sub. On higher levels, however, it takes a few more shots. Missiles have a relatively short range, so get close before opening fire. If the enemy gets a lock on you, speed up and dive deep. This will normally shake the torpedoes off your tail.

Mines are the small polygons on top of the square columns. You can pass through the columns without taking damage, but don't go too high. Be careful when you enter the sonar screen— you don't want to accidentally hit a nearby mine!

Use your sonar to help better prepare for what lies ahead and to help relocate the enemy submarines. If you lose track of an enemy on the sonar, exit and reenter the sonar screen. It's faster than waiting for the next sonar pulse. For winning a battle, you receive 20 GP and an item.

GP EXCHANGE

When you have a decent amount of GP, you can exchange it for a prize with the girl near the entrance to Wonder Square. Remember: The higher the cost, the better the item.

Potion *1 GP*; Ether *20 GP*; X-Potion *80 GP*; Turbo Ether *100 GP*; Gold Ticket *300 GP*; Carob Nut *500 GP*; Gil Plus Materia *1000 GP*; EXP Plus Materia *2000 GP*

GIL EXCHANGE

A man who can exchange Gil for GP at a rate of 100 to 1 will sometimes appear next to the little house at the back of the Gold Saucer's ropeway station. He's not always there, but if you enter and exit the Gold Saucer several times, he should appear. It may take a while so be patient.

FORT CONDOR BATTLES

In essence it's better to overwhelm the opposition rather than sitting back and letting them come to you. Take charge and move you troops south as soon as possible. You may even stop the enemy advance before the enemy Commander can reach the battlefield.

Place a line of Attackers, Fighters, and Defenders along the middle of the mountain. Back them up with Shooters and Repairers. As soon as the battle begins, move your troops south so that they meet the enemy as they arrive. This will keep the enemy hordes from regrouping and taking advantage of any weak spots in your defense. If any member of your team suffers serious damage, pull that person back and have a Repairer restore the character's HP. Slowly advance toward the bottom of the screen and eventually you'll have the entire path blocked. The enemy will soon give up and you'll have fewer casualties and a larger amount of Gil returned.

BESTIARY LEGEND

LVL	The monster's level
HP	Monster's Hit Point level
MP	Monster's Magic Point level
EXP	Experience points gained
GIL	Number of Gil received for defeating monster
AP	Experience gained for Materia Orbs

Symbol	Element
Fire	Fire
Ice	Ice
Lightning	Lightning
Earth	Earth
Poison	Poison

Symbol	Element
G	Gravity
Water	Water
Wind	Wind
Holy	Holy

Normal	Normal
Double Effect	Double Effect
Invulnerable	Invulnerable
Absorbs	Absorbs
Cuts damage in half	Cuts damage in half

Status	Status	Status
Slp Sleep	Trsfr Transform	SS Slowly stone
Ret Return	Stp Stop	Man Manipulate
Con Confusion	Bsk Berserk	Dth Death
Sil Silence	Psn Poison	Imp Impossible to fight
Slw Slow	Par Paralysis	No Effect
Drk Darkness	Stn Stone	Effects Monster

1ST RAY
Area—Reactor

LVL	HP	MP	EXP	GIL	AP
4	18	0	12	5	1

MORPH: n/a STEAL: n/a ATTACKS: Laser

2-FACED
Area—GS Prison

LVL	HP	MP	EXP	GIL	AP
18	330	80	100	156	10

MORPH: n/a STEAL: Phoenix Down ATTACKS: Self-Destruct, Cure3

8 EYE
Area—Temple of Ancients

LVL	HP	MP	EXP	GIL	AP
30	500	220	1000	720	100

MORPH: n/a STEAL: n/a ATTACKS: Life Drain

ACROPHIES
Area—Corral Valley

LVL	HP	MP	EXP	GIL	AP
35	2400	220	800	1200	90

MORPH: n/a STEAL: Water Ring ATTACKS: Claw, Huge Tidal Wave

ADAMANTAIMAI
Uses *Death Force* enemy skill.
Area—West Continent Beach

LVL	HP	MP	EXP	GIL	AP
30	1600	240	720	2000	100

MORPH: n/a STEAL: Adaman Bangle ATTACKS: Light Shell, Death Force, Barrier, Mbarrier

AERO COMBATANT
Area—Tower

LVL	HP	MP	EXP	GIL	AP
11	190	0	40	110	4

MORPH: n/a STEAL: Potion ATTACKS: Propeller Slash, Sword Rush

ANCIENT DRAGON
Area—Temple of Ancients

LVL	HP	MP	EXP	GIL	AP
34	2400	450	800	800	80

MORPH: n/a STEAL: n/a ATTACKS: Horn, Southern Cross

ALLEMANGE
Area—The Crater

LVL	HP	MP	EXP	GIL	AP
48	8000	200	1300	1360	100

MORPH: n/a STEAL: Eye Drop ATTACKS: Claw, L4 Death, L3 Flare

APS
Area—Sewers

LVL	HP	MP	EXP	GIL	AP
18	1800	0	240	0	22

MORPH: n/a STEAL: n/a ATTACKS: Sewer, Tsunami Tail

ARK DRAGON
Uses *Flame Thrower* enemy skill.
Area—Mythril Caves

LVL	HP	MP	EXP	GIL	AP
18	280	124	84	180	10

MORPH: Phoenix Down STEAL: Ether ATTACKS: Claw, Flame Thrower

ARMORED GOLEM
Area—The Crater

LVL	HP	MP	EXP	GIL	AP
41	10000	200	2500	2680	100

MORPH: n/a STEAL: Turbo Ether ATTACKS: Golem Laser

ATTACK SQUAD
Area—Junon

LVL	HP	MP	EXP	GIL	AP
34	1300	100	300	420	10

MORPH: n/a STEAL: 8-inch Cannon ATTACKS: Machine Gun, Grenade, Smoke Bullet

AIRBUSTER
Area—Reactor

LVL	HP	MP	EXP	GIL	AP
15	1200	0	180	150	16

MORPH: n/a STEAL: n/a ATTACKS: Counter Attack, Big Bomber, Rear Gun

BAD RAP
Area—Downed Plane

LVL	HP	MP	EXP	GIL	AP
38	9000	120	1050	2500	70

MORPH: n/a STEAL: Ink ATTACKS: None

BAD RAP SAMPLE
Area—Midgar

LVL	HP	MP	EXP	GIL	AP
50	13000	250	0	0	0

MORPH: n/a STEAL: n/a ATTACKS: Tentacles

BAGNARADA

Area—Mt. Corel

LVL	HP	MP	EXP	GIL	AP
16	450	60	110	120	11

MORPH	STEAL	ATTACKS
Guard Source	Diamond Pin	Horn, Claw, Poison Breath

BAHBA VELAMYU

Area—Rocket Town

LVL	HP	MP	EXP	GIL	AP
23	640	40	285	280	20

MORPH	STEAL	ATTACKS
Mute Mask	n/a	Bonecutter, Jumping Bonecutter, Magi-Bonecutter

BANDERSNATCH

Area—Bone Village

LVL	HP	MP	EXP	GIL	AP
30	860	100	510	600	40

MORPH	STEAL	ATTACKS
Ice Crystal	n/a	Fang, Bodyblow

BANDIT

Area—GS Prison

LVL	HP	MP	EXP	GIL	AP
17	360	0	99	220	10

MORPH	STEAL	ATTACKS
n/a	X-Potion	Mug, Hold up, Hit

BATTERY CAP

Area—Rocket Town

LVL	HP	MP	EXP	GIL	AP
24	640	58	270	386	32

MORPH	STEAL	ATTACKS
n/a	Dazers	Four Laser, Seed Shooting

BEACHPLUG

Uses *Big Guard* enemy skill.

Area—Costa Del Sol Beach

LVL	HP	MP	EXP	GIL	AP
16	200	100	95	155	10

MORPH	STEAL	ATTACKS
Turbo Ether	n/a	Bite, Big Guard, Ice

BEHEMOTH

Uses *????* enemy skill.

Area—Midgar

LVL	HP	MP	EXP	GIL	AP
45	7000	400	1500	2200	100

MORPH	STEAL	ATTACKS
n/a	Phoenix Down	Claw, Horn Lift

BIZARRE BUG

Area—West Continent

LVL	HP	MP	EXP	GIL	AP
28	975	0	420	340	40

MORPH	STEAL	ATTACKS
n/a	n/a	Toxic Power

BLACK BAT

Area—Mansion Basement

LVL	HP	MP	EXP	GIL	AP
25	550	0	270	80	24

MORPH	STEAL	ATTACKS
Vampire Fang	n/a	Blood Suck

BLOATFLOAT

Uses Spiky Hell when killed

Area—Mt. Corel

LVL	HP	MP	EXP	GIL	AP
18	240	0	90	125	9

MORPH	STEAL	ATTACKS
Hi-Potion	Soft	Body Blow, Vacuum, Spiky Hell

BLOOD TASTE

Area—Reactor2

LVL	HP	MP	EXP	GIL	AP
8	72	0	24	32	2

MORPH	STEAL	ATTACKS
n/a	n/a	Bite, Tentacle Drain

BLUE DRAGON

Area—Gaea's Cliff

LVL	HP	MP	EXP	GIL	AP
41	8800	500	1200	1000	200

MORPH	STEAL	ATTACKS
n/a	n/a	Great Gale, Blue Dragon Breath, Bite, Tail, Dragon Force

BLUGU

Area—Basement

LVL	HP	MP	EXP	GIL	AP
4	120	0	18	35	2

MORPH	STEAL	ATTACKS
n/a	n/a	Bite, Hell Bubbles

BOMB

Bomb Blast after hit 3 times

Area—Mt. Corel

LVL	HP	MP	EXP	GIL	AP
18	600	30	150	192	20

MORPH	STEAL	ATTACKS
Shrapnel	Right Arm	Ram, Bomb Blast, Fireball

BOTTOMSWELL

Area—Junon Harbor

LVL	HP	MP	EXP	GIL	AP
23	2500	100	550	1000	52

MORPH	STEAL	ATTACKS
n/a	n/a	Tail Attack, Moonstrike, Big Wave

LVL	The monster's level	
HP	Monster's Hit Point level	
MP	Monster's Magic Point level	
EXP	Experience points gained	
GIL	Number of Gil received for defeating monster	
AP	Experience gained for Materia Orbs	

Fire · Ice · Lightning · Earth · Poison

Gravity · Water · Wind · Holy

Normal · Double Effect · Invulnerable · Absorbs · Cuts damage in half

Slp Sleep · Ret Return · Con Confusion · Sil Silence · Slw Slow · Drk Darkness

Trsfr Transform · Stp Stop · Bsk Berserk · Psn Poison · Par Paralysis · Stn Stone

SS Slowly stone · Man Manipulate · Dth Death · Imp Impossible to fight · No Effect · Effects Monster

BULLMOTOR
Uses *Laser* enemy skill.

Area—GS Prison

LVL	HP	MP	EXP	GIL	AP
19	420	96	92	140	9

MORPH n/a — **STEAL** X-Potion — **ATTACKS** Body Blow, Mantra Magic

BOUNDFAT

Area—Bone/Shell Village

LVL	HP	MP	EXP	GIL	AP
27	500	80	420	350	40

MORPH Dazers — **STEAL** Dazers — **ATTACKS** Ice2, Dark Needle, Death Sentence

BRAIN POD

Area—Shinra Tower

LVL	HP	MP	EXP	GIL	AP
15	240	46	52	95	6

MORPH n/a — **STEAL** Antidote — **ATTACKS** Refuse, Ram

CACTUAR

Area—GS Prison Desert

LVL	HP	MP	EXP	GIL	AP
20	200	20	0	10,000	0

MORPH n/a — **STEAL** n/a — **ATTACKS** None

CAPPARWIRE

Area—Junon Forests

LVL	HP	MP	EXP	GIL	AP
15	210	20	60	103	6

MORPH n/a — **STEAL** Ether — **ATTACKS** Wire Attack, Grand Spark

CARRY ARMOR

Area—Underwater Reactor

LVL	HP	MP	EXP	GIL	AP
45	24000	200	2800	4000	240

MORPH n/a — **STEAL** n/a — **ATTACKS** Lapis Laser

CARRY ARMOR LEFT ARM

Area—Midgar

LVL	HP	MP	EXP	GIL	AP
	55	24000	400	0	

0
0

MORPH n/a — **STEAL** n/a

CARRY ARMOR RIGHT ARM

Area—Midgar

LVL	HP	MP	EXP	GIL	AP
	55	5000	300	0	

0
0

MORPH n/a — **STEAL** n/a

CASTANETS

Area—Mythril Caves

LVL	HP	MP	EXP	GIL	AP
15	190	0	65	113	7

MORPH n/a — **STEAL** n/a — **ATTACKS** 2-stage attack, Scissor Spark

CEASAR

Area—Sewers

LVL	HP	MP	EXP	GIL	AP
8	120	0	23	55	2

MORPH n/a — **STEAL** Tranquilizer — **ATTACKS** Ram, Bubble

CHEKHOV

Area—Wutai Village

LVL	HP	MP	EXP	GIL	AP
34	5000	210	2900	0	50

MORPH n/a — **STEAL** n/a — **ATTACKS** Absorb

CHRISTOPHER

Area—The Crater

LVL	HP	MP	EXP	GIL	AP
34	6000	200	1300	800	80

MORPH n/a — **STEAL** Earth Drum — **ATTACKS** Stardust March, High/Low Suite

CHUSE TANK

Area—Basement

LVL	HP	MP	EXP	GIL	AP
6	36	0	23	30	2

MORPH n/a — **STEAL** n/a — **ATTACKS** Rolling Claw, Slap

COKATOLIS

Area—Mt. Corel

LVL	HP	MP	EXP	GIL	AP
17	420	0	97	168	10

MORPH Soft — **STEAL** Soft — **ATTACKS** Beak, Bird Kick, Petrify Smog

CORNEO'S LACKEY

Area—Brothel

LVL	HP	MP	EXP	GIL	AP
8	42	0	8	10	0

MORPH n/a — **STEAL** n/a — **ATTACKS** Stab, Machine Gun

CORVETTE

Area—Water Tunnel

LVL	HP	MP	EXP	GIL	AP
36	3200	260	1050	2200	60

Slp	Ret	Con	Sil	Slw	Drk	Trsfr	Stp
Bsk	Psn	Par	Stn	SS	Man	Dth	Imp

MORPH — Light Curtain
STEAL — Hyper
ATTACKS — Bodyblow, Gash, Spinning Cut, Slap

CRAWLER

Area—Mythril Caves

LVL	HP	MP	EXP	GIL	AP
15	140	48	56	65	6

Slp	Ret	Con	Sil	Slw	Drk	Trsfr	Stp
Bsk	Psn	Par	Stn	SS	Man	Dth	Imp

MORPH — n/a
STEAL — n/a
ATTACKS — Bite, Cold Breath

CRAZYSAW

Area—Midgar

LVL	HP	MP	EXP	GIL	AP
44	39000	340	800	1300	80

Slp	Ret	Con	Sil	Slw	Drk	Trsfr	Stp
Bsk	Psn	Par	Stn	SS	Man	Dth	Imp

MORPH — Turbo Ether
STEAL — Mute Mask
ATTACKS — Uppercut, Rifle

CROMWELL

Area—Midgar

LVL	HP	MP	EXP	GIL/	AP
42	3500	120	800	1500	80`

Slp	Ret	Con	Sil	Slw	Drk	Trsfr	Stp
Bsk	Psn	Par	Stn	SS	Man	Dth	Imp

MORPH — n/a
STEAL — n/a
ATTACKS — Normal Shell

CRIPSHAY

Area—Trainyard

LVL	HP	MP	EXP	GIL	AP
8	100	0	26	53	3

Slp	Ret	Con	Sil	Slw	Drk	Trsfr	Stp
Bsk	Psn	Par	Stn	SS	Man	Dth	Imp

MORPH — n/a
STEAL — Potion
ATTACKS — Ram, Dual Spike, Fire

CROWN LANCE

Area—CC Beaches

LVL	HP	MP	EXP	GIL	AP
20	440	70	225	400	23

Slp	Ret	Con	Sil	Slw	Drk	Trsfr	Stp
Bsk	Psn	Par	Stn	SS	Man	Dth	Imp

MORPH — Dream Powder
STEAL — n/a
ATTACKS — Sleepel, Sting, Bolt

CUAHL

Area—Gaea's Cliff

LVL	HP	MP	EXP	GIL	AP
33	1300	60	720	800	70

Slp	Ret	Con	Sil	Slw	Drk	Trsfr	Stp
Bsk	Psn	Par	Stn	SS	Man	Dth	Imp

MORPH — Tranquilizer
STEAL — Tranquilizer
ATTACKS — Light Spell

CUSTOM SWEEPER

Uses *Matra Magic* enemy skill.

Area—Midgar

LVL	HP	MP	EXP	GIL	AP
15	300	100	63	120	7

Slp	Ret	Con	Sil	Slw	Drk	Trsfr	Stp
Bsk	Psn	Par	Stn	SS	Man	Dth	Imp

MORPH — X-Potion
STEAL — Atomic Scissors
ATTACKS — W Machine Gun, Smoke Shot, Mantra Magic

DARK DRAGON

Uses *Dragon Force* enemy skill.

Area—The Crater

LVL	HP	MP	EXP	GIL	AP
57	14000	600	5000	2500	350

Slp	Ret	Con	Sil	Slw	Drk	Trsfr	Stp
Bsk	Psn	Par	Stn	SS	Man	Dth	Imp

MORPH — n/a
STEAL — Dragon Armlet
ATTACKS — Laser, Dragon Force, Claw, Bite

DEATH CLAW

Area—GS Prison

LVL	HP	MP	EXP	GIL	AP
19	400	120	96	168	10

Slp	Ret	Con	Sil	Slw	Drk	Trsfr	Stp
Bsk	Psn	Par	Stn	SS	Man	Dth	Imp

MORPH — n/a
STEAL — Platinum Bangle
ATTACKS — Claw, Death Claw, Laser

DEATH CLAW

Area—The Crater

LVL	HP	MP	EXP	GIL	AP
48	7000	400	1800	1200	200

Slp	Ret	Con	Sil	Slw	Drk	Trsfr	Stp
Bsk	Psn	Par	Stn	SS	Man	Dth	Imp

MORPH — n/a
STEAL — Turbo Ether
ATTACKS — Death Roulette(22), Star, Spin Turn

DEATH MACHINE

Area—Junon

LVL	HP	MP	EXP	GIL	AP
35	2500	150	900	1200	80

Slp	Ret	Con	Sil	Slw	Drk	Trsfr	Stp
Bsk	Psn	Par	Stn	SS	Man	Dth	Imp

MORPH — n/a
STEAL — W Machine Gun
ATTACKS — W Machine Gun, 100 Needles, Matra Magic(11)

DEENGLOW

Area—Trainyard

LVL	HP	MP	EXP	GIL	AP
10	120	72	35	70	4

Slp	Ret	Con	Sil	Slw	Drk	Trsfr	Stp
Bsk	Psn	Par	Stn	SS	Man	Dth	Imp

MORPH — n/a
STEAL — Ether
ATTACKS — Slash, Demi, Ice

DEMONS GATE

Area—Temple of Ancients

LVL	HP	MP	EXP	GIL	AP
45	10000	400	3800	4000	220

Slp	Ret	Con	Sil	Slw	Drk	Trsfr	Stp
Bsk	Psn	Par	Stn	SS	Man	Dth	Imp

MORPH — n/a
STEAL — n/a
ATTACKS — Rock Drop, Cave In, Demon Crush

DESERT SAHAGIN

Shells protect from physical attacks.

Area—Cosmo Canyon

LVL	HP	MP	EXP	GIL	AP
20	580	0	230	300	21

Slp	Ret	Con	Sil	Slw	Drk	Trsfr	Stp
Bsk	Psn	Par	Stn	SS	Man	Dth	Imp

MORPH — Fire Veil
STEAL — Potion
ATTACKS — Harpoon, Sandgun

Legend

LVL	The monster's level
HP	Monster's Hit Point level
MP	Monster's Magic Point level
EXP	Experience points gained
GIL	Number of Gil received for defeating monster
AP	Experience gained for Materia Orbs

Elements: Fire, Ice, Lightning, Earth, Poison, Gravity, Water, Wind, Holy

Effect boxes: Normal, Double Effect, Invulnerable, Absorbs, Cuts damage in half

Abbrev	Meaning	Abbrev	Meaning
Slp	Sleep	Trsfr	Transform
Ret	Return	Stp	Stop
Con	Confusion	Bsk	Berserk
Sil	Silence	Psn	Poison
Slw	Slow	Par	Paralysis
Drk	Darkness	Stn	Stone
SS	Slowly stone	Man	Manipulate
Dth	Death	Imp	Impossible to fight

No Effect / Effects Monster

DEVIL RIDE

Area—Midgar

LVL	HP	MP	EXP	GIL	AP
13	240	0	60	100	6

- **Morph:** Hi-Potion
- **Steal:** Hi-Potion
- **Attacks:** Wheelie, Drift Turn

DIABLO

Area—Ancient Forest

LVL	HP	MP	EXP	GIL	AP
41	4000	200	1600	900	70

- **Morph:** n/a
- **Steal:** n/a
- **Attacks:** Horn Bomber, Flame, Cold

DOORBULL

Area—Temple of Ancients

LVL	HP	MP	EXP	GIL	AP
35	2800	160	760	680	50

- **Morph:** n/a
- **Steal:** Hi-Potion
- **Attacks:** Fire Shell, Fang, Slash, Light Shell

DORKY FACE

Area—Shinra Mansion

LVL	HP	MP	EXP	GIL	AP
23	520	80	300	202	35

- **Morph:** Mute Mask
- **Steal:** Echo Screen
- **Attacks:** Cutter, Curses, Funny Breath

DRAGON
Uses *Flame Thrower* enemy skill.

Area—Nibel Mountains

LVL	HP	MP	EXP	GIL	AP
32	3500	250	900	1400	110

- **Morph:** n/a
- **Steal:** Gold Armlet
- **Attacks:** Dragon Fang, Flame Thrower

DRAGON RIDER

Area—Whirlwind Maze

LVL	HP	MP	EXP	GIL	AP
35	3500	180	1000	690	80

- **Morph:** Mind Source
- **Steal:** Hi-Potion
- **Attacks:** Bite, Head Hunting, Dual Attack, Head Hunting2, Rider Breath

DRAGON ZOMBIE
Uses *Pandora's Box* enemy skill.

Area—The Crater

LVL	HP	MP	EXP	GIL	AP
54	13000	400	4000	2800	300

- **Morph:** n/a
- **Steal:** Cauldron
- **Attacks:** Poison Bite, Body Tail, Pandora's Box

DUAL HORN

Area—Setora Shrine

LVL	HP	MP	EXP	GIL	AP
30	2500	0	550	500	45

- **Morph:** n/a
- **Steal:** Pepio Nut
- **Attacks:** Angle Punch, Horn Lift

DYNE

Area—GS Prison Desert

LVL	HP	MP	EXP	GIL	AP
23	1200	20	600	750	55

- **Morph:** n/a
- **Steal:** n/a
- **Attacks:** Needle Gun, S-Mine, Molotov Cocktail

EAGLE GUN

Area—Coal Train

LVL	HP	MP	EXP	GIL	AP
46	17000	50	2000	3800	90

- **Morph:** n/a
- **Steal:** Warrior Bangle
- **Attacks:** Single Wing Fire, Dual Wing Fire

ELENA

Area—Midgar

LVL	HP	MP	EXP	GIL	AP
53	30000	100	6400	7000	800

- **Morph:** n/a
- **Steal:** Minerva Band
- **Attacks:** Flame Light, Confu

ELFADUNK

Area—Chocobo Farm

LVL	HP	MP	EXP	GIL	AP
14	220	34	64	140	7

- **Morph:** n/a
- **Steal:** Hi-Potion
- **Attacks:** Bodyblow, Shower

EPIOLNIS

Area—Frog Forest

LVL	HP	MP	EXP	GIL	AP
36	1800	90	950	1500	70

- **Morph:** n/a
- **Steal:** Wizard Bracelet
- **Attacks:** Bird Kick, Catapult, Acid Rain

EVILHEAD

Area—Gaea's Cliff

LVL	HP	MP	EXP	GIL	AP
28	740	45	650	400	50

- **Morph:** n/a
- **Steal:** n/a
- **Attacks:** Blood Suck, Ultrasound

FLAPBEAT

Area—North Cont./ Gold Saucer

LVL	HP	MP	EXP	GIL	AP
18	330	60	140	186	15

- **Morph:** T/S Bomb
- **Steal:** T/S Bomb
- **Attacks:** Tailbeat, Flying Sickle

FLOWER PRONG
Three different forms

Area—Gongaga

LVL	HP	MP	EXP	GIL	AP
19	550	68	240	400	24

Slp	Ret	Con	Sil	Slw	Drk	Trsfr	Stp
Bsk	Psn	Par	Stn	SS	Man	Dth	Imp

MORPH	STEAL	ATTACKS
n/a	n/a	Bio2

FORMULA

Area—Condor Mts

LVL	HP	MP	EXP	GIL	AP
16	240	100	65	120	7

Slp	Ret	Con	Sil	Slw	Drk	Trsfr	Stp
Bsk	Psn	Par	Stn	SS	Man	Dth	Imp

MORPH	STEAL	ATTACKS
Speed Drink	Boomerang	Swoop, Blue Impulse

FOULANDER

Area—Da-chao Statue

LVL	HP	MP	EXP	GIL	AP
27	800	100	440	460	34

Slp	Ret	Con	Sil	Slw	Drk	Trsfr	Stp
Bsk	Psn	Par	Stn	SS	Man	Dth	Imp

MORPH	STEAL	ATTACKS
n/a	n/a	Claw, Flame Dance

FROZEN NAIL

Area—Great Glacier

LVL	HP	MP	EXP	GIL	AP
28	1300	100	520	800	50

Slp	Ret	Con	Sil	Slw	Drk	Trsfr	Stp
Bsk	Psn	Par	Stn	SS	Man	Dth	Imp

MORPH	STEAL	ATTACKS
n/a	n/a	Continu-claw, Frozen Sickle

GAGIGHANDI

Area—CC, CC Jungle

LVL	HP	MP	EXP	GIL	AP
19	480	55	173	220	18

Slp	Ret	Con	Sil	Slw	Drk	Trsfr	Stp
Bsk	Psn	Par	Stn	SS	Man	Dth	Imp

MORPH	STEAL	ATTACKS
Remedy	Soft	Claw, Stone Stare

GARGOYLE
Temporarily stone

Area—The Crater

LVL	HP	MP	EXP	GIL	AP
43	2000	200	800	2500	80

Slp	Ret	Con	Sil	Slw	Drk	Trsfr	Stp
Bsk	Psn	Par	Stn	SS	Man	Dth	Imp

MORPH	STEAL	ATTACKS
n/a	n/a	Petrify, Bite, L4 Death

GARUDA

Area—Da-chao Statue

LVL	HP	MP	EXP	GIL	AP
29	1400	200	520	520	30

Slp	Ret	Con	Sil	Slw	Drk	Trsfr	Stp
Bsk	Psn	Par	Stn	SS	Man	Dth	Imp

MORPH	STEAL	ATTACKS
n/a	n/a	Rod, Ice2, Bolt2

GAS DUCTER

Area—Coal Train

LVL	HP	MP	EXP	GIL	AP
42	3000	200	900	1200	80

Slp	Ret	Con	Sil	Slw	Drk	Trsfr	Stp
Bsk	Psn	Par	Stn	SS	Man	Dth	Imp

MORPH	STEAL	ATTACKS
n/a	n/a	Punch, Smog Alert

GHIROFELGO

Area—Shinra Mansion

LVL	HP	MP	EXP	GIL	AP
26	1600	0	380	300	44

Slp	Ret	Con	Sil	Slw	Drk	Trsfr	Stp
Bsk	Psn	Par	Stn	SS	Man	Dth	Imp

MORPH	STEAL	ATTACKS
n/a	n/a	Slash

GHOST
Temporarily becomes invisible after being hit

Area—Trainyard

LVL	HP	MP	EXP	GIL	AP
10	130	80	30	22	3

Slp	Ret	Con	Sil	Slw	Drk	Trsfr	Stp
Bsk	Psn	Par	Stn	SS	Man	Dth	Imp

MORPH	STEAL	ATTACKS
n/a	Ghost Hand	Slap, Drain

GHOST SHIP

Area—Water Tunnel

LVL	HP	MP	EXP	GIL	AP
44	6600	100	1600	2000	60

Slp	Ret	Con	Sil	Slw	Drk	Trsfr	Stp
Bsk	Psn	Par	Stn	SS	Man	Dth	Imp

MORPH	STEAL	ATTACKS
Guide Book	Phoenix Down	CentoElmos Fire, Slap, Goannai

GI NATTAK

Area—Cave of the GI/CC Caves

LVL	HP	MP	EXP	GIL	AP
29	5500	200	1400	3000	150

Slp	Ret	Con	Sil	Slw	Drk	Trsfr	Stp
Bsk	Psn	Par	Stn	SS	Man	Dth	Imp

MORPH	STEAL	ATTACKS
n/a	n/a	Take Over, Aspil, Hit

GI SPECTOR
Uses *Death Sentence* enemy skill.

Area—Cave of the GI

LVL	HP	MP	EXP	GIL	AP
23	450	88	260	150	20

Slp	Ret	Con	Sil	Slw	Drk	Trsfr	Stp
Bsk	Psn	Par	Stn	SS	Man	Dth	Imp

MORPH	STEAL	ATTACKS
n/a	n/a	Death Sentence

GI SPECTOR

Area—Cave of the Gi

LVL	HP	MP	EXP	GIL	AP
23	450	88	260	150	20

Slp	Ret	Con	Sil	Slw	Drk	Trsfr	Stp
Bsk	Psn	Par	Stn	SS	Man	Dth	Imp

MORPH	STEAL	ATTACKS
n/a	n/a	Skewer, Hell Spear, Death Sentence

GIGHEE

Area—The Crater

LVL	HP	MP	EXP	GIL	AP
34	5500	100	700	600	60

Slp	Ret	Con	Sil	Slw	Drk	Trsfr	Stp
Bsk	Psn	Par	Stn	SS	Man	Dth	Imp

MORPH	STEAL	ATTACKS
n/a	Elixir	Stardust March, Kick

LVL	The monster's level
HP	Monster's Hit Point level
MP	Monster's Magic Point level
EXP	Experience points gained
GIL	Number of Gil received for defeating monster
AP	Experience gained for Materia Orbs

Icon	Element	Icon	Element
🔥	Fire	G	Gravity
❄	Ice	≈	Water
⚡	Lightning	🌀	Wind
⛰	Earth	✝	Holy
☠	Poison		

	Normal
	Double Effect
	Invulnerable
	Absorbs
	Cuts damage in half

Slp	Sleep	Trsfr	Transform
Ret	Return	Stp	Stop
Con	Confusion	Bsk	Berserk
Sil	Silence	Psn	Poison
Slw	Slow	Par	Paralysis
Drk	Darkness	Stn	Stone
SS	Slowly stone		
Man	Manipulate		
Dth	Death		
Imp	Impossible to fight		
	No Effect		
	Effects Monster		

GOBLIN
Uses *Goblin Punch* enemy skill.

Area—NE Island

LVL	HP	MP	EXP	GIL	AP
40	2000	80	20	20	20

MORPH: n/a
STEAL: Zeio Nut
ATTACKS: Fight, Goblin Punch(18), Sleepel

GODO
Uses *Trine* enemy skill.

Area—Wutai Village

LVL	HP	MP	EXP	GIL	AP
36	6000	240	5000	40000	60

MORPH: n/a
STEAL: n/a
ATTACKS: Confu, Beast Sword, Drain, Bio2, Demi3

GOLEM
Area—Cosmo Canyon

LVL	HP	MP	EXP	GIL	AP
24	1000	0	300	500	22

MORPH: n/a
STEAL: Turbo Ether
ATTACKS: Finger Shot, Megaton Punch

GORKI
Area—Wutai Village

LVL	HP	MP	EXP	GIL	AP
30	3000	150	1500	0	50

MORPH: n/a
STEAL: n/a
ATTACKS: Barrie, Regen, Demi2, Kick

GRAND HORN
Area—CC/Gongaga

LVL	HP	MP	EXP	GIL	AP
19	460	43	180	240	15

MORPH: Hi-Potion
STEAL: n/a
ATTACKS: Punch, Grand Punch

GRANGALAN
Opens to release Grangalan Jr.

Area—Costa Del Sol

LVL	HP	MP	EXP	GIL	AP
16	550	60	88	220	10

MORPH: n/a
STEAL: n/a
ATTACKS: Silver Wheel

GRANGALAN JR.
Opens to release Grangalan Jr. Jr.

Area—Costa Del Sol

LVL	HP	MP	EXP	GIL	AP
15	330	40	77	110	8

MORPH: n/a
STEAL: n/a
ATTACKS: Silver Wheel

GRANGALAN JR. JR.
Area—Costa Del Sol

LVL	HP	MP	EXP	GIL	AP
14	110	20	66	55	6

MORPH: n/a
STEAL: n/a
ATTACKS: Silver Wheel

GRASHTRIKE
Area—Subway

LVL	HP	MP	EXP	GIL	AP
8	42	0	20	20	2

MORPH: n/a
STEAL: n/a
ATTACKS: Silk, Slash

GREMLIN
Area—Whirlwind Maze

LVL	HP	MP	EXP	GIL	AP
36	1500	100	750	750	60

MORPH: X-Potion
STEAL: Tent
ATTACKS: Claw, Bad Mouth

GRENADE
Uses Bomb Blast after getting hit twice.

Area—Whirlwind Maze

LVL	HP	MP	EXP	GIL	AP
32	2000	0	900	400	100

MORPH: n/a
STEAL: Right Arm
ATTACKS: Bomb Blast, Bodyblow

GRENADE COMBATANT
Area—Shinra Tower

LVL	HP	MP	EXP	GIL	AP
10	130	0	42	72	4

MORPH: n/a
STEAL: Tranquilizer
ATTACKS: Gun, Hand Grenade

GRIFFIN
Area—Cosmo Canyon

LVL	HP	MP	EXP	GIL	AP
21	760	40	260	350	25

MORPH: Phoenix Down
STEAL: Phoenix Down
ATTACKS: Peacock, Slash

GRIFFON
Area—GS Prison Desert

LVL	HP	MP	EXP	GIL	AP
18	800	200	148	210	14

MORPH: n/a
STEAL: n/a
ATTACKS: None

GRIMGUARD
Area—Corral Valley

LVL	HP	MP	EXP	GIL	AP
31	880	120	600	560	45

MORPH: n/a
STEAL: Shrivel
ATTACKS: Grim Rod, Spin Shield, Bolt2, Ice2

GROSSPANZER

Area—Midgar

LVL	HP	MP	EXP	GIL	AP
46	4600	200	800	2100	80

Slp	Ret	Con	Sil	Slw	Drk	Trsfr	Stp
Bsk	Psn	Par	Stn	SS	Man		Dth	Imp

MORPH n/a **STEAL** n/a **ATTACKS** Midgar, Missile, Machine Guns, Ram

GRUNT

Area—Reactor

LVL	HP	MP	EXP	GIL	AP
7	40	0	22	15	2

Slp	Ret	Con	Sil	Slw	Drk	Trsfr	Stp
Bsk	Psn	Par	Stn	SS	Man	Dth	Imp

MORPH n/a **STEAL** n/a **ATTACKS** Punch, Beam Gun

GUARD HOUND

Area—Streets

LVL	HP	MP	EXP	GIL	AP
3	42	0	20	12	2

Slp	Ret	Con	Sil	Slw	Drk	Trsfr	Stp
Bsk	Psn	Par	Stn	SS	Man	Dth	Imp

MORPH n/a **STEAL** n/a **ATTACKS** Bite

GUARD SCORPION

If you attack when his tail is raised, he will use Tail Laser

Area—Reactor

LVL	HP	MP	EXP	GIL	AP
12	800	0	100	100	10

Slp	Ret	Con	Sil	Slw	Drk	Trsfr	Stp
Bsk	Psn	Par	Stn	SS	Man	Dth	Imp

MORPH n/a **STEAL** n/a **ATTACKS** Search Scope, Scorpion Tail, Rifle Tail

GUARD SYSTEM

Area—Junon

LVL	HP	MP	EXP	GIL	AP
35	2200	200	1100	1200	80

Slp	Ret	Con	Sil	Slw	Drk	Trsfr	Stp
Bsk	Psn	Par	Stn	SS	Man	Dth	Imp

MORPH n/a **STEAL** n/a **ATTACKS** None

GUARDIAN

Area—Underwater Reactor

LVL	HP	MP	EXP	GIL	AP
40	4000	340	940	500	60

Slp	Ret	Con	Sil	Slw	Drk	Trsfr	Stp
Bsk	Psn	Par	Stn	SS	Man	Dth	Imp

MORPH n/a **STEAL** n/a **ATTACKS** Jumping Blow, Rocket Punch, W Rocket Punch

GUN CARRIER

Area—Underwater Reactor

LVL	HP	MP	EXP	GIL	AP
39	3400	240	860	1600	75

Slp	Ret	Con	Sil	Slw	Drk	Trsfr	Stp
Bsk	Psn	Par	Stn	SS	Man	Dth	Imp

MORPH n/a **STEAL** n/a **ATTACKS** Normal Shell, Bodyblow

HAMMER BLASTER

Area—Shinra Tower

LVL	HP	MP	EXP	GIL	AP
12	210	0	43	80	5

Slp	Ret	Con	Sil	Slw	Drk	Trsfr	Stp
Bsk	Psn	Par	Stn	SS	Man	Dth	Imp

MORPH n/a **STEAL** Echo Screen **ATTACKS** Pound

HARD ATTACKER

Area—Underwater Reactor

LVL	HP	MP	EXP	GIL	AP
32	2500	150	750	600	58

Slp	Ret	Con	Sil	Slw	Drk	Trsfr	Stp
Bsk	Psn	Par	Stn	SS	Man	Dth	Imp

MORPH n/a **STEAL** n/a **ATTACKS** Bodyblow, Oil

HEAD HUNTER

Area—Southern Islands

LVL	HP	MP	EXP	GIL	AP
30	2000	100	650	450	80

Slp	Ret	Con	Sil	Slw	Drk	Trsfr	Stp
Bsk	Psn	Par	Stn	SS	Man	Dth	Imp

MORPH n/a **STEAL** Tranquilizer **ATTACKS** Sickle, Rising Dagger

HEADBOMBER

Area—Gaea's Cliff

LVL	HP	MP	EXP	GIL	AP
35	1600	200	640	460	64

Slp	Ret	Con	Sil	Slw	Drk	Trsfr	Stp
Bsk	Psn	Par	Stn	SS	Man	Dth	Imp

MORPH Tranquilizer **STEAL** Tranquilizer **ATTACKS** Dorsal Punch, Extreme Bomber

HEAVY TANK

Area—Gongaga

LVL	HP	MP	EXP	GIL	AP
21	1600	25	340	1300	45

Slp	Ret	Con	Sil	Slw	Drk	Trsfr	Stp
Bsk	Psn	Par	Stn	SS	Man	Dth	Imp

MORPH Power Source **STEAL** Phoenix Down **ATTACKS** Charge, Wheelie Attack, Big Spiral

HEDGEHOG PIE

Area—Church

LVL	HP	MP	EXP	GIL	AP
6	40	52	6	40	52

Slp	Ret	Con	Sil	Slw	Drk	Trsfr	Stp
Bsk	Psn	Par	Stn	SS	Man	Dth	Imp

MORPH n/a **STEAL** n/a **ATTACKS** Fire, Charge

HEG

Area—Cave of the Gi/CC Caves

LVL	HP	MP	EXP	GIL	AP
22	400	0	250	240	20

Slp	Ret	Con	Sil	Slw	Drk	Trsfr	Stp
Bsk	Psn	Par	Stn	SS	Man	Dth	Imp

MORPH n/a **STEAL** n/a **ATTACKS** Poison Fang, Holt Whip

HELI GUNNER

Area—Shinra Tower

LVL	HP	MP	EXP	GIL	AP
19	1000	0	250	200	25

Slp	Ret	Con	Sil	Slw	Drk	Trsfr	Stp
Bsk	Psn	Par	Stn	SS	Man	Dth	Imp

MORPH AB Cannon **STEAL** Firing Line **ATTACKS** C Cannon, Flying Drill

BESTIARY LEGEND

LVL	The monster's level
HP	Monster's Hit Point level
MP	Monster's Magic Point level
EXP	Experience points gained
GIL	Number of Gil received for defeating monster
AP	Experience gained for Materia Orbs

Symbol	Element
Fire	Fire
Ice	Ice
Lightning	Lightning
Earth	Earth
Poison	Poison
G	Gravity
Water	Water
Wind	Wind
Holy	Holy

Box	Meaning
Normal	Normal
Double Effect	Double Effect
Invulnerable	Invulnerable
Absorbs	Absorbs
Cuts damage in half	Cuts damage in half

Slp	Sleep
Ret	Return
Con	Confusion
Sil	Silence
Slw	Slow
Drk	Darkness
Trsfr	Transform
Stp	Stop
Bsk	Berserk
Psn	Poison
Par	Paralysis
Stn	Stone
SS	Slowly stone
Man	Manipulate
Dth	Death
Imp	Impossible to fight
No Effect	No Effect
Effects Monster	Effects Monster

HELL HOUSE
Area—Slums

LVL	HP	MP	EXP	GIL	AP
11	450	0	44	250	6

MORPH	STEAL	ATTACKS
n/a	n/a	Hell Bomber, Demi, Suicide Drop, Hell

HELL RIDER VR2
Area—Condor Mts

LVL	HP	MP	EXP	GIL	AP
18	350	50	72	165	8

MORPH	STEAL	ATTACKS
Hi-Potion	Hi-Potion	Stomp, Electromag

HELLETIC HOJO
Area—Midgar

LVL	HP	MP	EXP	GIL	AP
55	26000	260	0	0	0

MORPH	STEAL	ATTACKS
n/a	n/a	None

HELLETIC HOJO LEFT ARM
Area—Midgar

LVL	HP	MP	EXP	GIL	AP
—	55	24000	400	0	

MORPH	STEAL
n/a	n/a

HELLETIC HOJO RIGHT ARM
Area—Midgar

LVL	HP	MP	EXP	GIL	AP
—	55	5000	300	0	

MORPH	STEAL
n/a	n/a

HIPPOGRIFF
Area—Southern Islands

LVL	HP	MP	EXP	GIL	AP
37	3000	280	800	1500	80

MORPH	STEAL	ATTACKS
n/a	n/a	L2 Confuse, Peck, Peacock

HOJO
Area—Midgar

LVL	HP	MP	EXP	GIL	AP
34	11000	120	2000	2200	150

MORPH	STEAL	ATTACKS
n/a	n/a	Capsule

HUNDRED GUNNER
Area—Shinra Tower

LVL	HP	MP	EXP	GIL	AP
18	1600	0	330	300	35

MORPH	STEAL	ATTACKS
Aux Artillery	Hidden Artillery	Main Artillery, Wave Artillery

HUNGRY
Area—Bone/Shell Village

LVL	HP	MP	EXP	GIL	AP
33	2000	100	700	600	60

MORPH	STEAL	ATTACKS
n/a	n/a	Mini, Hit

ICE GOLEM
Area—Great Glacier

LVL	HP	MP	EXP	GIL	AP
40	4000	30	1000	1500	70

MORPH	STEAL	ATTACKS
n/a	Hi-Potion	Cold Snap, Wide Grazer, Bodyblow

ICICLE
Area—Gaea's Cliff

LVL	HP	MP	EXP	GIL	AP
30	3000	300	500	0	0

MORPH	STEAL	ATTACKS
n/a	n/a	Icicle Drop

IRON MAN
Area—The Crater

LVL	HP	MP	EXP	GIL	AP
46	20000	100	10000	600	150

MORPH	STEAL	ATTACKS
n/a	Elixir	Sword Slash, Grand Sword, Adrenaline

IRONITE
Area—Whirlwind Maze

LVL	HP	MP	EXP	GIL	AP
30	2400	100	900	680	48

MORPH	STEAL	ATTACKS
n/a	Phoenix Down	Bodyblow, Fry Upper, Sleepel

JAYJUJAYME
Area—Da-chao Statue

LVL	HP	MP	EXP	GIL	AP
28	640	20	410	350	35

MORPH	STEAL	ATTACKS
n/a	n/a	Bite, Confu-scales, Silk, Thread

JEMNEZMY
Area—Temple of Ancients

LVL	HP	MP	EXP	GIL	AP
24	800	80	510	400	50

MORPH	STEAL	ATTACKS
n/a	n/a	Cold Breath, Fascination

JENOVA-BIRTH

Area—Shinra Boat

LVL	HP	MP	EXP	GIL	AP
25	4000	110	680	800	64

Slp	Ret	Con	Sil	Slw	Drk	Trsfr	Stp
Bsk	Psn	Par	Stn	SS	Man	Dth	Imp

MORPH n/a **STEAL** n/a **ATTACKS** Tail Laser, W-Laser, Gas

JENOVA-DEATH

Area—Whirlwind Maze

LVL	HP	MP	EXP	GIL	AP
55	25000	800	6000	5000	400

Slp	Ret	Con	Sil	Slw	Drk	Trsfr	Stp
Bsk	Psn	Par	Stn	SS	Man	Dth	Imp

MORPH n/a **STEAL** n/a **ATTACKS** Silence, Red Light, Tropic Wind

---

JENOVA LIFE

Uses Aqualung enemy skill.

Area—City of the Ancients

LVL	HP	MP	EXP	GIL	AP
50	10000	300	4000	1500	350

Slp	Ret	Con	Sil	Slw	Drk	Trsfr	Stp
Bsk	Psn	Par	Stn	SS	Man	Dth	Imp

MORPH n/a **STEAL** n/a **ATTACKS** Blue Flame, Aqualung, Blue Light

---

JERSEY

Uses *????* enemy skill.

Area—Shinra Mansion

LVL	HP	MP	EXP	GIL	AP
25	500	100	320	384	30

Slp	Ret	Con	Sil	Slw	Drk	Trsfr	Stp
Bsk	Psn	Par	Stn	SS	Man	Dth	Imp

MORPH n/a **STEAL** Turbo Ether **ATTACKS** Spin Attack

JOKER

Area—North Cont./Gold Saucer

LVL	HP	MP	EXP	GIL	AP
18	370	0	150	260	30

Slp	Ret	Con	Sil	Slw	Drk	Trsfr	Stp
Bsk	Psn	Par	Stn	SS	Man	Dth	Imp

MORPH n/a **STEAL** n/a **ATTACKS** Heart, Club, Joker, Diamond, Spade

---

JUMPING

Area—Bone Village

LVL	HP	MP	EXP	GIL	AP
24	999	0	400	50	30

Slp	Ret	Con	Sil	Slw	Drk	Trsfr	Stp
Bsk	Psn	Par	Stn	SS	Man	Dth	Imp

MORPH Antarctic Wind **STEAL** n/a **ATTACKS** Dive Kick, Club Sword

---

KALM FANG

Area—Midgar

LVL	HP	MP	EXP	GIL	AP
10	160	0	53	92	5

Slp	Ret	Con	Sil	Slw	Drk	Trsfr	Stp
Bsk	Psn	Par	Stn	SS	Man	Dth	Imp

MORPH Hi-Potion **STEAL** Ether **ATTACKS** Fang, Bodyblow

KELZMELZER

Area—Certa Shrine

LVL	HP	MP	EXP	GIL	AP
30	800	0	410	400	35

Slp	Ret	Con	Sil	Slw	Drk	Trsfr	Stp
Bsk	Psn	Par	Stn	SS	Man	Dth	Imp

MORPH Antidote **STEAL** Antidote **ATTACKS** Claw, Liquid Poison

---

KIMARA BUG

Area—Gongaga

LVL	HP	MP	EXP	GIL	AP
19	700	25	190	278	19

Slp	Ret	Con	Sil	Slw	Drk	Trsfr	Stp
Bsk	Psn	Par	Stn	SS	Man	Dth	Imp

MORPH Hourglass **STEAL** Spider Web **ATTACKS** Butterfly Attack, Stop Web, Spider Web

---

KING BEHEMOTH

Area—The Crater

LVL	HP	MP	EXP	GIL	AP
60	18000	560	2000	950	250

Slp	Ret	Con	Sil	Slw	Drk	Trsfr	Stp
Bsk	Psn	Par	Stn	SS	Man	Dth	Imp

MORPH n/a **STEAL** Phoenix Down **ATTACKS** King Tail, Bite

KYUVILDENS

Area—Nibel Mountains

LVL	HP	MP	EXP	GIL	AP
24	800	0	340	368	34

Slp	Ret	Con	Sil	Slw	Drk	Trsfr	Stp
Bsk	Psn	Par	Stn	SS	Man	Dth	Imp

MORPH Hi-Potion **STEAL** n/a **ATTACKS** Lay Flat

KYUVILDUNS

Area—Rocket Town

LVL	HP	MP	EXP	GIL	AP
24	800	0	340	368	34

Slp	Ret	Con	Sil	Slw	Drk	Trsfr	Stp
Bsk	Psn	Par	Stn	SS	Man	Dth	Imp

MORPH Hi-Potion **STEAL** n/a **ATTACKS** Lay Flat

LAND WORM

Area—GS Prison Desert

LVL	HP	MP	EXP	GIL	AP
22	1500	80	400	256	40

Slp	Ret	Con	Sil	Slw	Drk	Trsfr	Stp
Bsk	Psn	Par	Stn	SS	Man	Dth	Imp

MORPH n/a **STEAL** Turbo Ether **ATTACKS** Earthquake, Sandstorm

---

LESSALOPLOTH

Area—Great Glacier

LVL	HP	MP	EXP	GIL	AP
34	2000	400	920	800	65

Slp	Ret	Con	Sil	Slw	Drk	Trsfr	Stp
Bsk	Psn	Par	Stn	SS	Man	Dth	Imp

MORPH Phoenix Down **STEAL** Phoenix Down **ATTACKS** Wing Cut, Scorpion's Tail, Avalanche

---

LEVRIKON

Area—Chocobo Farm

LVL	HP	MP	EXP	GIL	AP
14	200	0	65	128	7

Slp	Ret	Con	Sil	Slw	Drk	Trsfr	Stp
Bsk	Psn	Par	Stn	SS	Man	Dth	Imp

MORPH Hi-Potion **STEAL** Ether **ATTACKS** Bird Kick, Flaming Peck

LVL	The monster's level	
HP	Monster's Hit Point level	
MP	Monster's Magic Point level	
EXP	Experience points gained	
GIL	Number of Gil received for defeating monster	
AP	Experience gained for Materia Orbs	

Fire · Ice · Lightning · Earth · Poison
G Gravity · Water · Wind · Holy

Normal · Double Effect · Invulnerable · Absorbs · Cuts damage in half

Slp Sleep · Ret Return · Con Confusion · Sil Silence · Slw Slow · Drk Darkness
Trsfr Transform · Stp Stop · Bsk Berserk · Psn Poison · Par Paralysis · Stn Stone
SS Slowly stone · Man Manipulate · Dth Death · Imp Impossible to fight
No Effect · Effects Monster

LIFEFORM HOJO

Area—Midgar

LVL	HP	MP	EXP	GIL	AP
58	30000	100	25000	6000	2500

MORPH	STEAL	ATTACKS
n/a	n/a	Combo, Tentacle

LOST NUMBER

Area—Shinra Mansion

LVL	HP	MP	EXP	GIL	AP
35	7000	300	2000	2000	80

MORPH	STEAL	ATTACKS
n/a	n/a	Bolt2, Fire2, Quake2

MADOUGE

Area—Mythril Caves

LVL	HP	MP	EXP	GIL	AP
16	220	0	70	150	8

MORPH	STEAL	ATTACKS
Hi-Potion	Grand Glove	Iron Ball, Swamp Shoot

MAGIC POT

Area—The Crater

LVL	HP	MP	EXP	GIL	AP
41	4096	128	8000	8500	1000

MORPH	STEAL	ATTACKS
n/a	n/a	Bad Mouth

MAGNADE

Physical attacks almost always miss

Area—Great Glacier

LVL	HP	MP	EXP	GIL	AP
35	1000	100	980	1200	50

MORPH	STEAL	ATTACKS
n/a	Phoenix Down	Shield Throw, W-Shield Throw

MALBORO

Uses *Bad Breath* enemy skill.

Area—Gaea's Cliff

LVL	HP	MP	EXP	GIL	AP
44	4400	900	1000	100	100

MORPH	STEAL	ATTACKS
n/a	M-Tentacles	Frozen Beam, Bad Breath, Bio2

MALLDANCER

Area—Bone/Shell Village

LVL	HP	MP	EXP	GIL	AP
32	600	100	500	700	56

MORPH	STEAL	ATTACKS
X-Potion	Phoenix Down	Claw, Dance

MANDRAGORA

Area—Chocobo Farm

LVL	HP	MP	EXP	GIL	AP
10	120	0	55	135	6

MORPH	STEAL	ATTACKS
Ether	Lasan Nut	Grass Punch, Slow Dance

MANHOLE

Area—Midgar

LVL	HP	MP	EXP	GIL	AP
35	2500	110	900	3000	80

MORPH	STEAL	ATTACKS
n/a	n/a	Throw

MARINE

Area—Shinra Boat

LVL	HP	MP	EXP	GIL	AP
16	300	20	75	150	8

MORPH	STEAL	ATTACKS
n/a	Shin-Ra Defense	Sleep, Gun, Grenade

MASTER TONBERRY

Area—The Crater

LVL	HP	MP	EXP	GIL	AP
45	8000	400	6000	6800	200

MORPH	STEAL	ATTACKS
n/a	Elixir	Everyone's Grudge

MATERIA KEEPER

Uses *Trine* enemy skill.

Area—Nibelheim Mts

LVL	HP	MP	EXP	GIL	AP
38	8400	300	3000	2400	200

MORPH	STEAL	ATTACKS
n/a	n/a	Big Horn, Hell Combo, Trine

MIDGAR ZOLOM

Only performs Beta when low on HP
Uses *Beta* enemy skill.

Area—CF Swamp

LVL	HP	MP	EXP	GIL	AP
26	4000	348	250	400	25

MORPH	STEAL	ATTACKS
X-Potion	n/a	Bite, Push, Beta

MIGHTY GRUNT

Area—Shinra Tower

LVL	HP	MP	EXP	GIL	AP
12	230	0	50	98	5

MORPH	STEAL	ATTACKS
n/a	Grenade	Gun, Double Gun, Rollerspin

MIRAGE

Area—Shinra Mansion

LVL	HP	MP	EXP	GIL	AP
24	570	0	290	280	22

MORPH	STEAL	ATTACKS
n/a	n/a	Slice

Bestiary

MONO DRIVE
Area—Reactor

LVL	HP	MP	EXP	GIL	AP
2	28	28	18	8	3

MORPH	STEAL	ATTACKS
n/a	n/a	Ram, Fire

MOTH SLASHER
Area—Shinra Tower

LVL	HP	MP	EXP	GIL	AP
13	260	0	46	75	5

MORPH	STEAL	ATTACKS
n/a	Carbon Bangle	Speed, Slash, Ram

MOTOR BALL
Area—Shinra Tower

LVL	HP	MP	EXP	GIL	AP
19	2600	120	440	350	45

MORPH	STEAL	ATTACKS
Arm Attack	Twin Burner	Rolling Fire

MU
Uses *Suicide* enemy skill.
Area—Chocobo Farm

LVL	HP	MP	EXP	GIL	AP
12	210	52	54	130	6

MORPH	STEAL	ATTACKS
n/a	n/a	Hot Springs, Sinking, L4 Suicide

MP
Area—Reactor

LVL	HP	MP	EXP	GIL	AP
2	30	0	16	10	2

MORPH	STEAL	ATTACKS
n/a	n/a	Machine Gun, Punch

NEEDLE KISS
Area—Mt. Corel

LVL	HP	MP	EXP	GIL	AP
17	180	40	75	130	8

MORPH	STEAL	ATTACKS
Remedy	Soft	Chute Attack, Thunder Kiss

NEROSUFEROTH
Area—Junon

LVL	HP	MP	EXP	GIL	AP
16	150	20	53	146	5

MORPH	STEAL	ATTACKS
n/a	n/a	Beak, Heatwing

NIBEL WOLF
Area—Nibel

LVL	HP	MP	EXP	GIL	AP
23	700	0	265	260	24

MORPH	STEAL	ATTACKS
Hi-Potion	Luchile Nut	Bodyblow, Fang

PALMER
Area—Rocket Town

LVL	HP	MP	EXP	GIL	AP
38	6000	240	1800	5000	98

MORPH	STEAL	ATTACKS
n/a	n/a	Mako Gun

PARASITE
Uses *Level 5 Death* enemy skill.
Area—The Crater

LVL	HP	MP	EXP	GIL	AP
51	6000	300	1100	1000	100

MORPH	STEAL	ATTACKS
Remedy	Remedy	Head Attack, L5 Death, Magical Breath, Para Tail

POLLENSALTA
Uses *Angel Whisper* enemy skill.
Area—The Crater

LVL	HP	MP	EXP	GIL	AP
41	4000	220	1000	1000	100

MORPH	STEAL	ATTACK
n/a	Hyper	Cold Breath, Fire3, Angel Whisper, Fascination

POODLER
Area—Downed Plane

LVL	HP	MP	EXP	GIL	AP
42	6000	220	1000	2500	70

MORPH	STEAL	ATTACKS
n/a	Turbo Ether	None

POODLER SAMPLE
Area—Midgar

LVL	HP	MP	EXP	GIL	AP
42	10000	200	2000	2000	150

MORPH	STEAL	ATTACKS
n/a	n/a	Bodyblow

PROUD CLOD
Area—Midgar

LVL	HP	MP	EXP	GIL	AP
53	60000	320	7000	10000	1000

MORPH	STEAL	ATTACKS
n/a	n/a	Wrist Laser, Machine Guns, Materia Jammer, Beam Cannon

PROTO MACHINEGUN
Area—Reactor2

LVL	HP	MP	EXP	GIL	AP
4	100	0	16	15	2

MORPH	STEAL	ATTACKS
n/a	n/a	Machine Gun

LVL	The monster's level	
HP	Monster's Hit Point level	
MP	Monster's Magic Point level	
EXP	Experience points gained	
GIL	Number of Gil received for defeating monster	
AP	Experience gained for Materia Orbs	

Fire · Ice · Lightning · Earth · Poison
Gravity · Water · Wind · Holy

Normal · Double Effect · Invulnerable · Absorbs · Cuts damage in half

Slp Sleep · Ret Return · Con Confusion · Sil Silence · Slw Slow · Drk Darkness
Trsfr Transform · Stp Stop · Bsk Berserk · Psn Poison · Par Paralysis · Stn Stone
SS Slowly stone · Man Manipulate · Dth Death · Imp Impossible to fight
No Effect · Effects Monster

PROWLER
Steals items; kills to retrieve.

Area—Midgar

LVL	HP	MP	EXP	GIL	AP
12	150	0	55	160	5

Slp	Ret	Con	Sil	Slw	Drk	Trsfr	Stp
Bsk	Psn	Par	Stn	SS	Man	Dth	Imp

MORPH	STEAL	ATTACKS
Hi-Potion	Ether	Hit, Grind

RAPPS

Area—Da-chao Mountains

LVL	HP	MP	EXP	GIL	AP
39	6000	300	3200	20000	33

MORPH	STEAL	ATTACKS
n/a	n/a	Aero3, Scorpion's Tail

RAZOR WEED
Uses *Magic Hammer* enemy skill.

Area—West Continent

LVL	HP	MP	EXP	GIL	AP
27	1000	145	375	350	30

MORPH	STEAL	ATTACKS
n/a	n/a	Glasscutter, Spaz Voice, Magic Hammer

RED DRAGON

Area—Temple of Ancients

LVL	HP	MP	EXP	GIL	AP
39	6800	300	3500	1000	200

MORPH	STEAL	ATTACKS
n/a	n/a	Red Dragon Breath, Tail, Bite

RENO

Area—Midgar

LVL	HP	MP	EXP	GIL	AP
50	25000	200	5500	5000	600

MORPH	STEAL	ATTACKS
n/a	Tough Ring	Turk Light, Electropod

RENO

Area—Gongaga

LVL	HP	MP	EXP	GIL	AP
22	2000	80	660	1500	60

MORPH	STEAL	ATTACKS
n/a	n/a	Slap, Turk Light, Electropod

RILFSAK

Area—Frog Forest

LVL	HP	MP	EXP	GIL	AP
40	2000	500	750	1000	70

MORPH	STEAL	ATTACKS
n/a	n/a	Blood Suck, Autumn Leaves

ROCKET LAUNCHER

Area—Subway

LVL	HP	MP	EXP	GIL	AP
5	50	0	13	7	3

MORPH	STEAL	ATTACKS
n/a	n/a	Rocket Launcher

ROCKET LAUNCHER

Area—Junon

LVL	HP	MP	EXP	GIL	AP
20	1000	0	600	300	60

MORPH	STEAL	ATTACK
n/a	n/a	Missile

ROULETTE CANNON

Area—Junon

LVL	HP	MP	EXP	GIL	AP
38	3000	200	1200	1600	100

MORPH	STEAL	ATTACKS
n/a	n/a	Missile

RUDE

Area—Midgar

LVL	HP	MP	EXP	GIL	AP
51	28000	250	5500	5000	600

MORPH	STEAL	ATTACKS
n/a	Ziedrich	Punch, Grand Spark

RUDE

Area—Rocket Town

LVL	HP	MP	EXP	GIL	AP
42	9000	240	3400	3000	80

MORPH	STEAL	ATTACKS
n/a	Ziedrich	Punch, Grand Spark, Mbarrier

RUDE

Area—Gongaga

LVL	HP	MP	EXP	GIL	AP
23	2000	135	720	2000	70

MORPH	STEAL	ATTACKS
n/a	n/a	Punch, Fire, Cure

RUFUS

Area—Shinra Tower

LVL	HP	MP	EXP	GIL	AP
21	500	0	240	400	35

MORPH	STEAL	ATTACKS
Shotgun	n/a	n/a

SAHAGIN
Shell can protect from physical attacks

Area—Sewers

LVL	HP	MP	EXP	GIL	AP
10	150	0	30	89	3

MORPH	STEAL	ATTACKS
n/a	Hyper	Water Gun, Trident

SCHIZO (LEFT)
Area—Gaea's Cliff

LVL	HP	MP	EXP	GIL	AP
43	18000	350	2200	1500	120

MORPH	STEAL	ATTACKS
n/a	n/a	Frozen Breath, Earthquake

SCHIZO (RIGHT)
Area—Gaea's Cliff

LVL	HP	MP	EXP	GIL	AP
43	18000	350	2200	1500	120

MORPH	STEAL	ATTACKS
n/a	n/a	Flame Breath, Earthquake

SCISSORS
Area—The Crater

LVL	HP	MP	EXP	GIL	AP
33	2900	88	1000	1400	90

MORPH	STEAL	ATTACKS
n/a	Ether	Cross Scissors, Scissor Kick, Scissor Attack

SCOTCH
Area—Brothel

LVL	HP	MP	EXP	GIL	AP
11	150	0	22	60	0

MORPH	STEAL	ATTACKS
n/a	n/a	Machine Gun

SCREAMER
Area—Nibel Mountains

LVL	HP	MP	EXP	GIL	AP
26	800	40	400	400	33

MORPH	STEAL	ATTACKS
Power Source	n/a	Ironball, Iron Attack, War Cry

SCRUTIN EYE
Area—Shinra Boat

LVL	HP	MP	EXP	GIL	AP
15	240	60	80	120	8

MORPH	STEAL	ATTACKS
n/a	Ether	Fire2, Ice2, Ram

SEA WORM
Area—Southern Islands

LVL	HP	MP	EXP	GIL	AP
22	9000	200	1300	300	200

MORPH	STEAL	ATTACKS
Dragon Scales	Dragon Scales	Sandstorm, Crush, Earthquake

SEARCH CROWN
Area—Mt. Corel

LVL	HP	MP	EXP	GIL	AP
16	150	30	0	111	8

MORPH	STEAL	ATTACKS
Hi-Potion	Turbo Ether	Seed Shooting, Four Laser

SENIOR GRUNT
Area—Underwater Reactor

LVL	HP	MP	EXP	GIL	AP
35	2600	245	930	800	90

MORPH	STEAL	ATTACKS
n/a	n/a	Handclaw, Harrier Beam, Water Wave

SERPENT
Area—Downed Plane

LVL	HP	MP	EXP	GIL	AP
40	14000	290	1400	2500	70

MORPH	STEAL	ATTACKS
n/a	Water Ring	Viper Breath, Aqualung

SHADOW MAKER
Area—Midgar

LVL	HP	MP	EXP	GIL	AP
42	2000	120	500	500	25

MORPH	STEAL	ATTACKS
n/a	Graviball	Slow

SHAKE
Area—Wutai Village

LVL	HP	MP	EXP	GIL	AP
32	4000	180	2200	0	50

MORPH	STEAL	ATTACKS
n/a	n/a	Beak, Rage Bomber

SHRED
Area—Great Glacier

LVL	HP	MP	EXP	GIL	AP
32	900	100	500	950	40

MORPH	STEAL	ATTACKS
n/a	n/a	Tail, Crazy Claw, Cure3

SKEESKEE
Area—Cosmo Canyon

LVL	HP	MP	EXP	GIL	AP
20	540	0	222	222	22

MORPH	STEAL	ATTACKS
Hyper	Tranquilizer	Beak, Rage Bomber

SLALOM
Area—Junon

LVL	HP	MP	EXP	GIL	AP
37	1600	30	700	1500	70

MORPH	STEAL	ATTACKS
Hi-Potion	Smoke Bomb	Punch, Smog

Legend

LVL	The monster's level
HP	Monster's Hit Point level
MP	Monster's Magic Point level
EXP	Experience points gained
GIL	Number of Gil received for defeating monster
AP	Experience gained for Materia Orbs

Elements: Fire, Ice, Lightning, Earth, Poison, Gravity, Water, Wind, Holy

Effect key: Normal, Double Effect, Invulnerable, Absorbs, Cuts damage in half

Status: Slp Sleep, Ret Return, Con Confusion, Sil Silence, Slw Slow, Drk Darkness, Trsfr Transform, Stp Stop, Bsk Berserk, Psn Poison, Par Paralysis, Stn Stone, SS Slowly stone, Man Manipulate, Dth Death, Imp Impossible to fight — No Effect / Effects Monster

---

SLAPS

Area—Certa Shrine

LVL	HP	MP	EXP	GIL	AP
29	900	50	370	450	30

MORPH: Hyper
STEAL: n/a
ATTACKS: Bug Needle, Berserk Needle, Paralyzer Needle

SMOGGER

Area—Reactor2

LVL	HP	MP	EXP	GIL	AP
8	90	0	32	60	3

MORPH: n/a
STEAL: n/a
ATTACKS: Smog, Hit, Poison

SNEAKY STEP

Uses *Death Sentence* enemy skill.

Area—Cave of the GI/CC Caves

LVL	HP	MP	EXP	GIL	AP
21	600	65	270	330	24

MORPH: n/a
STEAL: n/a
ATTACKS: Triple Attack

SNOW

Area—Great Glacier

LVL	HP	MP	EXP	GIL	AP
32	4000	160	500	700	42

MORPH: n/a
STEAL: Circlet
ATTACKS: Cold Breath, Fascination, Ice2

SOLDIER: 1ST

Area—Midgar

LVL	HP	MP	EXP	GIL	AP
44	5000	400	960	2400	90

MORPH: n/a
STEAL: Shinra Alpha
ATTACKS: Sword of Doom, Slash

SOLDIER: 2ND

Area—Junon

LVL	HP	MP	EXP	GIL	AP
5	4000	340	1000	750	85

MORPH: n/a
STEAL: Remedy
ATTACKS: Fight, Sword of Doom

SOLDIER: 3RD

Area—Shinra Tower

LVL	HP	MP	EXP	GIL	AP
13	250	40	54	116	6

MORPH: n/a
STEAL: Hardedge
ATTACKS: Slash, Flying Sickle, Ice2

SONIC SPEED

Area—Nibel Mountains

LVL	HP	MP	EXP	GIL	AP
26	750	50	370	330	28

MORPH: Speed Drink
STEAL: Ether
ATTACKS: Harrier, Swoop

SOUL FIRE

Area—Cave of the GI/CC Caves

LVL	HP	MP	EXP	GIL	AP
21	1300	220	200	100	10

MORPH: n/a
STEAL: n/a
ATTACKS: Fire2

SPECIAL COMBATANT

Area—Reactor2

LVL	HP	MP	EXP	GIL	AP
9	60	0	28	40	3

MORPH: n/a
STEAL: n/a
ATTACKS: Hit, Wave, Beam Gun

SPENCER

Area—North Cont./Gold Saucer

LVL	HP	MP	EXP	GIL	AP
17	250	0	110	175	11

MORPH: n/a
STEAL: Saraha Nut
ATTACKS: Swordblade, Uppercutter

SPIRAL

Area—Southern Islands

LVL	HP	MP	EXP	GIL	AP
39	2800	100	700	200	80

MORPH: Guard Source
STEAL: X-Potion
ATTACKS: Spin, Charge

STANIV

Area—Wutai Village

LVL	HP	MP	EXP	GIL	AP
36	6000	240	3600	0	50

MORPH: n/a
STEAL: n/a
ATTACKS: Chain, War Cry

STILVA

Uses *Magic Breath* and *Trine* enemy skill.

Area—Gaea's Cliff

LVL	HP	MP	EXP	GIL	AP
40	2000	300	1000	1100	110

MORPH: n/a
STEAL: n/a
ATTACKS: Big Red Clipper, Trine, Magic Breath

STINGER

Area—Cave of the GI

LVL	HP	MP	EXP	GIL	AP
25	2200	60	290	358	25

MORPH: n/a
STEAL: Ether
ATTACKS: Hit, Sting Bomb

STINGER
Area—Cave of the Gi

LVL	HP	MP	EXP	GIL	AP
25	2200	60	290	358	25

Status immunities: Par, Man

MORPH	STEAL	ATTACKS
n/a	Ether	Hit, Sting Bomb

SUBMARINE CREW
Area—Junon

LVL	HP	MP	EXP	GIL	AP
32	1500	85	850	500	80

MORPH	STEAL	ATTACKS
n/a	8-inch Cannon	Machine Gun, Hand Grenade

SWEEPER
Area—Reactor

LVL	HP	MP	EXP	GIL	AP
8	140	0	27	30	3

MORPH	STEAL	ATTACKS
n/a	n/a	none

SWORD DANCE
Area—Shinra Tower

LVL	HP	MP	EXP	GIL	AP
11	160	0	39	90	6

Status immunities: Par

MORPH	STEAL	ATTACKS
n/a	Hyper	Slap, Sawback, Thrash

TAIL VAULT
Area—West Continent

LVL	HP	MP	EXP	GIL	AP
28	960	0	440	380	36

MORPH	STEAL	ATTACKS
n/a	n/a	Bite, Somersault

THUNDERBIRD
Area—West Continent

LVL	HP	MP	EXP	GIL	AP
28	800	80	385	420	36

Status immunities: Ret, Par

MORPH	STEAL	ATTACKS
Swift Bolt	Bolt Plume	Stab, Lightning

TONADU
Area—Setora Shrine

LVL	HP	MP	EXP	GIL	AP
30	1600	0	600	600	45

Status immunities: Ret, Par

MORPH	STEAL	ATTACKS
n/a	Bird Wing	Claw, Great Gale, Big Sound

TOUCH ME
Uses *Frog Song* enemy skill.
Area—CC Jungle

LVL	HP	MP	EXP	GIL	AP
18	300	74	170	180	23

Status immunities: Ret, Trsfr

MORPH	STEAL	ATTACKS
Remedy	Impaler	Frog Jab, Frog Song

TOXIC FROG
Uses Frog Song enemy skill.
Area—Temple of Ancients

LVL	HP	MP	EXP	GIL	AP
26	500	100	420	260	30

Status immunities: Ret, Trsfr

MORPH	STEAL	ATTACKS
Remedy	Impaler	Frog Jab, Frog Song, Poison

TRICKPLAY
Area—Icicle Area

LVL	HP	MP	EXP	GIL	AP
24	1500	100	480	800	35

Status immunities: Ret, Con, Trsfr

MORPH	STEAL	ATTACKS
n/a	n/a	Magma, Sewer, Gold Mountain, Sinking, L4 Suicide

TWIN BRAIN
Area—Nibel Mountains

LVL	HP	MP	EXP	GIL	AP
25	400	20	340	320	32

MORPH	STEAL	ATTACKS
Turbo Ether	Ether	Absorb, Stare Down

UNDERWATER MP
Area—Underwater Reactor

LVL	HP	MP	EXP	GIL	AP
34	1000	100	820	600	80

MORPH	STEAL	ATTACKS
n/a	Shinra Alpha	Machine Gun, Hand Grenade

UNKNOWN
Area—Downed Plane

LVL	HP	MP	EXP	GIL	AP
50	11000	110	1500	5000	150

MORPH	STEAL	ATTACKS
n/a	Fire Armlet	Tail, Tongue

UNKNOWN 2
Area—Downed Plane

LVL	HP	MP	EXP	GIL	AP
51	13000	130	3000	10000	300

MORPH	STEAL	ATTACKS
n/a	Aurora Armlet	Abnormal Breath, Tentacle, Needle

UNKNOWN 3
Area—Downed Plane

LVL	HP	MP	EXP	GIL	AP
52	15000	150	2000	7500	200

MORPH	STEAL	ATTACKS
n/a	Bolt Armlet	Poison Fang, Creepy Touch

BESTIARY LEGEND

LVL	The monster's level
HP	Monster's Hit Point level
MP	Monster's Magic Point level
EXP	Experience points gained
GIL	Number of Gil received for defeating monster
AP	Experience gained for Materia Orbs

🔥	Fire
❄	Ice
⚡	Lightning
⛰	Earth
✖	Poison
G	Gravity
≈	Water
🌀	Wind
✝	Holy

	Normal
	Double Effect
	Invulnerable
	Absorbs
	Cuts damage in half

Slp	Sleep	Trsfr	Transform
Ret	Return	Stp	Stop
Con	Confusion	Bsk	Berserk
Sil	Silence	Psn	Poison
Slw	Slow	Par	Paralysis
Drk	Darkness	Stn	Stone

SS	Slowly stone
Man	Manipulate
Dth	Death
Imp	Impossible to fight
	No Effect
	Effects Monster

VALRON

Area—Nibel

LVL	HP	MP	EXP	GIL	AP
24	950	80	300	300	30

Slp	Ret	Con	Sil	Slw	Drk	Trsfr	Stp
Bsk	Psn	Par	Stn	SS	Man	Dth	Imp

MORPH: Hi-Potion
STEAL: n/a
ATTACKS: Speed Punch, Jump Kick, Dive Kick, Mbarrier

VARGID POLICE

Area—Shinra Tower

LVL	HP	MP	EXP	GIL	AP
9	140	28	44	40	7

Slp	Ret	Con	Sil	Slw	Drk	Trsfr	Stp
Bsk	Psn	Par	Stn	SS	Man	Dth	Imp

MORPH: n/a
STEAL: Tranquilizer
ATTACKS: Needle, Suicide

VELCHER TASK

Area—Rocket Town

LVL	HP	MP	EXP	GIL	AP
26	900	28	320	350	31

Slp	Ret	Con	Sil	Slw	Drk	Trsfr	Stp
Bsk	Psn	Par	Stn	SS	Man	Dth	Imp

MORPH: Remedy
STEAL: Remedy
ATTACKS: Claw, Poison Blow

VICE

Area—Slums

LVL	HP	MP	EXP	GIL	AP
7	68	0	24	80	3

Slp	Ret	Con	Sil	Slw	Drk	Trsfr	Stp
Bsk	Psn	Par	Stn	SS	Man	Dth	Imp

MORPH: Potion
STEAL: Speed Drink
ATTACKS: Hit

VLAKORADOS

Area—Sensei's House

LVL	HP	MP	EXP	GIL	AP
33	33,333	333	510	460	40

Slp	Ret	Con	Sil	Slw	Drk	Trsfr	Stp
Bsk	Psn	Par	Stn	SS	Man	Dth	Imp

MORPH: Elixir
STEAL: Carob Nut
ATTACKS: Tail, Violent Advance, Bolt Ball

WARNING BOARD

Area—Shinra Tower

LVL	HP	MP	EXP	GIL	AP
12	270	0	38	75	4

Slp	Ret	Con	Sil	Slw	Drk	Trsfr	Stp
Bsk	Psn	Par	Stn	SS	Man	Dth	Imp

MORPH: n/a
STEAL: n/a
ATTACKS: n/a

WHOLE EATER

Area—Slums

LVL	HP	MP	EXP	GIL	AP
9	72	0	24	70	2

Slp	Ret	Con	Sil	Slw	Drk	Trsfr	Stp
Bsk	Psn	Par	Stn	SS	Man	Dth	Imp

MORPH: Potion
STEAL: Potion
ATTACKS: Sickle

WIND WING

Uses *White Wind* enemy skill.

Area—Whirlwind Maze

LVL	HP	MP	EXP	GIL	AP
36	1900	350	800	500	60

Slp	Ret	Con	Sil	Slw	Drk	Trsfr	Stp
Bsk	Psn	Par	Stn	SS	Man	Dth	Imp

MORPH: Phoenix Down
STEAL: Hi-Potion
ATTACKS: Tailbeat, Sham Seal, Aero3, White Wind

WOLFMEISTER

Area—Coal Train

LVL	HP	MP	EXP	GIL	AP
43	10000	200	10000	600	100

Morph	Steal	Attacks
n/a	n/a	Heavy Sword, Big Guard

YING / YANG

Area—Mansion Basement

LVL	HP	MP	EXP	GIL	AP
24	1200	220	350	400	35

Morph	Steal	Attacks
n/a	n/a	Bolt2, Ice2

ZENENE

Area—Shinra Tower

LVL	HP	MP	EXP	GIL	AP
14	250	93	58	60	6

Morph	Steal	Attacks
n/a	Deadly Waste	Ghengana, Tail, Piazzo Shower

ZEMZELETT

Uses *White Wind* enemy skill.

Area—Condor Mts

LVL	HP	MP	EXP	GIL	AP
17	285	36	70	165	7

Morph	Steal	Attacks
Hi-Potion	n/a	Thunderbolt, White Wind

ZOLKALTER

Area—Gaea's Cliff

LVL	HP	MP	EXP	GIL	AP
30	950	90	700	700	60

Morph	Steal	Attacks
Antidote	n/a	Bite, Toxic Barf

ZUU

Area—Nibel Mountains

LVL	HP	MP	EXP	GIL	AP
27	1200	40	450	430	38

Morph	Steal	Attacks
Bird Wing	Bird Wing	Great Gale, Slash

Status abbreviations (per card): Slp, Ret, Con, Sil, Slw, Drk, Trsfr, Stp / Bsk, Psn, Par, Stn, SS, Man, Dth, Imp

WEAPONS

LEGEND

ABBREV.	WHAT IT MEANS
Name	Name of Weapon
Cost	How much Weapon costs
Atk	Attack power
A%	Attack percentage
Un	Unlinked Materia holes
Ln	Linked Materia holes
Mg	Growth
Location	Where you find it
Notes	Unique info concerning Weapon

CLOUD

Name	Cost	Atk	A%	Un	Ln	MG	Location
Buster Sword		18	96		2	1	Initially Equipped
Hardedge	1500	32	98	2	2	1	Stolen from SOLDIER: 3rd in Shinra Tower
Mythril Saber	1000	23	98	1	2	1	Shop in Kalm Town
Force Stealer	2200	36	100	3		2	150+ Performing in Junon, shop in North Corel
Butterfly Edge	2800	39	100		4	1	Shop in Cosmo Canyon
Rune Blade	3800	40	108	4		2	Nibelheim Mountains
Yoshiyuki		56	100	2		1	Man outside of Item Shop in Rocket Town
							NOTE—Sword is used when an ally is down
Murasame	6500	51	100	1	4	1	Shop in Wutai
Nail Bat	2800	70	100			0	Temple of the Ancients (underneath clock)
Organics	12000	62	103	2	4	1	Shop in Icicle Inn
Enhance Sword	12000	43	107		8	1	Gaea's Cliff
Crystal Sword	18000	76	105		6	1	Shop in Mideel
Heaven's Cloud		93	100	6		1	Downed Shinra Plane
Apocalypse		88	110	3		3	Ancient Forest
Ragnarok		97	105		6	1	After defeating Proud Clod in Midgar
Ultima Weapon		100	110		8	0	After defeating Ultimate WEAPON

AERIS

Name	Cost	Atk	A%	Un	Ln	MG	Location
Guard Stick		12	99	1		1	Initially Equipped
Striking Staff	1300	32	100	2	2	1	Stolen from Eligor in Trainyard
Mythril Rod	370	16	100		2	1	Shop in Wall Market
Full Metal Staff	800	22	100	1	2	1	Shop in Kalm Town
Wizard Staff		28	100	3		2	After falling (left) from Mt. Corel Railroad Tracks
Fairy Tale	2500	37	103	7		1	After defeating Turks outside of Gongaga Village
Prism Staff	2600	40	105		4	1	Shop in Cosmo Canyon
Wiser Staff		33	100	4		2	After defeating Gi Nattak in Cave of the Gi
Aurora Rod	5800	51	110	1	4	1	Shop in Wutai
Princess Guard		52	111	1	6	1	Temple of the Ancients (Door 4)
							NOTE—Raises power and protects others nearby
Parasol		58	118				Speed Square in Gold Saucer

TIFA

Name	Cost	Atk	A%	Un	Ln	MG	Location
Leather Glove		13	99	1		1	Initially Equipped
Metal Knuckle	320	18	102		2	1	Shop in Wall Market
Mythril Claw	750	24	106	1	2	1	Shop in Kalm Town
Grand Glove	1200	31	110	2	2	1	Steal from Madouge in Mythril Cave
Motor Drive		27	106	3		2	Costa Del Sol
Tiger Fang	2500	38	110		4	1	Shop in Cosmo Canyon
Platinum Fist	2700	30	108	4		2	Tifa's House in Nibel
Powersoul	4200	28	106	4		2	Nibelheim Mountians
Diamond Knuckle	5800	51	112	1	4	1	Shop in Wutai
Work Glove	2200	68	114			0	Temple of the Ancients (Door 6)
Dragon Claw	10000	62	114	2	4	1	Shop in Icicle Inn
Kaiser Knuckle	15000	44	110	6	2	1	Whirlwind Maze
Crystal Glove	16000	75	115		6	1	Shop in Mideel
God's Hand		86	255		4	1	After defeating Carry Armor in Submarine Bay
Premium Heart		99	112		8		Abandoned Item Shop in Wall Market

BARRET

Name	Cost	Atk	A%	Un	Ln	MG	Location
Gattling Gun		14	97	1		1	Initially Equipped Note—Long Range
Assault Gun	350	17	98		2	1	After defeating Guard Scorpion in Shinra Reactor Note—Long Range
Atomic Scissors	1400	32	99	2	2	1	Steal from Custom Sweeper outside of Midgar
Cannon Ball	950	23	98	1	2	1	Shop in Kalm Town
W Machine Gun	18000	30	100	3		2	Mt. Corel Railroad Tracks Note—Long Range
Heavy Vulcan	2700	39	100		4	1	Shop in Cosmo Canyon Note—Long Range
Enemy Launcher	3200	35	100	3	2	1	Treasure chest in Nibelheim Mansion Note—Long Range
Drill Arm	2000	37	97	4		2	Cid's House
Chainsaw	6300	52	100	1	4	1	Shop in Wutai
Rocket Punch		62	110			0	Temple of the Ancients
Microlaser	12000	63	101	2	4	1	Shop in Icicle Inn Note—Long Range
AM Cannon	12000	77	103		6	1	Shop in Mideel Note—Long Range
Solid Bazooka	3300	61	100		8		Costa Del Sol
Max Ray		97	98		6		Sector 8 Note—Long Range
Missing Score		98	108		8		Before fighting Hojo on Mako Cannon Note—Long Range

YUFFIE

Name	Cost	Atk	A%	Un	Ln	MG	Location
4-Point Shuriken		23	100	2	1	1	Initially Equipped
Boomerang	1400	30	101	2	2	1	Steal from Formula near Junon Note—Long Range
Wind Slash		30	103	3		1	Shinra Boat Cargo Hold
Pinwheel	2600	37	104		4	1	Shop in Cosmo Canyon
Twin Viper		36	108	4		2	Nibelheim Mansion Note—Long Range
Razor Ring	6000	49	105	4	1	1	Shop in Wutai
Hawkeye	12000	61	107	4	2	1	Shop in Icicle Inn
Crystal Cross	18000	74	110		6	1	Shop in Mideel
Conformer		96	112		8	0	Downed Shinra Plane
Oritsuru		90	116	4	4	1	Da-chao Mountains
Magic Shuriken	14000	68	110	2	6	1	Costa del Sol
Super Ball	3000	68	120				Fort Condor (Battle #4)

RED XIII

Name	Cost	Atk	A%	Un	Ln	MG	Location
Mythril Clip	800	24	100	1	2	1	Initially Equipped
Magic Comb	3500	37	100	3		2	First victory at Fort Condor
Diamond Pin	1300	33	102	2	2	1	Steal from Bagnadrana on Train tracks
Silver Barrette	2500	40	110		4	1	Shop in Cosmo Canyon
Seraph Comb		68	110	4		1	After Cosmo Canyon Caves Note—Memento of father
Plus Barrette	6000	39	104	4		2	Nibelheim Mountains
Hairpin	6000	57	120			0	Hidden Passage in Wutai House
Gold Barrette	6000	50	104	1	4	1	Shop in Wutai
Adaman Clip	11000	60	106	2	4	1	Shop in Icicle Inn Note—Long Range
Crystal Comb	17000	76	108		6	1	Shop in Mideel
Spring Gun Clip		87	100		6	1	Frog Forest
Centclip		58	108	8			Costa Del Sol
Limited Moon		93	114		8		Bugenhagen's dying gift

VINCENT

Name	Cost	Atk	A%	Un	Ln	MG	Location
Quicksilver	1000	38	110	2	2	1	Initially Equipped
Peacemaker		38	118	1	2		Kalm Town
Sniper CR	3000	42	255		4	1	Nibelheim Mountains
Shotgun	3100	48	112		4	1	Shop in Rocket Town
Shortbarrel	6400	51	118	1	4	1	Shop in Wutai
Silver Rifle	3000	62	120			0	Temple of the Ancients
Lariat	12000	64	120	2	4	1	Shop in Icicle Inn
Winchester	18000	73	120		6	1	Shop in Mideel
Outsider		80	120	4	4	1	Downed Shinra Plane
Supershot ST		97	120		6	0	Ancient Forest
Buntline		48	124		4		Bone Village
Long Barrel R		66	255		8		Costa Del Sol
Death Penalty		99	115		8		Waterfall Cave

NOTE—All of Vincent's weapons are Long Range

CAIT SITH

Name	Cost	Atk	A%	Un	Ln	MG	Location
Yellow M-Phone	500	36	100	2	2	1	Initially Equipped
White M-Phone	2300	35	102	3		2	House in Gongaga Village
Green M-Phone	2400	41	100		4	1	Shop in Cosmo Canyon
Black M-Phone	2800	31	104	4		2	Cave of the Gi
Silver M-Phone	3300	28	106	8		1	Nibelheim Mansion
Blue M-Phone	5500	48	100	1	4	1	Shop in Wutai
Trumpet Shell	3000	68	118			0	Temple of the Ancients (Door 7)
Red M-Phone	11000	60	100	2	4	1	Shop in Icicle Inn
Crystal M-Phone	18000	74	100		6	1	Shop in Mideel
Gold M-Phone		58	103		8		Costa Del Sol
Battle Trumpet		95	95		6	1	Underwater Reactor
Starlight Phone		88	102		8		Sector 8
Marvelous Cheer		95	110		8		Shinra Corporate Tower (Gym)

CID

Name	Cost	Atk	A%	Un	Ln	MG	Location
Spear	1200	44	97		4	1	Initially Equipped
Slash Lance	6500	56	98	1	4	1	Wutai
Trident	7500	60	105	6		1	Temple of the Ancients
Viper Halberd		58	102	4		2	Coral Valley
Mast Ax	13000	64	99	2	4	1	Shop in Icicle Inn
Javelin		62	104	1	4	2	Inside of Gaea's Cliff
Partisan	19000	78	100		6	1	Shop in Mideel
Scimitar		86	102		2	3	Underwater Reactor
Dragoon Lance		66	100	8		1	Wutai Mountains
Mop		68	118				Temple of the Ancients
Venus Gospel		97	103		8		Rocket Town

Armor

Name	Cost	D	D%	MD	M%	Un	Ln	Mg	Location
Bronze Bangle		8	0	0	0	0	0	0	Initially Equipped
Iron Bangle	160	10	0	2	0	1		1	Beginner's Shop
Titan Bangle	280	14	2	4	0	2		1	After defeating Airbuster in Shinra Reactor
Mythril Armlet	350	18	3	6	0		2	1	Shop in Wall Market
Carbon Bangle	800	27	3	8	0	1	2	1	Stolen from Moth Slasher in Shinra
Four Slots	1300	12	0	10	0	8		1	Exchange for Item Coupon A in Shinra Tower
Shinra Beta		30	0	0	0		2	2	1	Stolen from Marine on Shinra Boat
Platinum Bangle	1800	20	0	12	0	2		1	Shop in Costa Del Sol Bar
Silver Armlet	1300	34	4	14	0	2	2	1	After defeating Dyne in Gold Saucer
Gold Armlet	2000	46	4	22	0	0	4	1	Steal from Dragon in Nibel Mountains
Edincoat		50	0	33	0	8		1	After defeating Palmer in Rocket Town
Diamond Bangle	3200	57	6	37	0	1	4	1	Shop in Bone Village
Rune Armlet	3700	43	5	24	0	4		2	Shop in Bone Village
Dragon Armlet		58	3	0	7		6	1	After defeating Red Dragon in Temple of the Ancients
Gigas Armlet		59	0	0	0	1		0	After defeating Demons Gate in Temple of the Ancients
Aurora Armlet		76	8	54	3		4	1	Forgotten City Shrine
Wizard Bracelet	12000	6	3	85	3		8	1	After defeating Jenova Life in Forgotten City
Bolt Armlet		74	8	55	3		4	1	Corral Valley Caves NOTE—Nullifies Lightning Attacks
Fire Armlet		72	8	52	3		4	1	Inside of Gaea's Cliff NOTE—Nullifies Fire Attacks
Crystal Bangle	4800	70	8	45	1		6	1	Shop in Mideel
Warriors Bangle		96	0	21	0		4	1	Defeating Eagle Gun on Coal Train
Shinra Alpha		77	0	34	0		6	1	Steal from Underwater MP in Underwater Reactor
Ziedrich		100	15	98	18	0	0	0	Steal from Rude on Shinra No. 26 NOTE—Decreases all elemental attacks by 1/2
Escort Guard		62	5	55	0	0	6	1	Sunken Shinra Air Ship NOTE—Man's Armlet nullifies, Lightning/Earth/Water/Poison
Aegis Bracelet		55	15	86	50		4	1	Invasion of Midgar
Imperial Guard		82	0	74	0		6	1	Reno
Minerva Band		60	8	57	0	0	6	1	Steal from Elena in Midgar Subway NOTE—Woman's Armlet nullifies, Fire/Cold/Gravity/Holy
Mystile		65	50	72	60	0	6	1	Invasion of Midgar
Chocobracelet		35	10	38	10	4	0	1	Chocobo Racing Gift

LEGEND
ABBREV.   WHAT IT MEANS
Name   Name of accessory
Price   How much the accessory costs
Description   The effect the accessory has
Location   Where you can find the accessory

ACCESSORIES

NAME	PRICE	DESCRIPTION	LOCATION
Star Pendant	4000	Protects against Poison	Exchange for Item Coupon B in Shinra Tower
Talisman	4000	Spirit +10	After defeating H0512 in Shinra Tower
Protect Vest	3500	Vitality +10	After defeating Rufus on Shinra Tower Balcony
Poison Ring		Absorbs Poison Attacks	After defeating Motorball on Midgar Highway
Power Wrist	7500	Power +10	After defeating Bottomswell in Junon Harbor
Silver Glasses	3000	Protects against Darkness	Shop in Junon
Headband	3000	Protects against Sleep	Shop in Junon
White Cape	5000	Protects against Frog/Small	After defeating Jenova-BIRTH on Shinra Boat
Fire Ring	8000	Nullifies Fire attacks	Basement of Costa Del Sol House
Fury Ring	5000	Automatically puts you in Berserk	Shop in Gongaga Town
Fairy Ring	3500	Protects against Poison/Darkness	Cosmo Canyon Caves
Jem Ring	7500	Protects against Paralyze/Petrify/Slow Numb	After defeating Scorpion in Nibelheim Mountains
Earrings	7500	Magic +10	Shop in Rocket Town
Choco Feather	10000	Dexterity+10	Shop in Wutai
Peace Ring		Protects against Berserk, Fury, and Sadness	After defeating Rapps on the Da-chao Statue
Champion Belt		Power+10, Strength+10	16,000 BP at Battle Square
Ribbon		Immune to all status attacks	Cetra Shrine (Door 5)
Water Bracelet		Drains water attacks	Corral Valley
HypnoCrown		Increases Manipulation Rate	Corral Valley Cave
Safety Bit		Immune to Sudden Death/Petrify/Slow Numb	Great Glacier
Reflect Ring		Automatically sets up Reflect	After defeating Jenova-DEATH in Whirlwind Maze
Ice Ring	8000	Nullifies Cold attacks	After defeating Chekhov, shop in Mideel
Amulet	10000	Luck +10	Shop in Mideel
Bolt Ring	8000	Nullifies Lightning attacks	Shop in Mideel
Tough Ring		Vitality & Spirit +50	Steal from Reno in Midgar Sewers
Tetra Elemental		Absorb Fire, Ice, Thunder and Earth and converts to HP	Final Dungeon
Sneak Glove		Increase Stealing % Rate	Sector 6 Slums (Weapon Shop)
Cat's Bell		Restores HP as you walk	Gold Saucer (Chocobo Race)

216

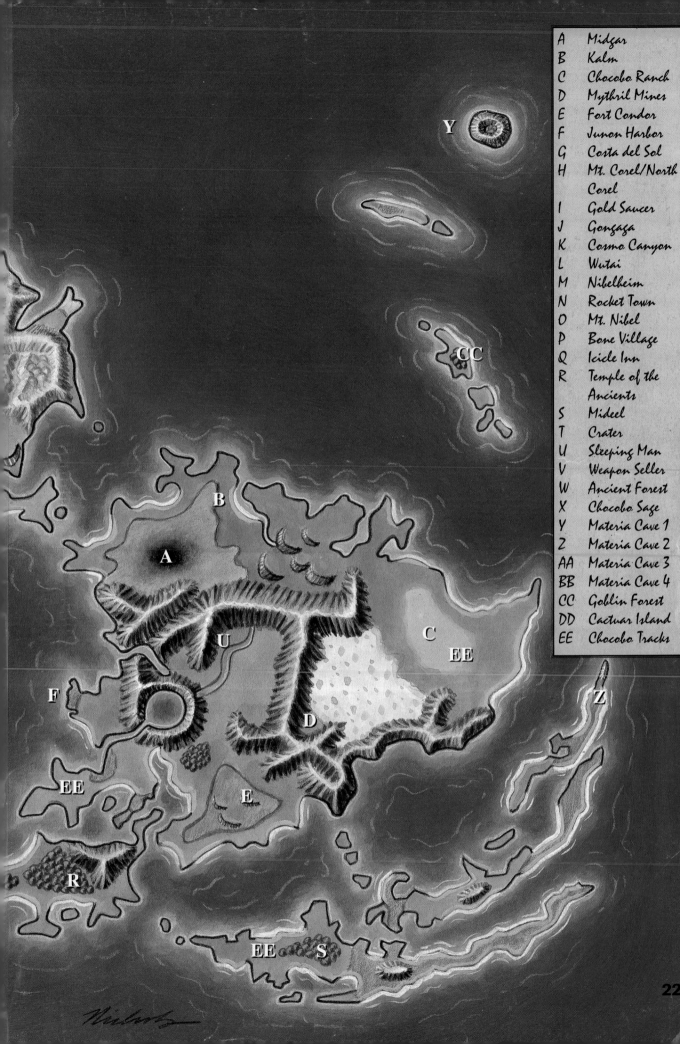

A	Midgar
B	Kalm
C	Chocobo Ranch
D	Mythril Mines
E	Fort Condor
F	Junon Harbor
G	Costa del Sol
H	Mt. Corel/North Corel
I	Gold Saucer
J	Gongaga
K	Cosmo Canyon
L	Wutai
M	Nibelheim
N	Rocket Town
O	Mt. Nibel
P	Bone Village
Q	Icicle Inn
R	Temple of the Ancients
S	Mideel
T	Crater
U	Sleeping Man
V	Weapon Seller
W	Ancient Forest
X	Chocobo Sage
Y	Materia Cave 1
Z	Materia Cave 2
AA	Materia Cave 3
BB	Materia Cave 4
CC	Goblin Forest
DD	Cactuar Island
EE	Chocobo Tracks